Frauds

Books by Richard Aldington

—

Biography

VOLTAIRE
WELLINGTON
FOUR ENGLISH PORTRAITS
THE STRANGE LIFE OF CHARLES WATERTON
PORTRAIT OF A GENIUS, BUT . . . (Life of D. H. Lawrence)
PINORMAN
LAWRENCE OF ARABIA: A BIOGRAPHICAL ENQUIRY
INTRODUCTION TO MISTRAL
FRAUDS

Novels

DEATH OF A HERO
THE COLONEL'S DAUGHTER
ALL MEN ARE ENEMIES
WOMEN MUST WORK
VERY HEAVEN
SEVEN AGAINST REEVES
REJECTED GUEST
THE ROMANCE OF CASANOVA

Short Stories

ROADS TO GLORY
SOFT ANSWERS

Poetry

A DREAM IN THE LUXEMBOURG
COMPLETE POEMS

Essays

FRENCH STUDIES AND REVIEWS
LITERARY STUDIES AND REVIEWS
D. H. LAWRENCE

Anthologies

POETRY OF THE ENGLISH-SPEAKING WORLD
FIFTY ROMANCE LYRIC POEMS
THE RELIGION OF BEAUTY (the English Aesthetes)

Translations

EURIPIDES: Alcestis
MEDALLIONS: Anyte, Meleager, Anacreontea, Renaissance Latin Poets
BOCCACCIO: Decameron
FIFTEEN JOYS OF MARRIAGE (15th Century French)
MYSTERY OF THE NATIVITY (15th Century Liégeois)
CYRANO DE BERGERAC: Voyages
VOLTAIRE: Candide
CHODERLOS DE LACLOS: Dangerous Acquaintances
JULIEN BENDA: The Great Betrayal
A WREATH FOR SAN GEMIGNANO

RICHARD ALDINGTON

Frauds

WILLIAM HEINEMANN LTD
MELBOURNE :: LONDON :: TORONTO

FIRST PUBLISHED 1957

PRINTED IN GREAT BRITAIN
AT THE WINDMILL PRESS
KINGSWOOD, SURREY

Contents

Illustrations

ONE

Introduction

SOME FLAGRANT IMPOSTORS AND FRAUDS

A friend who has looked over the following pieces suggests that my title may mislead some potential readers since "for the average citizen who hasn't time to bother about niceties of language 'fraud' means 'financial fraud'." He goes on to suggest that perhaps 'impostors' would be the better word.

I should not wish anyone to borrow this book in the expectation of finding what is not in it. True, there are one or two financial frauds included, but financial frauds tend so much to fall into well-known or even conventional patterns that fresh cases are immediately classified by the police under a few headings of typical examples. I should think a whole book of financial frauds would inevitably turn out to be monotonous, not only because of the repetition of methods but because of the similarity of the dupes—and one of the interests in the investigation of successful frauds is the psychology of the dupes.

This query sent me to my Shorter Oxford Dictionary, where I find this entry under the word 'Fraud':

"1. The quality of being deceitful. Now *rare*. 2. Criminal deception; the using of false representations to obtain an unjust advantage of another. 3. An act or instance of deception, a dishonest trick. 4. A fraudulent contrivance;

in mod. colloq. use, a spurious or deceptive thing, 1658.
b. *colloq.* of a person: An impostor, a humbug, 1850.
5. State of being defrauded or deluded. Milton."

And this under the word 'Impostor':

"One who imposes on others; a deceiver, swindler, cheat;
now chiefly, one who passes himself off as someone other
than he is."

English, thanks be, is still a living language, in the sense
that the literary or standard speech is constantly being
modified or added to unconsciously by the people, the real
creators and transmitters of language in a state of "creative
evolution". In a popular piece of writing on something of
topical or general interest, even if it happens to be historical,
I would far rather use colloquial language or even slang than
be stiff or pedantic. The recent use of 'impostor' is shown
by the dictionary to be mainly "one who passes himself off
as someone other than he is", and so I use it in, for example,
the obvious case of Arthur Orton pretending that he was Sir
Roger Tichborne. The colloquial use of 'fraud' includes that
as well as any spurious or deceptive thing or person. Thus,
every impostor (i.e. impersonator) is a fraud, but every fraud
(i.e. cheat, spurious person, deceiver) is not an impersonator
in the sense that Orton fraudulently tried to impersonate the
deceased Sir Roger.

Of course 'impostor' has been, and no doubt still is, used
in a more extended meaning than I give it, indeed rather
tending towards what I mean by 'frauds'. There is an
amusing example in the lively memoirs of Mr. Creevy, whose
cheerful irreverence towards 'Prinney' and other pompous
characters so much infuriates modern snobs. After recording
his regret that the great Duke of Wellington in 1818 was
going to descend from his eminence as "the soldier of Europe"
to occupy a minor post in a Tory Cabinet, Mr. Creevy
continues:

". . . considering the impostors that most men in power
are—the insufferable pretentions one meets with in every
jack-in-office—the uniform frankness and simplicity of
Wellington in all the conversations I have heard him engaged
in, coupled with the unparalleled situation he holds in the
world for an English subject, make him to me the most
interesting object I have ever seen in my life."

Mr. Creevy, it will be noted, used the word 'impostor' in
a sense different from that in which we now generally employ
it. Jacks-in-office are 'impostors', not because they pretend
to an identity which is not theirs, as if for instance an Under-
Secretary of State under the Prince Regent had tried to
convince people that he was really Napoleon Bonaparte,
which would have led to an obvious but lamentable end. But
they are 'impostors' because they pretend to wisdom, dignity,
knowledge, popularity, indispensability and the like, which
character they try to support by what we, with a wider
colloquial vocabulary, should call bluffing and high-hatting
—posturings which the poor but irreverent Whig seldom fails
to deride mercilessly when he comes upon them.

For his antithesis of "uniform frankness and simplicity"
he could hardly have chosen a more striking and illustrious
example among great Englishmen of action. The co-
existence in Wellington of military and administrative
abilities of the highest order, with exceptional honesty,
common sense and a sardonic wit which invariably exposed
pretences, makes him a standard to measure the Englishman
at his best. He failed as a politician mainly because he did
not know how to tell lies, like the great Queen Elizabeth; and
there was such simplicity in him that he was disappointed to
find that not one of his rather numerous mistresses really had
loved him. A nation has a right to be judged by its best, and
not by its worst, men, even if the latter inevitably enormously
exceed in number. Wellington is an antithesis not only to
'impostors' in Mr. Creevy's sense of the word, but to the

curious specimens of 'frauds' and 'impostors' we shall look over in these pages.

Is it really true that "the English dearly love a Fraud"? This is "a newspaper question", which is as much as to say that it is no question at all because it is too vague and there is no exact way of measuring the degrees of gullibility of different nations. When I have been taunted by foreigners with this supposedly well-recognised trait I have urged that, while no doubt the English do succumb with incredible alacrity to the most obvious impostors and frauds, other peoples are far from exempt. I have discovered two quite staggering examples in sceptical France, on whose *escrocs* I might be encouraged to expatiate at some future time. But the reason why we hear apparently so much more about English frauds and impostors is that while the English may dearly love a fraud for a time, they even more dearly love to find him out. It is typical of that character of 'doubleness', of wanting to have a thing both ways, which is so common in Englishmen and all men. "The Anglo-Saxon is essentially dishonest," said Robert Louis Stevenson, a hard saying which goes too far, but he is speaking of the bilking of French hotel-keepers by the English and American bohemians of his day. Unluckily that much-quoted little proverb "Honesty is the best policy" rather gives the game away for its quoters, by suggesting that if honesty didn't pay then presumably they wouldn't be honest. I must reluctantly admit that when I have returned to England after a long absence, wearing foreign clothes and perhaps a slightly more friendly air which caused me to be mistaken for an American or a 'Colonial', I have been amazed by the well-nigh universal attempts to over-charge and to exploit a supposed ignorance of a clumsily out-of-date coinage by trying to short-change and pass bad money. On the other hand it is only fair to admit that these practices exist almost everywhere, and usually become worse the farther you get away from the

sophisticated haunts of over-population. North Africa. . . .
The West Indies. . . . Sicily . . .

If there is any truth in this belief that the English are
exceptionally gullible and it is not a mere libel of envious
foreigners, a possible reason might lie in a misplacing of the
supernatural. Walking in Palermo I passed an elderly
woman of the people who turned and blew a kiss with her
fingers to an image of the Santissima, just as her Greek
predecessors did to the Erycine or the Magna Mater so
many centuries ago. A sacred image weeps or sheds blood or
bows the head; a holy tomb sweats scented oil; a shepherdess
and her half-witted younger brother mistake a fashionably
dressed Englishwoman wandering for cyclamen beyond the
usual tourist orbit for a celestial apparition; astonishing
cures of stubborn diseases are effected by exposure to a
thirteenth-century Byzantine picture painted by St. Luke.
All these and other supernatural occurrences in the South
cause much pleasurable excitement and eerie titillation;
pilgrimages are organised; thriftily calculated offerings
—sprats to catch whales—are made; and the world
goes on as usual. The supernatural has been kept in its
place, and these same people (whom we pity or despise as
credulous and superstitious) show a tremendously virile
aggressiveness in salesmanship. They would not knock a
franc off their prices for any number of celestial apparitions,
and as a matter of fact celestial apparitions never do advise
them to charge less.

Hard-headed haberdashers with both feet on the pavement
are quite sincerely shocked by this puerile parody of sacred
things which are conveniently kept by them at a distance so
remote that they practically never need to be thought about.
But it seems that we all have a certain amount of credulity
which must be employed somehow, so that the practical man
and the rationalist are singularly liable to be taken in by
frauds and impostors. Of course they are not the only

victims, though peculiarly appropriate ones. There are persons, apparently a great many, who are so abundantly gifted with credulity that they can be persuaded to believe in anything which able and unscrupulous persons find profitable. It certainly looks as if we should be more prudent to invest our stock of credulity in the supernatural of a harmless kind, and to keep our reason and scepticism for mundane situations and contingencies. The fact is curious that a long series of English secular 'impostors' and 'frauds' begins at the eve of the Reformation in the reign of Henry VII. Doubtless there were other causes, and of course it is obvious that some of the most important historical frauds and impostures had religious as well as political motives. But then bigotry and superstition are only dangerous when they leave their proper sphere of credulity and become political, when they misuse the essential and proper power of the State to try to enforce unwanted beliefs and to save souls despite the wishes of their owners.

Looking at a few of the historical cases of fraud and imposture we cannot help noticing first of all that they are more varied than the mere financial cheatings which now are supposed to occupy everybody's attention. Strange that two epochs of English history have been disturbed by claimants or pretenders to the throne. But how different! On the theory of the divine right of kings, that only the legitimate heirs are the lawful Kings, then of course the exiled Stuarts were the true Kings of England and the Hanoverians usurpers. But then there are the theory and the fact that the people and Parliament could and did intervene. And still more potently, *force majeur*. The fact is that the last purely English King died with his house carls defending the country against an invader who, being a natural child, could have no legitimist claim to the throne whatever. It was indeed a "Protestant lie" to say that Prince James was not the true legitimate son of James II and his wife, but then the sticklers

for pure legitimist descent had to trace it back to William
I. And of course there had been usurpations by members
of the Royal Family who were not the lawful *jure divino* heirs.
Henry IV was a usurper, so was Richard III, and so was
Richard's slayer and successor, Henry Tudor.

Strictly speaking, on the death of Richard III—or indeed
when Richard murdered Edward V and his brother—the
true heir was the Princess Elizabeth of York. When she
married Henry Tudor she should have been Queen regnant,
and he a prince consort. But the prejudice in favour of the
male ruler, which had made Matilda's reign so disastrous,
still operated. So there was the strange position that though
the Queen's heir—Arthur, and later Henry—was unquestionably true King after his father's and mother's death,
her husband Henry VII was not. The true male heir was
Clarence's son, Edward Earl of Warwick, who was kept a
close prisoner. Hence the impostors Lambert Simnel,
Perkin Warbeck and Ralph Wilford.

They were, of course, simply the puppets of discontented
Yorkists, exasperated tax-payers, and foreign princes who
knew that they were impostors but used them in the end-
lessly dirty game of power politics. Nobody seems to know
where Simnel came from, but he was produced to an always
discontented Ireland as the true Edward of Warwick, who
was in fact in the Tower, and was paraded through the
streets of London to show the citizens that the Irish Edward
was an impostor. Yet Simnel managed to land in Lancashire
with a small army of foreign bandits, aided by the Queen's
cousin, Lord Lincoln, who knew perfectly well that Simnel
was an impostor. The invaders were defeated in a short but
bloody fight, and Simnel was captured. The King wisely
and humorously spared the 'prince' to serve in the royal
kitchen, and later made him a falconer.

Supposing the rebels had won, what would the Yorkists
have done with the impostor, assuming, as is most likely, that

B

the true Edward of Warwick would have been killed before
they could get to London? Probably he would have disappeared, and John of Lincoln would have inherited a
usurper's troubles.

Undeterred by Simnel's menial disgrace, another and
more dangerous impostor, named Perkin Warbeck, started
up—again in Ireland. Who he really was is uncertain. In the
end he 'confessed' that he was the son of a Flemish trades-
man, but he looked so much like a real Plantagenet that
many think the likeness could not be accidental, and that
Perkin may or must have been one of Edward IV's natural
children. It was given out that he was Prince Richard, the
younger of *"les enfants d'Édouard"*. At all events he kept up
the imposture until he was summoned to the Court of
Margaret of Burgundy, Richard III's sister, who of course
was able to tutor a clever, imitative, ambitious young man
far more effectively than poor silly Lady Tichborne tutored
the butcher she hoped was her dead son. He lasted longer
than Simnel, and seems actually to have convinced James IV
of Scotland of his *bona fides*. Otherwise it is hard to see why
the King married him to Lady Katherine Gordon, who was
related to the Scottish Royal Family. However carefully
Perkin had been tutored, you would think that a King could
not be so credulous as to be taken in by so obvious an
impostor who showed his plebeian instincts by protesting
against the ferocity of Border warfare, to the huge contempt
of both English and Scotch. Eventually Perkin was captured,
but instead of being made a kitchen servant was allowed to
live under guard. After an attempt to escape, he was sent to
the Tower, and then Henry heard of yet another impostor,
Ralph Wilford, pretending to be Edward of Warwick. In
1499, some eight years after his imposture began, Perkin was
hanged and Edward beheaded. Wilford disappeared.
Luckily for Henry these impostors were supported only by
foreign princes, conspirators, and Cornishmen who refused

to pay taxes to keep the Scots from invading Cornwall, and not by the mass of the people. If they in any numbers had been as credulous as the King of Scots, another civil war might have resulted. Doubtless they knew that, and doubtless they did not care much who was the King they never saw so long as they were not too abominably oppressed and robbed by officials, landlords' deputies, and clergy.

Lambert Simnel, Perkin Warbeck, Ralph Wilford. They are quaint names but sound authentic English (though 'Simnel' like so many English words is a French derivative and 'Warbeck' should be Flemish), far more so to a native English ear than Plantagenet, Orange Nassau, or even Saxe-Coburg-Gotha. Their careers as royal impostors are a curious episode in English history which left some mark on the people's memory, for long afterwards John Ford wrote a play *Perkin Warbeck* (printed 1634) which revived the character. Ford makes Warbeck a dignified and stout-hearted person who persists in his assumed part to the end (in spite of the 'confession' which historically he made), but then Orton did the same. Ford would not have dared to make a hero of Warbeck in the lifetime of Elizabeth Tudor, but was there merit in doing so under a Stuart whose ancestor had recognised Warbeck as Richard IV of England? A strange fact which (one would suppose) the Stuart Kings would not have been specially eager to see mimed before their loving people.

In that epoch nearer to ourselves which goes from Elizabeth to William of Orange Nassau, there are, of course, plenty of frauds and impostors of various types, as well as rogues and vagabonds of the Marlowe-Shakespeare tribe. It was an epoch of religious change and controversy, when, however, politics failed to show any traces of the religion professed, and religion became if possible even more political. Moreover, there was a remarkable increase in the shift of the realm of credulity from the organised to the heterodox and carnal realms of belief. The paid charlatan or fanatic or perjurer appeared on the scene. Obviously they had existed in Europe and England in the Middle Ages, but there is a breath-taking impudence in Edward Kelley the fortune-telling fraud, Matthew Hopkins the witch-hunting fraud, and Titus Oates the world's record false witness which, joined to the eminence of some of their supporters, makes necessary a glance or two at these well-known figures.

Kelley, whose real name was Talbot, practised and financially exploited alchemy (which has lately been re-habilitated by the infinitely more dangerous 'Modern Science') crystal-gazing, spirit-raising, astrology, and similar methods of foretelling the future. Therein he was merely one of an almost infinite flock of frauds who have deceived man-kind (and often no doubt themselves) for money for millennia. Men have yet to devise any organisation or even single-handed cultivation of the supernatural which does not involve either a subsidy or sending round the hat, or both.

In addition to these activities Kelley (born 1555) spent a year at Oxford and is said to have been both "a London attorney and a deft forger". He began his career as a mage by violating graves in search of information about the future, but was insufficiently warned, as is proved by the fact that he soon after had his ears cut off for forgery. In Wales he bought (so the tale runs) a bottle of powder and a mysterious manuscript (probably on alchemy and doubtless written by himself) from a Welsh innkeeper. With these Kelley hastened to the celebrated Dr. Dee, a Cambridge man of much mathematical and astronomical learning, who also practised astrology and was visited by spirits. The angel Gabriel once brought him the philosopher's stone, which after the lapse of ages was bought by Horace Walpole, who found it was not 'a crystal' as stated but a round piece of polished cannel coal. It is not surprising then to learn that Dee was consulted by explorers such as Frobisher and Sir Humphrey Gilbert, by statesmen such as Cecil and Walsingham, and was visited (and doubtless consulted) by the Queen's Majesty.

This learned and important person was so much impressed by Kelley and his tales that he adopted the wanderer (who is said to have devised a particularly venerable and impressive bonnet to hide the loss of his ears) as a 'skryer', i.e. he peered into the lump of polished coal,* saw the visions Dr. Dee wanted him to see, and told the doctor what he wanted to hear and what Kelley wanted him to believe. There was no difficulty about the latter, for the doctor's credulity stopped short of no absurdity or unconventionality. Only, he had such extensive interests and wanted instant information about so many recondite subjects that Kelley had to work very hard to catch up. The way of the medium is often hard. His own interests at this time seem to have been devoted mainly to the potentially lucrative but elusive science of changing cheap metals into gold. Meanwhile, having acquired a decisive hold on Dee's credulity, Kelley pretended he was going away in dissatisfaction at the honorarium he received as hard-working medium, taking care of course that Dee should find it out in time. He consented reluctantly to remain in consideration of his full keep and pocket-money of fifty pounds annually—a fair income at that time.

So far the brace of mages had done no particular harm, unless getting married is so considered, since it is hard to believe they had much influence on the actions of Burleigh and the Queen, whatever the explorers did. It would not be fair to blame Dee and Kelley for the drowning of Gilbert, for their advice on his voyage may not have been decisive. But now another dupe appeared on the scene, in the shape of a Polish nobleman named Albert Laski, whose preposterous credulity joined to his presence on a visit to England seemed designed by Providence to take away the reproach that the

---

* The 'speculum' said to be Dee's at the British Museum is a ball of solid rose-coloured glass.

English hold any monopoly in gullibility. A special crystal-spirit named Madimi was invented for this silly Pole, who was easily persuaded that it was his destiny to be the king, not of one, but of two kingdoms. Eventually, Madimi or some other spirit commanded Laski to take Dee and Kelley at once to his estates in Poland, and not only to pay their expenses on the journey but to entertain them honourably for an indefinite time. The spirit or spirits obviously would not mention so delicate a *contretemps*, but the fact is that Kelley had just learned there was a warrant out against him for making counterfeit money. As Kelley had no ears left to be cut off by the soothing hand of Justice, he might have been hanged for this crime, so it was just as well to change climates.

Strange to relate, in spite of the unpleasant charge hanging over Kelley, the two mages corresponded with Burleigh and the Queen, and seem to have initiated, or far more probably to have continued, the custom of acting as spies in the countries they visited, for Poland was not the only one. From Laski's hospitable home it was that the pair sent to the Queen, as evidence of Kelley's progress in alchemy, an iron frying-pan from which a small piece had been cut and transmuted to gold by Kelley's transcendent science. Here, it seems to one influenced by the modern spirit of scepticism, Kelley and Dee erred in their view of the Queen's Majesty and her character. What they should have done was to send her a small piece of iron to fit the hole in the accompanying solid gold frying-pan. She might have been really interested in that.

When the pair had spent most of Laski's money they moved on, frequently quarrelling and even separating, but always joining up again. Antwerp, Cracow and Prague are mentioned. The relations between Dee and Kelley became complicated. As was natural, Kelley in time became bored with the esoteric, learned and high-falutin stuff he had to invent continually as a 'skryer'; and, as sometimes happens in these mediumistic performances, the spirits began to display carnal interests and appetites we associate rather with the gross flesh than with pure spirit. Madimi, a female spirit, eventually manifested herself without clothes. Mrs. Kelley was plain and Mrs. Dee was pretty. So it is not surprising that Madimi on behalf of God informed the philosophic mages that henceforth they were to enjoy their wives in common. It is perhaps a little more surprising that Dee consented to this, but then what can the uninitiated know of the solemnity and weight of celestial orders?

This quaint spiritual event surely goes to show that Dee may have been Kelley's dupe and not an accomplice, as much of the available evidence seems to suggest. And yet perfect harmony was not established even by obedience to Madimi's communications, and in 1589 Kelley and Dee parted, Dee returning home to an honoured old age, and Kelley remaining in Prague, as trusted 'skryer' (it appears) to a Bohemian nobleman named Rosenberg and potential gold-maker to the Emperor Rudolf. Meanwhile Dr. Dee back in England warmly recommended Kelley to Lord Burleigh as "a man of the highest intelligence and utmost value for gathering information respecting the secret counsels of foreign States". What, if anything, Kelley received from the Secret Service funds is not known, but he proceeded to justify Dee's praise by denouncing "one Parkyns, a Jesuit come from Rome to Prague," as guilty of a diabolical plot "of murthering her Majesty". Kelley had neither the effrontery nor the luck of Oates in plots and perjury. Parkins, it is true, had been a Jesuit, but in Rome he had saved the life of Burleigh's son from an anti-Protestant mob, and was in 1598 (though apparently Kelley did not know it) a Secret Service agent far more trusted than Kelley and employed on really important errands—at this time to the King of Poland. But zealous lying is often more than its own reward, for Burleigh continued to write most friendly letters to Kelley, only exhorting him sarcastically to send to England enough of his alchemical powder to make the gold needed for the cost of the Navy that year! For some reason Kelley neither sent the powder nor accepted an urgent invitation to return to England.

He would have been wiser to do so. Failure to produce gold awoke the Emperor's Catholic conscience, and he decided that Kelley was a necromancer and must be punished accordingly. Kelley tried to escape, but was captured. Set at liberty (reluctantly, at the request of the Queen's Majesty), he was again arrested when Rudolf found he was planning a return to England. In a fit of rage Kelley murdered one of his warders and, realising that this was a fatal error, again tried to escape on the usual impromptu rope of knotted bed-clothes, which broke. The fall was so violent he broke a rib and both legs, of which injuries he died, bequeathing to us the pious hope that:

". . . my name and character will so become known to posterity that I may be counted among those who have suffered much for the sake of truth."

If the story as told us is true there are one or two rather curious points involved. Did Mrs. Kelley—and later on Mrs. Dr. Dee—never notice the lack of ears and comment on it? Such is the scientific interest of ladies in all such matters that they seldom refrain from urgent enquiry, and then, in the purest spirit of scientific research, hasten to pass on their knowledge to others. Did Dr. Dee in all those years never hear the fact from one or other of the ladies or 'skrye' it for himself? In those days the question: "How did you come to lose your ears?" must have been awkward, since it was almost invariably due to the rough but ready workings of a barbarous legal system. The spirits, including Madimi, must have had to do some explaining. Further, how did it happen that the warrant for counterfeiting money was executed in so dilatory a manner that Kelley was able to leave the country openly and apparently at leisure? How did it happen that Kelley was able to communicate with the Queen—indirectly, no doubt—and to correspond with the Lord Treasurer? Of course the most scrupulous Government cannot enquire too closely into the habits and past of its agents, but it seems remarkable that Burleigh should have personally committed himself in writing to such a fraud and actual criminal. Possibly Kelley was covered by the prestige of Dee, who received a pension as the Queen's 'intelligencer', but why after the two parted was the Government so anxious to get Kelley back to England that it sent an emissary with the rank of captain to try to get him back? But the questions are endless—among them, how did this vagabond and vulgar exploiter of the credulous come to be called "Sir Edward"?

As for Dr. Dee, who can state definitely whether he was dupe or accomplice? At times as one reads the accounts of their doings Dee seems as bad a charlatan as Kelley. And, after all, he was the scholar protected by the friendship of the great. You might well suppose that a man who for years accepted the more and more preposterous inventions of Kelley would hardly be the person to ferret out and supply accurate information of the secret intentions and plottings among the Queen's enemies; and if Burleigh went on the principle that such loons might by accident hit on some valuable fact in the midst of their random reportings he must have wasted a good deal of time and money. The doctor's alchemical style in his *Fasciculus Chemicus* is so mystic and symbolical (no doubt to baffle the idle curiosity of the profane) that if it were submitted to an enlightened jury of modern American psychiatrists they would doubtless find the author insane and recommend his incarceration. One of his sublime directions begins thus:

"Take a red dragon, courageous, warlike, to whom no natural strength is wanting, and afterwards seven or nine noble eagles (virgins), whose eyes will not wax dull by the rays of the sun, cast the birds with the beasts into a clean prison, and strongly shut up, and under which let a bath be placed, that they may be incensed to fight by the warm vapour. In a short time they will enter into a long and harsh contention, until at length about the day forty-five or fifty, the eagles begin to prey upon and tear the beast to pieces; and his dying, it will infect the whole prison with its direful poison, whereby the eagles being wounded, they will also be constrained to give up the ghost. From the putrefaction of the dead carcasses, a crow will be generated . . ."

It seems strange, though perhaps not, that the author of that and much like it, far from being "strongly shut up", was appointed Warden of Manchester College, Oxford.

Whatever benefit of the doubt may be allowed Dee, it seems clear that Kelley was a criminal as well as a fraud. The case of the three bogus but pathetic pretenders is different. True, in aspiring to a throne which was already occupied they were guilty of attempted usurpation and high treason; but, however deplorable, treason does not necessarily offend the basic sentiments of right and wrong which used to be thought common to all mankind. Treason is one of those emigrant crimes depending on which side wins; and Henry VII would have gone down to history as a traitor and would-be usurper if he had lost the battle and his life at Bosworth. Legitimist fomenters of rebellion in England do not seem to have registered the fact that success mainly depended, not on divine right by birth, but on how much the country was exasperated against what it thought a tyrant and his bad government.

It is inconceivable that anyone should doubt the vileness of the two ruffians we are now to glance at, both of whom abused human credulity, fanaticism and stupidity to commit judicial murders, mainly for the sake of a little money and much notoriety, but also out of what is flatteringly called "the spirit of Puckishness", the love of mischief for mischief's sake. Titus Oates is in every school history, but the infamous Matthew Hopkins is half-forgotten.

"Oliver Cromwell," says Carlyle with his customary studious moderation, "whose body they hung on their Tyburn gallows because he had found the Christian Religion inexecutable in this country, remains to me by far the remarkablest Governor we have had here for the last five centuries or so."

One muses a little over that apocalyptic sentence, especially the bit about the Christian religion, wondering if Carlyle knew that during the Long Parliament and Oliver's reign more than three thousand innocent persons, many of them poor old women, were hanged or burned to death for witchcraft, and that in the space of three years at least two hundred of these victims owed their dreadful doom to the paid professional witch-taker, Matthew Hopkins? Of course, with the exception of the self-appointed paid witch-hunter, there was nothing new about this, for the Parliamentary saints were but carrying on the tradition of their predecessors, particularly of James I. It is worth noting that they who wished to change so much in so many respects here made no change, except perhaps to intensify the persecution, of 'malignants' and all other enemies of the "Christian Religion", including the burning alive of epileptics and of senile paupers crazed with misery and solitude. One novelty in this pursuit of Christianity under difficulties is that the witches were prosecuted before the secular courts under an Act of Henry VIII of 1541 making witchcraft felony, which was renewed by Elizabeth in 1562. Before that, witchcraft came under the ecclesiastical courts (Joan of Arc's case among them) and we learn that during a period of 150 years they burned about 30,000 witches, and even had a famous witch-hunter named Sprenger. Since this pre-Reformation 30,000 in 150 years presumably included England, it will be seen that the zeal of the neo-Christians in punishing witches was proportionately even more rewarded. Indeed we are told that Parliament entirely approved of Hopkins and his proceedings, and even sent a committee "to assist" him by intimidating juries and judges.

Hopkins lived in complete obscurity until he discovered this method of exploiting the credulity, stupidity and cruelty of authority and public. He is supposed to have been born early in the seventeenth century, the son of a 'minister', by which presumably is meant a Nonconformist divine or preacher. He himself was a lawyer, but perhaps not a very successful one, since he found it worth while to destroy the lives of innocent persons by fraud and perjury at a fee of one pound per district visited, plus one pound per head for every witch convicted. He must have made a close study of witch-craft before his active career began, since he re-organised and, as it were, codified the methods of investigating and added a few sprouts of his own invention.

Hopkins borrowed from Scotland his sadistic and popular test of 'pricking'. Suspected or self-denounced women were stripped naked, shaved and examined for the presence of "a third teat" which was decisive proof of a pact with the Devil. In the absence of this, the woman's body was repeatedly pricked, for if there seemed to be no pain or if any puncture did not bleed—then guilty. Another 'test' invented by Hopkins was as follows. The suspected witch was tied to a chair, and for twenty-four hours received nothing to eat or drink. Any insect which flew into the room was pursued by the 'watchers', and if they failed to catch it, then it was the devil come to suck the witch's blood. A 'test' more often used with men, whom it was no particular fun to strip naked and torture, was to compel the suspect to walk until he was completely exhausted and ready to confess to anything. But 'swimming' appealed to the gentle Hopkins as much as 'pricking'. The victim, having been stripped, had the right hand bound to the left foot, the left hand to the right foot, was then wrapped in a sheet, and carefully placed on the surface of a pond or river. If she sank she was innocent, but of course was drowned; if by any accident she was not drowned, she was a witch, and was burned alive.

On top of this revolting sadism and stupidity Hopkins showed an imbecile vulgarity of invention in the 'devils' he invented as familiars to his victims. Here, from his book *The Discovery of Witches* (1647), is the list of the devils he observed in the house of a poor old woman in Essex:

"Holt, who came in like a white kitling. Jarmara, who came in like a fat spaniel without any legs at all. Vinegar Tom, who was like a long-legged greyhound with a head like an ox . . . who when this Discoverer spoke to and bade him go to the place provided for him and his angels, immediately transformed himself into the shape of a child of four years old without a head and gave half a dozen turns about the house and vanished at the door. Sack and Sugar, like a black rabbit. News, like a polecat."

That last devil was perhaps more shrewdly chosen than Hopkins knew, but who can fail to see that these are nothing but the malignant distortions of the pet animals which any lonely old woman might keep? But this pamphlet was Hopkins's last shot. It was written in an attempt to answer a denunciation of him and his methods published by a Huntingdonshire vicar named John Gaule who, strange to say, was also a strong believer in witches. He objected to Hopkins's methods and especially to his intruding on the functions of the ministry which Mr. Gaule ornamented. Other clergymen followed, and Hopkins was denounced at the Norfolk assizes as himself a wizard. In Essex, where he had created a reign of terror and was detested, he was accused of sorcery and attacked by a mob. For long it was believed that Hopkins was himself 'swum' by a mob and then hanged, but there seems to be no evidence for this. It is known that he was buried in Essex, near the scene of some of his crimes, on the 12th August, 1647. Of course, his brief but

bloody life as a witch-finder could not have existed without
the credulity of Government and people; it was the dupes who
made the fraud so easy. Very likely Hopkins was 'sincere' to
the extent that he half-believed in his own horrible deceptions.
Fanatics often do, but invariably accede openly or tacitly to
the morally fatal doctrine of the end justifying the means.
According to the credulity of the age, witches existed—the
Bible says "Thou shalt not suffer a witch to live"* and King
James I had published a feeble book elaborating the text.
So long as persons, mainly women, could be tortured and
judicially murdered as witches, and Hopkins got his gold
pieces, that was all that was required. What more do you
want? Genuine proof? But an imaginary crime must surely
be proved by imaginary evidence? Which was what Hopkins
supplied, and a good deal of sadistic excitement along with it.

Perhaps the only plea that can be made for Hopkins—and
it is weak indeed—is that his dreadful total of two hundred
mostly female victims takes off some of the horror of the ten
or twelve unfortunate men sacrificed to the ambitions of
Titus Oates and to one of the worst fits of collective panic and
hysteria which ever afflicted our nation. The reader will not
expect to find here anything fresh about Titus Oates, still
less a summary of an episode or squalid tragedy which has
been so often and so adequately studied. Partly because
Oates himself is such a repulsive figure, partly because of
their intrinsic interest, other figures and aspects of this
sinister sink of perjuries inevitably attract the attention. The
question: Who murdered Sir Edmund Godfrey? is bound to
be asked by anyone who hears the story, and in spite of the
twelve possible and in some cases less than possible solutions
propounded, the mystery is not solved, and probably never
will be. Again, was there a Popish Plot, and, if so, what was
it? Oates's very title of the 'Popish' Plot suggests a lie. If one
fact is certain in this imbroglio it is that Innocent XI (Bene-

* *A mistranslation!*

detto Odeschalchi) knew nothing about it and was far too high-minded to do anything but put under arrest anyone proposing a plan to assassinate the King of England. He was no friend to the Jesuits, and when later an emissary of James II outlined his master's plans for the restoration of Roman Catholicism in England, Innocent strongly opposed them as more likely to have the opposite effect. If there was a genuine "Jesuit Plot" (apart of course from Oates's inventions) was there not also a "Protestant Plot"? Much has been written and debated about these topics, and such characters as the future King James, Shaftesbury, and the judges Scroggs and Jeffreys. Above all there is the character and the part played by King Charles II, who, in spite of the Whig calumnies, stands out more and more clearly as far more able, civilised and humane than most of his subjects, even the most eminent. It is unlucky that he thought that Protestantism is not the religion for a gentleman, since it meant that he dissembled and even prevaricated from his conversion until his death-bed, and one cannot accept the casuistry that Charles Stuart's religion was no business of the King of England. He was descended through his mother from a once Protestant King who thought that Paris was worth a Mass; why should not London have been worth a Prayer Book?

Actually, the King was as sceptical as Elizabeth, and perhaps even more so. At all events the Restoration led to a welcome decline in the persecution and torture of 'witches' such as had disgraced the preceding decades—not that the persecution wholly ceased, but the jesting of "deboshed cavaliers" undoubtedly helped people to pluck up courage against this monstrosity. Unluckily, no amount of jesting and scepticism could remove at once the fanaticism, stupidity and cruelty of the mob which made witch-hunts possible. There was a curious contradiction between their excessive religious claims for themselves and the outlets found by over-repressed impulses and disorderly passions. They were half

God's toadies, and half the Devil's bullies. And then something or other always found mischief for their godly hands to
do. The "deboshed cavalier" drinking with wenches and
good companions had no mind or time for the burning of
witches. It was far better—and healthier—to kiss a young
woman than stick pins in an old one.

As the purely superstitious or mainly theological motives
for fear and persecution of the weak died down, there was a
strengthening of the politico-religious mania. A violent and
unscrupulous anti-Catholic and anti-Jesuit propaganda,
much of which must have emanated from Shaftesbury and
the Puritans, kept the popular mind, particularly in London,
in a state of fear and anxiety when any outburst of homicidal
hysteria became possible. The great plague of 1665 could
hardly be openly attributed to Roman Catholic malice, but
the great fire of the next year was, and this quite untrue
statement was included in the inscription on the Monument.
In 1678, twelve years only after the fire which came on top of
the sufferings and terrors of the plague, the sensational news
of this alleged 'Popish' or 'Jesuit' or 'Catholic' plot to murder
the King, as the prelude to a forcible conversion of the nation,
was launched by Tonge and Oates. Almost certainly, if Sir
Edmund Berry Godfrey—the magistrate to whom Oates
made a formal deposition of his knowledge of the 'plot'
before publicising it—had not been found murdered a few
days later, the 'plot' would not have had the enormous and
deplorable effect it did have. The 'plot' threatened the
murder by Jesuit emissaries of the highest personage in the
land, and lo! almost at once a well-known, much-respected,
Protestant London magistrate disappears, and is found dead
with a broken neck and his sword stuck in him. The resultant
frenzy of panic terror and wild clamour for reprisals would
have been difficult to control if all in a position of authority
or eminence in the country had collaborated to try to soothe
and remove these maddened feelings, but there was a power-

ful party with Shaftesbury at its head who did all they could
to inflame passions and increase the confusion. In addition
to the King, all "the Protestants" were to be murdered,
according to Oates, though it has been estimated that they
outnumbered the Catholics by about forty to one.

When we turn from the general situation which made the
panic of the Plot possible, if not inevitable, to Oates himself,
we have to remember the principle that if the English dearly
love a fraud they also dearly love exposing him—too late.
Facts and evidence are never regarded by mobs and parties,
and the very persons who are most credulous in believing the
fraud during his period of success may later be found among
those most bitter in denouncing him or her. In the register
of Merchant Taylors' School (where Oates was a pupil for a
year) his name is followed by a hand-written note: "The
Saviour of the Nation, first discoverer of that damnable
hellish plot in 1678." A little later is another note: "Perjured
upon record and a scoundrel fellow." From which I infer
that while the reports and opinions of a fraud during his
glory are obviously wildly exaggerated in his favour, so in the
period of discredit the evidence against him may be exaggerated, and injustice done. As the living Oates was
literally flogged through the streets of old London and made
to stand in the pillory, so he has been flogged metaphorically
through the pages of books and made to stand in the pillory
of History.

If we accept no more than can be proved or reasonably
inferred about Oates we soon notice that, as often happens
with frauds, his deceptions and tales of himself and others
began early, while his propensity to alter facts to suit himself
was supported by boundless impudence and a remarkable
"tenacious memory". It is obviously not the only way to
equip a fraud or impostor, but it is frequent—the reader will
find that much the same is related of "George Psalmanazar"
and Arthur Orton, who are treated later in this book in more

c

detail. The Psalmist, evidently subject to fits of melancholy and pessimism, thought that "all men are liars"; but some are born liars, some achieve lying and some have lying thrust upon them. Clearly, when Titus Oates was born at Oakham in 1649 he was born a liar of exceptional and pestilential prowess. Thomas Seccombe remarks pleasantly but untruly: "Though he is stated by more than one writer to have had a brother, William, who achieved some distinction as a horse-stealer, it is more probable that he was an only as well a unique child." He had in fact two brothers and two sisters.

Nothing is known of Titus's early education, if any, but in 1664, (at the then late age of fifteen, he was entered at Merchant Taylors' School, and showed his mettle at once by cheating his form-master, William Smith, of his entrance-money. In justice to Oates, let it be added that many years later he repaid the money. A year later (1665) he was expelled, and, after about two years obscurely passed in a small school, was entered at Gonville and Caius, Cambridge. After only two terms he was thrown out of Caius, but managed to transfer to St. John's as a servitor, only to be expelled by that College in 1669 because (it is alleged) he cheated a tailor and was detected in lying. If so, it seems strange that with so defective an education he should have been admitted to Holy Orders in the Church of England by the influence of a great noble, the Duke of Norfolk. He had a curacy at Sandhurst, then was given the living of Bobbing, Kent, but in less than a year for various ill-deeds (doubtless exaggerated by the anti-Titus pamphleteers) he was inhibited by the Archdeacon of Canterbury, and thrown out of the living by his patron. Whereupon Titus became curate to his father, Samuel Oates, who like his son after him had changed his sect with the times, and from a Baptist 'dipper' renowned for baptising his converts by total immersion at night had become a divine of the Church of England at All Saints' Rectory, Hastings.

In 1675 Titus is said to have coveted a schoolmaster's post held by William Parker, son of a Captain Parker, a man of influence in Hastings who did not like the Oates family. In furtherance of his views Titus is said to have laid information before the Mayor accusing young Parker of homosexual practices with "a young and tender man-child" in the church of All Saints. While young Parker lay in prison awaiting trial, Titus then charged the father, Captain Parker, with treasonable talk. In those days both were capital charges. Either Titus had not then perfected his system of bragging, lying, and malice, or people were less credulous in 1675 than in 1678, or, more likely, he had not yet the backing of militant Protestant politicians, for both charges were dismissed and a suit for damages brought—of course they were never paid.

Titus Oates next appears in the post of Naval Chaplain on H.M.S. *Adventurer*. This was not as astonishing a promotion for a man of Titus's record as would appear. The post of Naval Chaplain was usually sought by parsons in financial difficulties, for its one advantage was immunity (while at sea) from arrest. The Naval Chaplain was a despised person, receiving an A.B.'s pay of nineteen shillings monthly plus fourpence a month from every sailor; and Cromwell's efforts to Christianise England had not included any efforts to see that Naval Chaplains were properly chosen. Not until 1677, two years after Oates's appointment, did the Sea Lords of godless Charles place the Chaplains under the authority of the Bishop of London. Even so, the hellish conditions on British ships of that epoch must have made a Naval Chaplaincy most unattractive to any decent man. The pamphleteers assert that Oates's service was marked by his being "caught in the crime of sodomy" and that he "narrowly escaped a hanging at the yard-arm" in consequence. At any rate when H.M.S. *Adventurer* returned to England Titus certainly hurriedly left the service, 'expelled', so it is said. But though he hid in London lodgings he was arrested on a charge of perjury at the instance of the injured Parker, but contrived to escape from custody, and then found somebody to bail him. In spite of all, in 1677 we find him appointed as Chaplain to the Duke of Norfolk! In all this fantastic imbroglio the fact that Titus Oates was actually in the service of the Dukes of Norfolk is not the least astonishing. The anomaly of the greatest noble in England entertaining such a Chaplain was no doubt the result of benevolence, but clearly the Duke might in contempt confer the reluctant benefit on the worst parson he could find. He certainly nourished a viper on this occasion.

And then Titus lost even this job—why, is not known. After so many dismissals and expulsions this was a formidable difficulty, but he met it by an admirable turn of dexterity which most people would not have thought of. The future saviour of Protestant England turned Catholic, arguing no doubt that the conversion of a Church of England parson complete with cassock and bands would be gratifying to Catholics who knew nothing about him. Father Berry, who received him, was a Jesuit who had also been a Protestant, but was generally considered more or less insane. It is a charitable explanation. Titus's statement that he was immediately received into the Society of Jesus "to pass the time of my Novitiate abroad in dispatching business for the Society" is obviously untrue. But they certainly befriended him by sending him to study at the English College in Valladolid, where, of course, the standard of studies (the lectures were in Latin) was so far above his ignorance that he was bored to death. As the best liars often like to start from a basis of fact, Titus made this brief stay at Valladolid the pretext for his assertion, persisted in years later, that he had been to the University of Salamanca, which he never saw, and had been made a Doctor of Divinity, which he never was. The persistence, even in the face of the House of Lords' refusal to accept it in the days of his disgrace, is a curious fact, due perhaps to Titus's living so long in a fictitious world of his own invention that he came to believe his own lies. He was always a braggart, and even at Valladolid boasted to chance English acquaintances of his knowledge of Jesuit secrets which unquestionably were never confided to him.

Naturally, Titus was expelled from Valladolid, four months after he arrived. According to him, between that date and his return to England he travelled extensively in Europe, meeting many important persons and of course "Jesuit plotters". In this case the liar can be confuted, for there still exists the deposition of a post-boy who took him direct to Bilbao, where he remained until he sailed for England. From there he was sent to the Jesuit College at St. Omer, which was a school for boys. He was placed in Rhetoric, the highest class, not because of his knowledge but because of his age—he was getting on for thirty. Obviously he could not there claim to be a D.D. of Salamanca, so he boasted that he had been Bursar of St. John's. A report on him by Father Watten shows much penetration, for it describes Oates as "rash, indiscreet, turbulent, and vindictive, a great flatterer, boaster and liar." And once more the inevitable happened. When the English Provincial made his visitation in June 1678 he ordered the immediate expulsion of Titus Oates, who returned again penniless to London. And there, after long consultations with the fanatical anti-Jesuit, Tonge, he at last successfully (though with ups and downs) solved the problem of how to make a living, by launching on a credulous London of "rabid Protestantism and raucous patriotism" the great lie of the "Popish Plot".

For these facts about the pre-Plot life of Oates I am indebted, like everyone else, to the careful researches of Jane Lane, whose admirably documented book has virtually superseded all predecessors. While nearly all generalisations

are necessarily inaccurate, it seems fair to say that though
some of the accusations—perhaps many of them—brought
against the pre-Plot Oates are traceable to seventeenth-
century party writers, the unbroken series of dismissals is well
attested. There must have been some reason for them. If
only half of what is attested against Oates was true, the
mystery to us is how he managed to obtain any credit at all,
still more how he was able to convulse a nation, capture by
perjury and insolence the credulous belief of most of the
Lords, Commons, Clergy, Bench, Universities and Dissenters,
and cause the judicial murder of a dozen innocent men
as well as the imprisonment of scores if not hundreds of
others.

To answer that in a few paragraphs is impossible. We can
only note, first, that Oates was not the original inventor of
the 'Plot'. That was the fanatical anti-Jesuit, Dr. Israel
Tonge, who used Oates at first as a puppet advertiser, only
to have his invention stolen by a more impudent liar than
himself. How far Tonge was himself utilised and tutored by
Shaftesbury and the other Whig lords will never be known
for certain, but he and Oates must have been guided to some
extent by persons more crafty and better informed than they.
It was clever, for instance, of Tonge to take Oates to swear
his deposition before Godfrey. He was a convinced Protestant, but no fanatic, and a friend of Catholics, and therefore a far better depositary than any of the fanatical Protestant magistrates to whom Tonge and Oates on their own
would almost certainly have gone. The 'Plot' itself was a
long-winded re-vamping of former 'scares'—murder of the
King and the Duke, armed insurrections, massacre of
Protestants, re-burning of London, triumphant re-establish-
ment of "Popery and persecution" and so forth. All this
'supported' by a rigmarole of lies and false witnesses which
ought to have been detected at once, as the King detected it.
The 'Plot' was a move in the war between Monarchy and

Money fought on politico-religious lines during that uneasy truce between the Great Rebellion and the 'Glorious' (or 'Commercial') Revolution. Even so the Tonge-Oates 'Plot' would very likely have fizzed out like its predecessors, but for the hysterical condition of the public and the episodes of Godfrey and Coleman. Oates threatened a massacre of Protestants, 'revealed' (from memory) treasonable correspondence with foreign Jesuits. And lo! the known and respected Protestant magistrate, Sir Edmund Godfrey, is found murdered, after he had expressed fears that his life was in danger! Either through accident or the skill of the Plot's secret managers the first person examined was Edward Coleman, a fanatical Catholic convert, who was found with what then were considered treasonable papers, although Godfrey had warned him to destroy them.

Godfrey's murder may have been a providential (for the plotters) accident or it may have been part of the Plot, but on whose side? The Jesuits, repeatedly accused, had nothing to gain and much to lose by so spectacular a piece of violence, and Pollock's theory that Godfrey was murdered because Coleman had told him of the Jesuit 'Consult' in the Duke of York's apartments is inadequate. The murder cannot be brought home to Shaftesbury and his friends, who seem the more likely culprits. Muddiman's theory, afterwards developed and strengthened by J. D. Carr, is that Godfrey was murdered from motives of private vengeance by that homicidal maniac, Lord Pembroke, who was in fact related to Shaftesbury. The timing may have been a coincidence, or it may have been cunningly suggested to the madman.

On the perjured testimony of Oates, three innocent men were convicted and hanged for the murder of Godfrey. Oates, assisted by another perjurer, Bedloe, swore away the lives of Father Ireland, Pickering and Grove; of five Jesuits, Whitebread, Harcourt, Fenwick, Cavan and Turner, and of a well-known Catholic lawyer, Richard Langhorne. His first check came when he failed to secure the conviction of the Queen's physician, Sir George Wakeman, on a charge of conspiring with her to poison the King! Yet even after that he continued to receive money from the Government, and secured the conviction of a Catholic peer, Lord Stafford. In February 1681 when Oates's false testimony secured the conviction of a priest named Atwood, the popular frenzy had flagged enough for the King to be able to grant a reprieve. And Court writers, particularly L'Estrange and Dryden, were turned against him. The villain sank slowly, yet sank. In April 1682 he was arrested for debt, but was bailed by his "rich City friends", who also bailed him when he was arrested in a slander suit which went against him, with damages and costs. The plaintiff was only a poor parson, the Rev. Adam Elliot, but in the spring of 1684 nemesis really began to catch up with Oates, for he was arrested for slandering the Duke of York, found guilty with damages of £100,000, to be kept in prison until he paid the impossible sum. In February 1685 he was brought from prison and indicted on two charges of perjury. The sentence was as follows. On each indictment he was fined 1,000 marks. On the first, he was condemned to be stripped of his canonical robe, and to stand an hour on Monday in the pillory at Westminster Hall Gate. On the second, to be pilloried on Tuesday for one hour at the Royal Exchange, to be whipped on Wednesday from Aldgate to Newgate, and on Friday from Newgate to Tyburn. So long as he lived he was to be pilloried every year for an hour at Tyburn on April 24th, at Westminster, Charing Cross and Temple Gate on August 9th, 10th and 11th.

Much has been made of the behaviour of Scroggs and Jeffreys at these trials, including that of Oates, though, in the case of Oates, Jeffreys was unusually restrained and not anything like as unfair as he had been to many innocent people. But the really disquieting thing is that, with the change of dynasty, Oates was pardoned and released, received by William III personally, and awarded a pension of ten pounds a week "from the Secret Service". This was in September 1689. In July 1698 he received a grant of £500 to pay his debts, and a pension of £300 a year (for the lifetime of himself and the wife he had wedded, to everyone's amazement) from the post office revenues. It is said that when Queen Anne succeeded, she struck the name of Titus Oates from the pension list. The fact cannot be proved, but Miss Lane says there is no record of payments to Oates under the Queen's reign, and he died unmourned and unmissed in 1705.

We have now reached the eighteenth century, when the "glorious Constitution" was gloriously defended by the mughouse riots and pleasantly championed by the midnight pranks of the Mohocks. Even these were an improvement on the times of Hopkins and Oates, for if the Mohocks to some extent carried on the tradition by assaulting women and defenceless pedestrians under cover of night and the immunity of noble birth, the mug-house rioters were political fanatics who mostly fought each other either for the pleasure of the exercise or because it was their habitual mode of discussion. The Riot Act did little to check them, and in the end the mug-houses were declared illegal and closed down. Unfortunately, this did not abolish mob violence, which reached a new paroxysm of destruction in the 'Protestant' riots of Lord George Gordon, and still later flared up in the window-smashing of the Reform Bill partisans. Nor does it appear that there was much improvement in the general level of intelligence, at least in the early part of the eighteenth century:

"The easy credulity and superstition of the English people at this period, cherished and increased by the preaching and writings of a number of fanatical sectarians, was exhibited in many other circumstances beside their belief in quack medicines, and made them the dupes of several practical jokes, and intentional or involuntary impostures."

Such was the situation which George Psalmanazar was able to exploit with an imposture and a set of imbecile stories which you would think could scarcely have deceived a congress of the feeble-minded.

TWO

George Psalmanazar

BOGUS PRINCE OF FORMOSA

No collection of that ignoble company of frauds and impostors can omit some notice, however slight, of the nameless
impostor from the Midi who in spite of his alleged repentance
never revealed his true name, but always passed as George
Psalmanaazaar or George Psalmanazar. To the usual
ingredients of vanity, notoriety-hunting and the need for
money Psalmanazar added a strong dose of religious
hypocrisy and sectarian time-serving. The people of the
Midi are noted both for their ingenuity in devising *galéjades*
(fantastic hoaxes) and their credulity in believing those
invented by others. Yet, however credulous the Midi, it can
hardly be thought more credulous than the considerable and
in some cases learned and pious section of Queen Anne's
England which believed the wild tales of Psalmanazar the
Formosan. In defence we can plead that he would probably
never have been listened to if he had not been presented by
an alleged confederate(?), the Rev. Alexander Innes, in the
character of a high-born son of Formosa, abducted by a
wicked Jesuit, and after sundry vicissitudes of fortune and
temptations to rival sects a convinced convert to the pure and
superior doctrines of the Church of England as interpreted at
that time by the Right Reverend Father in God, by Divine
Providence, Henry Compton, Lord Bishop of London. There

was the bait that caught the silly fishes! There was the appeal to ignorant wonder—he came from the almost unknown island of Formosa; the appeal to snobbery—he was son of a king; and, above all, the appeal to sectarian conceit—he had been sought after by Jesuits, Lutherans and Calvinists, but to his noble savage mind all had seemed wrong except the Church of England.

It is, perhaps, worth noting that, like Oates in the seventeenth century, and Orton the "Tichborne claimant" in the nineteenth, Psalmanazar played on that irrational fear and hatred of the Jesuits which was so potent in creating moods of hysterical frenzy and prejudice in Protestant England.

The first part of Psalmanazar's book on Formosa is mainly theological, with a display of piety and zeal for the Church most obviously aimed at the clergy and especially at his patron the Bishop. This precedes an absurd and lying account of Formosa, which the author (after getting all he could out of the swindle in kudos and money) 'repentantly' admitted was a fraud, since he was not a Formosan as he had claimed, had never been to Formosa, nor indeed ever travelled out of Europe. But he did not make this admission or feel the prick of remorse and penitence until he had long been exposed as an impostor. Now, if the *Description of Formosa* is a pack of lies, as it unquestionably is, what guarantee is there that the religious hypocrisy which recommended it was not transferred along with the mendacity to the *Memoirs*? The *Memoirs* were not published until sixty years after the *Description* and Psalmanazar's brief career in London and Oxford as a Formosan convert, when there could have been very few living eye-witnesses to contradict him. It looks as if he thus scored a double success. After a temporary imposition on their credulity as an Oriental Mandeville he turned round and imposed himself for the rest of his life as the repentant sinner or the London literary

Tartuffe. Of course, parts of the *Memoirs* may be true, for the human mind is not inventive enough to fabricate continuously but merely embroiders. Parts even of the *Description* are taken from a genuine geographical writer, G. Candidius. How can we rely on the narrative of such a man?

The fact that Psalmanazar could not remember the year of his birth, or at any rate gave different dates, might simply be due to forgetfulness or the fact that he was early separated from his family. But why was it necessary to conceal his real name, long after his parents were dead, as well as the place and even the province in which he was born and brought up? We have a statement at second-hand that a certain "Rev. Mr. Vilette", who was long a friend of Psalmanazar, says he spoke French with a slight accent of Gascony and that his knowledge of the "dialect of Languedoc" suggested he must have come from that province. Gascony is not Languedoc, and in any case, as no Englishman at that time knew anything about the *langue d'oc* and its dialects, a confusion between the language and the province might easily have occurred. Psalmanazar's record and character suggest that the vicinity of Marseille is at least a possibility, especially as the first town he names is Avignon, and not Montpellier, which would be the obvious centre for a student born in Languedoc.

We can probably accept as true his statement that his parents were poor, that his father had left his mother, that he was brought up in poverty, and that his education was ecclesiastical and inconsecutive. The date of his birth is somewhere between 1679 and 1684. He says he studied with Franciscans, Jesuits and Dominicans. He must have known Latin, since the *Description* was written by him in Latin and translated into English, and his fake Formosan alphabet seems to indicate some knowledge of Greek and Hebrew. His 'Kaphi' is only one place from where kappa would come, and his 'Xatara' falls in the place of 'xi', while the "Formosan writing" seems vaguely imitated from Hebrew. He certainly studied Hebrew in England after his 'repentance', found work as a translator and contributed extensively to the *Universal History*. He spoke seven European languages. This suggests that his education may not really have been as defective as he asserted, and it is always possible that his refusal to tell his real name may mean that it was of a known family.

He says that he went from the Dominican school of theology in a university to Avignon, and found employment in the neighbourhood as a boys' tutor, but had to leave because of his virtuous repulse of their mother's advances. Finding himself destitute he set out on a life of wandering vagabondage with various adventures which may or may not be true. He says that he secured a passport as an Irish pilgrim, managed to beg his way back to his mother, and was advised by her to go to his father, who was living in Germany. Undoubtedly he did make his way north, having changed himself by then from an Irish pilgrim to a Japanese. He was conscripted for one army, rejected as a heathen; joined another and was discharged; and finally got into a regiment of Germans in the Dutch service under the name 'Salmanazar'. If this is true, then he had already transformed himself into an Oriental,; and he claims that he pretended to worship the sun and moon, and that he argued successfully with the Lutheran soldiers on theological topics.

Towards the end of 1702 his regiment was moved to Sluys, and we now get on rather firmer ground. If we may believe him, by this time he had developed his Japanese impersonation into the inevitable 'hoax' on his comrades, and for the sake of the notoriety he made up a book of gibberish in the invented writing which was afterwards palmed off as Formosan but at this time as Japanese. His antics became known to the Scottish governor, General Lauder, who

examined him in the presence of several other officers and
two clergymen, one of whom was the General's kinsman, the
Rev. Alexander Innes. If what we are told of Innes is true
he must have been as big a rogue as Psalmanazar and a good
deal cleverer, though it is very hard to see how, if he did all
the shady things Psalmanazar says he did, Innes escaped his
Bishop's disciplinary action, lax as that may have been in the
days of good Queen Anne.

Anyway, the tale is that Innes was the only one present at
this gathering with sense enough to guess that Psalmanazar
must be an impostor. He detected him by very simple means.
Having invited the 'Japanese' to a private interview, Innes
asked him to translate a passage of Cicero (imagine an
eighteenth-century Japanese knowing Cicero!) into his
native language. Innes took the version from him, and told
him to write it out again. Then was seen the cogency of the
old saying that a liar needs a very good memory, for Psalmanazar was quite unable to remember the extempore
gibberish he had scribbled down at random, and had to
confess his imposture. According to the *Memoirs* this Cicero
test and exposure were used by Innes to force Psalmanazar
to do what Innes had been urging him to do for some time,
namely, to allow himself to be baptised as a convert to the
Church of England. Innes, says Psalmanazar, had already
written to the Bishop of London about him as a Formosan, or
did so later. At all events, the change to Formosa from
Japan was supposed to be Innes's idea because he realised
that something was known in England of Japan but practically nothing of Formosa. His idea in planning this conversion was simply to advance his own career in the Church.
Psalmanazar says Innes suggested to the Bishop that, when
converted and baptised, Psalmanazar should be sent to
Oxford to instruct some of the clergy in 'Formosan', whereupon they would all set out and convert the inhabitants of
Formosa to the doctrines of the Church of England. It is

certain that Psalmanazar (who really was a Catholic of the Midi) submitted to baptism by a heretic with General Lauder as his godfather.

It would be very interesting to know if by any chance the archives of the see of London have preserved these letters from Innes to Bishop Compton. The story as we have it comes solely from Psalmanazar. Of course, if you believe that his later repentance was sincere and that after being a shameless liar for years he suddenly became entirely reliable and truthful, there is nothing more to be said. But if you suspect, as anyone reasonably may, that the unctuous hypocrisy and religious acting of the *Description* may have passed into the *Memoirs*, then it is reasonable to ask how much of all this plausible tale is true. All the moral guilt is thrown on Innes, whose motive is presented as a base kind of simony—he forced Psalmanazar to simulate a conversion to Christianity (knowing he already was a Christian) and into making his living out of an imposture which hitherto had been harmless, simply for the advancement of Innes in the Church on the strength of this valuable acquisition of a ragged recruit in the Dutch Army who said he was an Oriental. We are told that Innes later published as his own work a book which had been lent him in manuscript by its author and that he was forced to retract. This, if true, is a point against him, though literary property hardly existed in those days and nobody thought much of stealing it whenever feasible; but might not the publisher be to blame for a mistake? Is it certain that the Church preferment Innes received was due to the 'conversion' of Psalmanazar? Is it not possible that Innes may have been taken in, like his betters, and that the change from Japan to Formosa was staged by Psalmanazar himself when he realised that if he went to England he would meet people who knew something of Japan? It would explain why he made the absurd statement that Formosa belonged to Japan when in fact it was then held by the Chinese. The Cicero story sounds convincing, and if that is true then of course Innes did know Psalmanazar was an impostor, and himself became an accomplice of an ignominious kind. Those who suspect that the saintly old Psalmanazar of popular legend may have been a saintly old humbug will keep an open mind and feel that without additional and objective proof Innes may just as well have been a dupe as his Lordship of London. When the *Memoirs* were published Innes was dead.

At all events it can hardly have been the suggestion of Innes that when they proceeded to Rotterdam on their way to London he should convince doubters he was a Formosan by the unanswerable demonstration of his nationality in living on "raw flesh, roots and herbs", which he contrived to choke down with the aid of plenty of spices and pepper. This was only one of the absurdities and monstrosities Psalmanazar foisted on his Formosans, which Innes must have seen would weaken Psalmanazar's case. If they were accomplices why did Innes not warn him against such blunders? With the result of the Cicero test in his possession Innes could have exposed the charlatan at any moment, and therefore had him in his power. Moreover, Innes's conduct when they reached England seems often more explicable as that of a dupe than of an accomplice. And if Innes really did make the suggestion that his convert should be sent to Oxford "to teach the gentlemen Formosan" then it was surely a very unlikely and silly suggestion on the part of a supposedly wily and scheming confederate. Oxford was the one place in England where a fraudulent language was most likely to be detected. On the other hand, if Innes really was an accomplice then he was a careless and stupid one who ought to have been found out, which makes his subsequent preferment in the Church all the more remarkable.

Soon after they reached London, the pair had an audience of the Bishop of London. Presumably the conversation

between Psalmanazar and the Bishop was conducted in
Latin, but the actual conduct of the talk must have been
entirely in the control of Innes, for we learn that when later
the impostor was received by the Archbishop of Canterbury
their pronunciations of Latin were so different that Innes
had to interpret!

Presumably what the Bishop and Archbishop were told
about the 'Formosan' did not substantially differ from what
was published soon after in the *Description*. The change from
'Japanese' to 'Formosan' is said to have been suggested by
Innes, but Psalmanazar may just as well have been lying
about that as all the rest. His was the inventive mind, and he
may quite well have made himself a Formosan and have
transferred Formosa to "the Japanese Empire" when he
found that General Lauder and his staff knew more about
Japan than was desirable for his purpose. In any case such a
change was prudent in Holland, for however closely the
Dutch 'factory' in the island off Nagasaki was restricted, some
knowledge of Japan as well as Japanese goods must have
come through.

Naturally the tale of Psalmanazar the Formosan differs
entirely in its beginnings from the tale of Psalmanazar the
child of the Midi as published sixty years later. From the
first paragraph of his book Psalmanazar plays up to the
Protestant dread of the Jesuits. According to him Jesuit
missionaries were trained in Oriental languages, particularly
Japanese, at Goa, until they were able to pass themselves as
native Japanese—a manifest impossibility. These pseudo-
Japanese Jesuits were alleged to act as tutors to the sons of
wealthy men or princes in Japan and Formosa for a period of
four years; but as they had to conceal their religion and could
make no converts, there seems no particular point in this
perilous exile. A "certain Jesuit of Avignon, whose true
name was Father de Rode" (no such person was known to
other Jesuits) came to Formosa about 1694, and was

eventually employed by Psalmanazar's father as Latin tutor. The boy was to "give over the learning of the Greek Tongue"(!) and concentrate on Latin. At the end of four years this singular Jesuit persuaded his charge to steal money from his father, and to run away in order to see the world in this distinguished company. From Formosa they got away to the Philippines in a boat belonging to the fugitive's father, and thence to Goa, where they remained six weeks "very civilly and nobly treated". Thence after a long sea voyage they came to Gibraltar, and eventually to Avignon by way of Toulon, Marseille and Aix-en-Provence.

Naturally also, having got his Formosan to Avignon, Psalmanazar starts to prepare the way for a gradual mingling with his other self, and to invent some explanation to account for a penniless recruit being really the son of a Formosan noble or king, who had fled with a large sum of gold. It is perhaps worth noting that this dejected scion of Formosan royalty did not then demand, as a 'Japanese' subject, to be restored to his country, his bereaved family and his ancestral wealth. (In much the same way the "Tichborne Claimant" suffered poverty and menial occupations in Australia, quite forgetting he had an income of £1,000 a year in England!) The wicked Jesuits, of course, supply the necessary bridge between the two Psalmanazars. Father de Rode "confess'd ingeniously" that he was a native of Avignon and invited the Formosan to become a convert, at the same time giving out publicly that he was "the Son of a King". Since the account was aimed at Protestant England, the reader will hardly be surprised to learn that the noble savage easily refuted all the theological arguments of the Fathers, and was particularly destructive to the Doctrine of Transubstantiation, discovering on his own and without any help all the arguments against it urged by Protestant divines!

The Formosan stayed at the monastery for six months, and then, leaving the Jesuits "a great part" of his money, he

rambled about the South of France for another six months.
But some three months later, as he still triumphantly refuted
their arguments, he was told that he would be put into the
Inquisition unless he "would embrace the Christian
Religion". After a good deal of suspense, he manages of
course to escape from Avignon by bribing a sentry, and for
no particular reason the Formosan Psalmanazar follows the
track north of the French Psalmanazar, and like him is
conscripted for a German regiment. Here again he enters
into controversy with Jesuits, and even proves to them that
the religion of the Formosans is superior to theirs, and that in
fact "there were greater Absurdities in their Religion than
they could show in mine"—a statement which would not
displease the hearty zealots of Geneva and Canterbury.

It is scarcely necessary to add that the Formosan eventually
gets to Holland, meets Lauder and "my learned and
judicious guide, Mr. Innes," at which point the fusion
between the Formosan of the *Description* and the Provençal or
Occitanien of the *Memoirs* was complete.

Within a few weeks of his arrival in London, Psalmanazar
had become the most publicised novelty of the day, and
everyone wanted to meet him. He claims that he met Sir
Hans Sloane, Lord Pembroke, the Minister for Prussia, Dr.
Mead, a fashionable doctor of the time, Bishop Burnet and
numbers of the clergy. There were of course sceptics from the
beginning, particularly because of his white skin, which he
tried to explain away by saying that in Formosa the upper
classes always kept out of the sun in "cool shades or apartments underground". In view of his high ecclesiastical
patrons, Psalmanazar naturally found most support among
the clergy, particularly of the Tory High Church section,
whose views were closer to those in which he had been
brought up than those of the Whigs such as Burnet. His
greatest danger came from a Jesuit missionary named Father
Fountenoy who was in London after spending eighteen years

in China. He must have known that Formosa then belonged to China, and in fact said so in one of his conferences with Psalmanazar, adding correctly that it was called Taiwan— spelled as Tyowan by the 'Formosan' in the preface where he attempts to refute and sneer at the Jesuit. Father Fountenoy was something of an ironist, for when at a second conference the Prussian Minister asked who owned Formosa, the priest waved a hand towards Psalmanazar and said: "Here is a young man who is a native of the country, he can better inform you than I, who have only been in China!" Psalmanazar records this stinging irony as an admission of his claim! At a third encounter the missionary contented himself with saying that he had never heard of Father Rode of Avignon. Apparently Father Fountenoy was less restrained in other company, for in this preface Psalmanazar complains that "I am well informed he takes a great deal of freedom in aspersing me," as well he might, while Psalmanazar has the effrontery to say (in Latin) that the Jesuit "lied most impudently". Yet on the very same page he prints the impudent lie that he was "a raw and unpolish'd Japanese" while asserting with an effrontery it is hard to exaggerate that it is "much more becoming a man of probity to speak openly, and face to face, than thus clandestinely to backbite and calumniate"! He rounds this off on the next page with a staggering piece of hypocrisy in which he regrets having to publish his arguments against "those religions which I could not conform to" and winds up by thanking God he is not as other men are inasmuch as he has joined "that Christian communion which is most conformable to the institutions of our Saviour."

Some weeks after his arrival at London he made a further bid for the support of the clergy by putting out an alleged Formosan translation of the catechism. As a specimen of this ridiculous jargon I give what is supposed to be the opening phrases of the Lord's Prayer:

"Amy Pornio dan chin Ornio viey, Gnayjorhe sai Lory, Eyfodere sai Bagalin, Jorhe sai domion apo chin Ornio, kay chin Badi eyen . . ."

This is supposed to take us down to ". . . on earth as it is in Heaven". Whether this gibberish was the cause of Psalmanazar's being sent to Oxford to teach the gentlemen Formosan, or whether it was simply a reminder to Dr. Compton of a previous promise to that effect, is impossible to say; but it is certainly true that he did go to Oxford and that the Bishop paid for him for a period of six months, during which he resided at Christ Church. Part of his time was spent in drafting out the Latin version of the *Description*, and there is a tradition that he left behind a treatise on Roman coins. But of course the impostor could not be at peace even in that academic quietude, but must needs cultivate the amazement and admiration of his bedmaker by pretending to sit up all night for a week, hard at work at his studies. He left a candle burning all night and slept in his easy-chair, taking care of course to be at his work-table when the servant arrived in the morning and observed with awe that once again the bed had not been touched all night.

Years after Psalmanazar's death there was published what purported to be some contemporary notes on Psalmanazar at Oxford. They may be authentic, and if so they show he was as eager to *épater* the ladies and gentlemen of Oxford as the guileless bedmaker. Some of these tales might have been taken from the *Description*, but there is an improvement here on the laws against adultery recorded in that veracious narrative. When Formosan husbands grow tired of their wives (he told a horrified Oxford lady) they have merely to accuse them of adultery, and may then cut off their heads and eat them. He admitted that to accuse a wife wrongly was deplorable, but as to the cannibalism he would only go so far as to say that he would "own it is a little unmannerly"! He talked of a grandfather who lived to be 117 by sucking the blood of snakes, and regretted that English snakes could not be made such loving pets as those of Formosa. Possibly to keep up the myth of teaching the Oxford gentlemen Formosan so that they could go out as missionaries, Psalmanazar now declared that he would return home and convert his father!

If these Oxford notes are genuinely contemporary (i.e. 1704) then we must admit that Oxford society seems to have been even more credulous than that of London. True, the ladies objected to the ferocious methods of 'Formosan' divorce, but appear to have been silenced by Psalmanazar's equally absurd evasions. It may have been at Oxford that he first had to defend what he later admitted was one of the most preposterous of his blunders, namely his assertion that the Formosan religion called for the annual sacrifice of 18,000 males of nine years old or less. He tells us that no matter what absurd statement he happened to make in the course of conversation, he made a rule always to stick to it and to justify it. No doubt this is an essential rule for all charlatans, though in Psalmanazar's case the justification seems usually as absurd as the statement. When it was objected that such a fearfully high annual consumption of infant males would lead inevitably to depopulation, he stoutly denied it, because the 'Formosans' practised polygamy. A man might have as many wives as he could support —a poor man two or even three, a rich man ten or a dozen. The idea was doubtless suggested to him by those sinister passages in the Bible hinting at the sacrifice of children to Moloch in Judæa, while the Romans accused the Carthaginians of similar practices. But these Semitic atrocities were rare and limited, and Psalmanazar's main literary source must have been the Elder Pliny. Apparently nobody asked, and Psalmanazar certainly does not try to explain, why the parents of Formosa did not rise in furious revolt against so wholesale and murderous an outrage. But why

discuss such idiotic statements, except indeed to wonder that
people in their senses could have listened to such nonsense
without kicking the fellow out of the house? But there—how
often must it be said that the English dearly love a fraud?

In March 1704 a British fleet sailed for Portugal carrying
an expeditionary force to the War of the Spanish Succession,
and, according to the *Memoirs*, Innes went with them as
Chaplain-General to the Forces, which post (Psalmanazar
asserts) was the reward for his conversion of the 'Formosan'.
Psalmanazar goes on to state that this was a blow to him
because he needed the help of his confederate, for whom
however he had no esteem, since Innes was a drunkard and
had been mixed up in scandalous affairs with women to
such an extent that he had been turned out of one set of
lodgings and was threatened with dismissal from another.
Now, here we meet once more with the questionable statements of the repentant *Memoirs* which are in some ways as
suspicious as the self-confessed lies of the *Description*. In the
modern British Army a Chaplain-General ranks as a Major-
General and of course holds a commission, though whether
this was the case in the days of Queen Anne I don't know.
But surely it stands to reason that if Innes had been half as
notorious for unclerical behaviour as Psalmanazar pretends
he would never have been appointed to so dignified and
important a post either by his Bishop or the Secretary of
State. The outcry of the godly and of disappointed candidates would have been terrific, and even if the appointment had been made by some accident it would necessarily
have been cancelled. And why was it so important for
Psalmanazar to have Innes always by him as a prompting
confederate and accomplice? He had just completed six
months as a wholly successful impostor at Oxford, without
any help from Innes, and apparently without being in touch
with him, if Innes was spending his life in open debaucheries
and his appointment came as a surprise to the 'Formosan'.

And these accusations seem all the more suspicious since, with his usual smug hypocrisy, Psalmanazar goes on to compare Innes's behaviour very unfavourably with his own, though he admits vaingloriously that he was a favourite with the women. Failing some objective proof that Innes was the scoundrel, humbug and debauchee Psalmanazar makes him out to be, we ought at least to keep an open mind. The loss caused by his absence from England may not have been his guidance as an accomplice, but his support as one of the clerical dupes.

The downfall of Psalmanazar the Formosan may possibly date from the departure of Innes, but as he managed to keep up some sort of fight for his imposture until 1711—seven years later—the loss cannot have been so fatal. The real reason for the exposure is that educated men had the chance to study his statements more closely than when they were made in conversation or in lectures, through the *Description*, which was first published just before he went to Oxford, while a second and 'improved' edition came out in June 1705. He received only £22 as payment for both editions. It was poor compensation indeed for a collection of lies which made him ridiculous and dishonourable. And what is to be thought and said of a man who in a book which he knew and subsequently confessed was a mass of lies has the effrontery to say: " 'Tis certain that God will not exert his Almighty Power to confirm a Lye, and justifie an Imposture"? The High Church parsons who bought the book, partly for its pious sentiments and arguments in favour of their sect, would surely have been outraged and angered if they had realised the religion was all humbug to help pass off the Formosan fraud on which Psalmanazar lived for several years. Even later writers who were perfectly well aware that Psalmanazar was a fraud seem to have been taken in by this mock piety to the extent of condoning the *Description* as an amusing production which harmed nobody but its author,

while others have gone so far as to praise it as one of the best
if not the best book of imaginary travels ever written! They
cannot have paid much attention to Cyrano de Bergerac and
Swift, though of course the latter must have known Psalmanazar's book.

One cannot help feeling that, since he was giving himself
carte blanche in the matter of lies, he might have invented something either more amusing or more satirical or more graceful
that the poor absurdities he turned out. On the whole his
account of 'Formosa' is the product of a rather ignorant,
silly and ill-bred fellow whose ideas of what was interesting
and instructive dwelt on cannibalism, hecatombs of murdered
children, eating raw meat, a woman smoking six ounces of
tobacco a day, the manifestation of the Formosan 'God' as a
lion, a bear or some other living animal, and the gibberish of
which I have quoted a few sentences. It is depressing to think
that our forefathers were taken in by such rubbish. But all
along he was cunning enough to slip in supposed traits of
'Formosan' morals which would meet with the approval of
pious chumps after they had been thrilled by atrocious
yarns of sacrifice. Thus we are informed that:

". . . the manners of the Formosans are not so Corrupt as
the People are in other Places; and the reason is because they
are strictly oblig'd to observe the Laws of their Policy and
Religion under severe Penalties, with which the Laws are
enforc'd against the Commission of any Villainy or Impiety,
so that none dare to violate them . . ."

This was comfortable and acceptable doctrine for non-
juring clergymen and high-flying Tories, and one can
imagine an approving underlining by the clergy, especially
of the admirable statement that "they Salute an High-
Priest as they do a King" while "Superiors do not Salute an
Inferior, but by a nod of their Head they signify that they
have seen him Saluting them." Though it is an obvious
anachronism, this last sentence calls up a vision of Trollope's

Mrs. Proudie—one can visualise her practising that "nod of
the Head" to an inferior the moment she heard her husband
had a mitre. In the 1700s it might have been thought a little
strait-laced that "no Conversation is allow'd between any
Man and another Man's Wife, nor between a Batchelor and a
Maid". That these ceremonious moralists were also poly-
gamists, cannibals, eaters of raw fowls, epicures in the
enjoyment of broiled snakes and murderers of their own
children apparently evoked no sense of absurdity, and years
elapsed before the impostor had to acknowledge defeat. It is
said that Halley tried to catch him out by asking him to say
how many days the sun shone down the chimneys in Formosa, which Psalmanazar evaded (so he says) by answering
that the chimneys were pipes with an angle in them and a
turn-up at the end so that the sun could never shine down
them.

While still trying to keep up the Formosan fraud Psalmanazar published a dialogue "between a Japonese and a
Formosan", and of course on the religious topics he had
found went down so well. He also made a bold attempt to
answer some of the many criticisms made of him in a
pamphlet which contained a letter, almost certainly forged by
Psalmanazar, purporting to show that a 'Chinese' had been
brought to the Jesuits at Avignon and turned out later to be a
"Japponese from Formosa".

Psalmanazar's final discomfiture as a Formosan is said to
date from a satirical note on him published in the *Spectator* for
March 16th, 1711. He then states that for over ten years he
lived a life of "the most shameful idleness, vanity and
extravagance". How he could have been 'extravagant' when
he was driven to all sorts of shifts for a livelihood is hard to
imagine, but of course the subsequent 'repentance' of this
vagabond Tartuffe looked all the more dramatic if it was
supposed to follow on a long period of conventional wickedness. He tried to pretend that he was rather a dog with the

women. In fact, he and another man tried to put on the market a white paint under the name of "The White Formosan Work", but this failed. He also says he gave lessons in modern languages he knew very slightly, and at one time set up as a quack doctor. (He ought to have succeeded there, if he didn't try to make his patients sacrifice their children and eat raw venison.) He got through a couple of years by teaching Latin, but was glad to serve as clerk to a cavalry major during the Jacobite rebellion of 1715. As late as 1717 he found a guileless clergyman who still believed in the Formosa story, and raised a fund for Psalmanazar to study theology! This, if true, is an amazing example of credulity, but unluckily all this comes from the *Memoirs*, which in its own way is probably as much a pack of lies as the *Description* and even more hypocritical.

His next efforts to earn a living landed him in Grub Street, where he seems to have remained for the rest of his life, turning out translations and anonymous books, including the contributions to the *Universal History* already mentioned. He became a laudanum addict, but derived much ghostly comfort and edification from various works of piety such as somebody's *Reformed Devotions* and Law's *Serious Call*, a famous work in its day. (Law, by the way, was the spiritual guide of one of Gibbon's aunts, and died in her house.) But in spite of his repentance and the saintly life he was supposed to be living, Psalmanazar did not make a public admission of his imposture until 1747, forty-four years after he had started it, and then only anonymously and in the third person.

According to Smollett, the last years of Psalmanazar were very penurious, as he lived meagrely on what was really the charity of the booksellers. Yet he enjoyed apparently a reputation for sanctity, and Dr. Johnson made the astounding statement that Psalmanazar's "piety, penitence and virtue exceeded almost all what we read as wonderful even in the lives of the saints", and on another occasion asserted that he would no more have contradicted Psalmanazar than he would have contradicted a bishop! Some critics have even thought that Johnson helped him with the *Memoirs*. He had strange notions of what qualifies a man to be considered a saint or even an honorary bishop. On the face of it one would hardly apply either flattery to a man who on his own showing had been a most impudent impostor and liar, profiting by his false reputation in every way he could, and making no public acknowledgement of his deception for over forty years, until, in fact, the imposture had long ceased to pay the smallest dividends. Moreover, at the time Johnson cultivated his company with such reverence Psalmanazar was a Tartuffe playing the part of the contrite sinner. He was a drug-addict, whose intake of laudanum at one period was as high as seven to eight fluid ounces a day, though he says he eventually reduced it to as many drops—which may or may not be true. Laudanum does not kill off its victims early (witness Coleridge and De Quincey), but like other drugs makes them inert, neglectful of responsibilities, and above all most unreliable in matters of fact and truth. Of course, the action of such habit-forming drugs as laudanum was not understood in Johnson's day, and he may well have mistaken for 'virtue' the fact that Psalmanazar had ceased to have any active vices out of sheer inertia. Moreover, Johnson was a man of violent prejudices, which in controversies often, indeed usually, put him on the wrong side. Politics and theology picked up from the High Church, with the addition of pious expressions and practices remembered from the monks and Jesuits of Psalmanazar's youth, might easily have deceived a man who was more learned than intelligent. It is typical of the English love of frauds that the literary dictator who insulted Dr. Percy at table and raved against Macpherson and Voltaire should have picked out Psalmanazar as a saint.

In his will Psalmanazar desired that he should be buried "in some obscure corner" of the graveyard and "without any further ceremony or formality" in the "lowest and cheapest manner possible". As he knew he was practically insolvent, that was making a virtue of necessity with a vengeance. In the same will he deplores his "base and shameful imposture" in the matter of Formosa, "all or most of it hatched in my own brain, without regard to truth or honesty." But as this had been proved long before, there was not very much merit in a posthumous acknowledgement. He goes on to say that he has left a manuscript—the *Memoirs*—which explains while deploring that "scandalous imposition on the public". The question is how far this explanation or apology is to be credited, coming as it does from a man who admitted he was a fraud, especially when he tries to exculpate himself at the expense of his one-time friend and benefactor, Innes. Probably it is far too late now ever to discover the facts, but it might be worth the while of some curious researcher to try to discover from old records whether Innes really was the scoundrel Psalmanazar says he was. If so, it must be a rare occurrence in the long history of the Church of England for a clergyman to receive benefices, the honours of a D.D. and appointment as Chaplain-General to an expeditionary force for having foisted an impudent impostor on the public while himself being a notorious scandal as a person of drunken and debauched habits for which he was kicked out of his lodgings. That is surely hard to believe even of the golden days of good Queen Anne.

Obviously Psalmanazar's real name can never be known. But as the author of a serious of preposterous but successful *galéjades* at the expense of the credulous British public, it ought surely to have been Marius, *Marius de Marseille à votre service!*

THREE

Thomas Griffiths Wainewright

FORGER AND POISONER

Until 1938 when Mr. Jonathan Curling published his *Janus Weathercock*—by far the best book on Wainewright ever written or likely to be written—no portrait of Wainewright was known to the public. There were written descriptions, but they were so vague and contradictory that nothing very much could be visualised, except that Wainewright wore a moustache and looked younger than he really was. Then Mr. Curling found and published a self-portrait in pencil which had belonged to Dr. R. K. Nuttall, who had known Wainewright during his convict life in what was then Van Diemen's Land, seeing the artist-criminal every day for a period of four years.

Now, it is notoriously unsafe to found any judgment or even impression of a man's character and temperament on a mere portrait. Such impressions are apt to be no more than a projection of one's prejudices, so that the same portrait may for one person look like a hero and for another be simply the likeness of a charlatan. Moreover, in this case we have to be especially cautious. Wainewright, who had that craving for notoriety of any kind so long as it is notoriety which goes so often with gifted failures, cultivated a kind of spurious Byronism, especially after his downfall, trying to shock respectable visitors with the cynical wickedness they seemed to expect from him. As the reproductions of his drawings and paintings show, he had some skill as an artist; and it was quite possible for him to produce a recognisable portrait of himself and yet give it the evil expression of a suburban Cesare Borgia.

Very possibly that is the explanation of the sketch, especially since Wainewright has written underneath it: "Head of a *Convict*, very characteristic of *low cunning* & *revenge!*" This is meant as heavy irony, perhaps; but may have been intended to back up, however clumsily, the impression intended by the portrait. At all events, when I first came upon it I looked with interest on this portrait of a man whom I had read about in Wilde's sketch when I was a boy, and had heard discussed from time to time all my life. Though the face as sketched is certainly not ugly, the effect it had was to create a feeling of instinctive repulsion, as if one were looking straight into the glassy eyes of a poisonous snake. Very likely that is exactly the impression he wanted to create; but it is interesting to learn that one of the persons who knew him in Australia says that he "looked like a snake"! The coincidence is surely worth noting.

If the words scribbled by Wainewright under his self-portrait were really intended ironically, they are not very convincing. It is true that he was never even indicted for his murders, but it was surely not very 'high' cunning which caused him to leave such obvious evidence of his forgeries, and then to fall so stupidly into the clutches of the Bow Street runner? And the implication that he was not actuated by any feeling of revenge in Australia is contradicted by a story of his malignant conduct towards a dying convict whom for some reason he hated (a story which comes from Dr. Nuttall) and the fact that the main motive for his application for a ticket-of-leave was that he hoped to return to England and murder his cousin, Edward Foss, whose evidence at the trial had convicted him. Of course Foss may have given his evidence vindictively, but it is now too late to clear up that point. But whether he was or was not vindictive, he could not help giving the evidence which convicted his cousin. After all, he was a trustee; Wainewright had forged his cousin's signature to get money; Foss must have been forced under subpœna to give evidence. Was Wainewright's egotism so insane that he expected his cousin to commit perjury for his sake? And quite uselessly, since the truth must have come out? Yet there exists a letter written from Australia soon after Wainewright's death, which says:

"He certainly was a wonderful man, full of talent and fuller still of wickedness. The last time I saw him he said all he wished to live for was to go home and murder the person who had transported him—of course I affected to think he was jesting, but I am quite sure he was in earnest."

Of course, as we all know, highly respectable women whose husbands have official posts are apt to be sensational and censorious in their judgments on the conduct and motives of the unfortunate and condemned. Who can say? But looking at that snake-like face one can hardly think that such a pilgrimage of disgrace was improbable for Waine-wright. His egotism knew no limits, and when it was involved he knew no limits of pity, of human decency or of self-control. How right he was when he gave himself the literary pseudonym of "Egomet Bonmot", except of course that 'Malfait' would have been a more accurate surname than an unearned 'Bonmot'. Was it really so witty to pretend that he had poisoned Helen Abercromby because her ankles were so thick, when in fact Wainewright and his wife murdered their relative for the ignoble purpose of trying to collect the insurance policies they had taken out on Helen's life— so obviously and stupidly faked that the marvel to this day is why they were not both hanged for murder.

When, during these literary metamorphoses, Wainewright

E

changed his pseudonym of "Egomet Bonmot" temporarily
for "Janus Weathercock" he chose a symbolical nickname
which could not be bettered. Whether intentionally or not, it
explained him as 'Egomet' did not. After all, most men are
egotists. But "Janus Weathercock"! There could not be a
more felicitous symbolism of that split personality and its
continually changing aims. There is unfortunately no symbolism to express the fact that he tried to excuse his un-
willingness to do any real work on the ground that he was "a
gentleman".

Wainewright's most distinguished relative was his maternal
grandfather, Ralph Griffiths, a bookseller, who lived from
1720 to 1803. It is said that he gave Cleland twenty guineas
for *Fanny Hill*, and made ten thousand pounds out of it,
though what evidence there is for this story I cannot discover. If true, it would go to show that he had the makings
of a splendid publisher. He also founded *The Monthly
Review*, but eventually had to sell a fourth share to one B.
Collins, who before long got control of the journal. However,
Griffiths continued as editor, and was able to buy the property back in 1780. His greatest pride was a suburban
mansion called Linden House, at Turnham Green, near
London. His second daughter, Ann, married Thomas
Wainewright, the son of a Gray's Inn solicitor; and "Janus
Weathercock" was their child. She died on October 11th,
1794, in giving birth to her son; the father died a few years
later; and the grandfather when T. G. Wainewright was ten.
The boy was then brought up by his grandmother and his
uncle, George Edward Griffiths. Under his grandfather's
will he inherited an annuity of £250 a year secured on
£5,000 Navy Five Per Cents, in the keeping of trustees—
whose names Wainewright eventually forged to get possession
of the capital.

At the age of nineteen Wainewright was taken as a pupil by
Thomas Phillips, a portrait-painter, and as the grandson of the

editor of *The Monthly Review* had already made the acquaintance of many literary characters of the time. It is even
rumoured that as an art student he was allowed to paint a
portrait of Lord Byron; but where is it? Much more to be
noted is the fact, which he himself put on record much later,
that he was of "a giddy, flighty disposition", suddenly
abandoned painting, and in April 1814 bought a commission as Ensign in the 16th Foot. He sold out during the
Hundred Days and was not with the regiment when it was
ordered to France in August 1815. Wainewright returned
to London, and became an æsthete, a gentleman about town,
and a distinguished amateur. Moreover, after his experiences as an artist and a soldier, he now had two or three
years as a writer, under the name of Van Vinkbooms, as well
as the two already quoted, in the *The London Magazine*. It is
perhaps worth noting that Van Vinkbooms published an
interview with Janus Weathercock. Between January 1820
and January 1823 he had twenty-three articles published.

Wainewright's connection with the writers of these two
reviews naturally lead to the suspicion that at such an early
age the knowledge of books, particularly new books, and of
the newest fashionable art fads, was in him largely a matter of
"reviewer's culture"—i.e. knowledge and enthusiams picked
up *ad hoc* according to what was being boosted at the time.
With a person so "giddy and flighty" as Wainewright this
was very likely the case, since he would hardly have had the
qualities needed to work such things out for himself. But
without going to the extremes of Oscar Wilde, who identified
himself as a sympathetic æsthete with the better side of
Wainewright, one cannot help thinking that some of the
enthusiasm was genuine. He even edited an edition of the
Hero and Leander by Marlowe and Chapman, which I have
not seen, though I certainly agree with Wainewright in
thinking that Lamb did not sufficiently praise Marlowe.
What is rather staggering, considering from whom it comes,

is Wainewright's assertion (quoted by Mr. Curling) that he was disgusted by "the unrestrained prostitution of the person which seems considered so venial by Percy B. Shelley and Co." Against that let us put the fact that in the early 1820s he had the wit to write that Turner was "the only man of real genius in landscape now existing". If only Ruskin had never existed, this truth would be far more generally accepted. Put a first-rate Turner among the French Impressionists (as I have seen myself in Paris) and he makes them all look amateurs, even Manet. Moreover, Wainewright admired Blake, and bought two of his books. And Gilchrist has (quite independently) given us a glimpse of Blake at the Royal Academy saying that a skied picture of Wainewright's was "very fine". This was a large picture illustrating 'The Milk-maid's Son' in Walton's *Compleat Angler*. What has happened to it?

I do not find—but I have not looked very hard—that Wainewright's painter friends left any remarks on him. On the other hand, the writers have made up for them. Mr. Justice Talfourd was more successful as a lawyer than as an author, and his remarks on Wainewright are severe:

"His tastes appreciated only the most superficial beauty; his vanities were the poorest and most empty; yet he fancied himself akin to greatness."

And again:

". . . flaunting vivacity . . . luxuriated in artistic im-pertinence . . . terrible deeds have since invested with frightful interest his true name of Wainewright."

These virtuous judgments on Wainewright after the sentence of transportation are natural enough, and no doubt perfectly just, but it is more interesting to find those which were recorded *before* people knew what he really was. Very possibly they may be as much biased in his favour as the later pronouncements and recollections seem biased against him. The best-known person who has left contemporary testimony in Wainewright's favour is of course Charles Lamb, with whom Wainewright dined, and who was a fellow-contributor to *The London Magazine*, in which Wainewright flattered both him and his sister. Unfortunately Lamb is not so good a witness as he might be, either to Wainewright as a person or as a writer. In the last century it was the fashion to over-praise Lamb, and he has remained the divinity of literary journalists; but his own writings of the Elia kind contain mannerisms if not downright affectations, while he was of a temperament so convivial that he can hardly have been in a position for cool judgment on a man whose obvious interest was to flatter him, since Lamb had considerable influence with *The London Magazine* people.

Still, there is no reason to doubt the esteem on both sides. Lamb liked out-of-the-way people; and he and Wainewright certainly had common ground for sympathy in their taste for painting, engravings and Elizabethan drama. Lamb admitted that he also was a scatter-brain, and he seems to have liked the idea of a dandy being also a wit and a con-noisseur. Although Lamb's own hard-earned income was really larger than Wainewright's annuity, he probably imagined him wealthy and living the kind of life Lamb himself would have wished to live if he had not so honour-ably sacrificed himself to others. Writing to one of the owners of *The London Magazine* in 1822, Lamb said:

"What is gone* of the Opium Eater, where is Barry Cornwall, and above all what is become of Janus Weather-cock—or by his worse name of Vink—something? He is much wanted. He was a genius of the Lond. Mag. The rest of us are single Essayists."

This is generous praise, even if it must be qualified by the fact that Lamb thought the periodical was getting too serious,

* 'Become'?

and needed the liveliness of frivolity. Wilde also admired
Wainewright's articles, but I for one cannot help subscribing
to G. A. Allen's remark that "neutralising his knowledge and
his merit" there is "an all-pervading affectation of a
peculiarly irritating character, and a sense of individual
importance almost boundless. His cleverness does not avert a
sense of tediousness and annoyance, and he is difficult to read
except in homœopathic doses." That seems to me just and
admirably expressed, and the final judgment on Wainewright as a writer. But Lamb must also have liked Wainewright as a person, since in his *Letter to Mr. Southey* he speaks
of "the light, and warm-as-light hearted, Janus of the London". That was in October 1823, and a month earlier he had
used similar words in another letter where he speaks of
"kind, light-hearted Wainwright (*sic*), their Janus". Now, by
that time Wainewright was so harassed for money that he had
already committed the first of his forgeries, and, however
supple or callous, his conscience could hardly have been
really 'light-hearted'. And, with what was to come, 'kind'
and 'warm' seem singularly infelicitous guesses at character.
Coming from Lamb such a judgment must be recorded,
though I cannot avoid a suspicion that he may have been
teasing the solemnity and righteousness of friends who dis-
approved of Wainewright's flamboyance and self-absorption.

It was surely no modest self-effacement which led "Janus
Weathercock" and his other pseudonymous selves to entertain the capital with details of Mr. Wainewright's style of
living and his collections of *bric-à-brac*. This has naturally
attracted the attention of his biographers. Oscar Wilde
seems to have detected in Wainewright a kindred interior
decorator, and praises him as "one of the first to recognise
what is, indeed, the very keynote of æsthetic eclecticism, I
mean the true harmony of all really beautiful things, irre-
spective of age or place, of school or manner."*

* "Only an auctioneer should admire all schools of art" (Oscar Wilde).

He then proceeds to detail Wainewright's application of these principles. "The delicate fictile vase of the Greek" was supported by engravings from Michelangelo and Giorgione, by majolica ware, and "a rude lamp" from a Roman tomb, a Book of Hours "cased in a cover of solid silver gilt, wrought with quaint devices and studded with small brilliants and rubies," "a Lar" said to be Sicilian, a crucifix of ivory and another of wax, trays of gems, a sweet-box of the age of Louis XIV, brown-biscuit teapots, a pomona-green chair, Marc Antonio prints and the *Liber Studiorum* of Turner!

This was well-enough for a young man whose income was an annuity of £250 a year, with journalistic and art earnings which were so occasional they cannot have exceeded another £100 a year—and in 1821 he had married a beautiful but penniless girl, Eliza Frances Ward, whose mother had married again and had two other daughters, Madeleine and Helen Abercromby.

While he was living in the suburbs, we hear that Wainewright kept his horse and gig, and that the reins if not the whole harness were white. He was fashionably and therefore expensively dressed, often wearing the blue undress of an officer, at other times "braided surtouts" with lemon-coloured kid gloves, and variously coloured neck handkerchiefs. He wore diamond rings, breast-pins with antique cameos, and carried a quizzing-glass though his sight did not require it.

The Oscar Wilde *bric-à-brac* was installed in the apartment Wainewright took for himself and his wife at Great Marlborough Street, rooms which had belonged to Mrs. Siddons. The living-room was furnished with a "gay Brussels carpet", a silver inkstand, a piano, a couch, a Damascus sword, prints, a picture by Fuseli, a cast of the Venus de' Medici, finely-bound books, china, a cat and a Newfoundland dog. The study and inner rooms had Persian carpets, bronzes after Gian Bologna, framed prints which he said had cost twenty guineas, and illustrated books on art and antiquities which were supposed to have cost about 250 guineas. There was a suit of armour, and a footman in "drab coat and crimson breeches".

And his occupations? Anything but work, for like so many hangers-on he had discovered as the perfect excuse for idleness that he was "a gentleman"—and indeed he had held His Majesty's commission, though dropping it when a battle was imminent. He has given us a glimpse of his aristocratic distractions in one of his essays:

". . . engaged to meet some prime coves at twelve; then to the Fives Court; must be at the Royal Institution by half-past two; take my twentieth peep at Haydon's picture on my way back; letters to Belzoni till five; dinner *chez moi* with the little philosopher and the doctor at six; don our azure hose for the Lady Cerulea Lazuli's *Conversazione* at half-past nine; opera—applaud Milanie, and sup with the Corinthians in St. James's Square at two Sunday morning:—good-bye,—hope to see you at church to-morrow, if up in time,—or meet ye at Sir Joseph's to-night."

This was the life of a gentleman of wit and fashion about town, such as it had been lived only a few years before by Lord Byron, with the result that during the year his unhappy marriage lasted the bailiffs were continually in his Piccadilly house, and he only escaped imprisonment for debt because of his immunity as a peer. All who have written about Wainewright and even his contemporaries appear to have accepted his boasting at its face value. It is one more example of the credulity which seems so often to accept the confident assertions of 'frauds'. But with a good-looking and extravagant young wife, with expensive lodgings, could any man possibly live the fashionable life described on £250 and what he could raise as heir to his uncle Griffiths? Unfortunately, all we know is that he got into serious financial difficulties, so that with his impudence and cunning he may have achieved the seemingly impossible.

Similar doubts are aroused by the glowing descriptions of his furnishing and bibelots, which Oscar Wilde accepted so enthusiastically. But, in the first place, may not Vinkbooms have intentionally exaggerated the luxury and opulent surroundings of his friend Janus Weathercock, if only in the hope of maintaining a financial credit which in December 1821 badly needed support? And since the Great Marlborough Street lodgings were *furnished*, surely most of the furniture and even some of the bibelots really belonged to the landlord? No doubt the carefully priced books and prints belonged to Wainewright, if he had ever paid for them. In the matter of prints a squalid story came out after the crash. This relates that Wainewright bought on credit (and apparently never paid for) some very expensive engravings by Bonasone and Marc Antonio. He got these from the well-known dealer, Dominic Colnaghi, who had made notes of the high prices asked in his own handwriting on the mounts. Wainewright sold or pledged these engravings, but retained the mounts, on which he fixed cheap copies of the same prints. He then showed them to friends, who had presumably no expert knowledge of engravings and their prices, and pointed out the sums marked on the mounts in Colnaghi's handwriting. As a special act of friendship Wainewright would allow a friend to buy a print at less than the price marked! If that is not "low cunning", what is? This story comes from "Barry Cornwall" (B. W. Procter), an honest though rather careless witness in dates and details. He goes on to say that Wainewright had been "dealing with scarce old prints and etchings to a great extent," which suggests that he had been trying to raise money by trade in spite of being such a gentleman, and that *The London Magazine* articles which Lamb and Wilde liked so much may have been at least partly intended as advertisements for his wares.

Here we are touching on the realm of conjecture, since there is so little evidence of Wainewright's activities as a dealer, which he naturally kept secret, in much the same way that Thomas J. Wise, the 'forger' of first editions, pretended that his profitable sales of genuine old books were simply acts of friendship to his American millionaire friends. What is certain is that in 1822, the year after his marriage, Wainewright was so pressed for money that he committed a felony. In those days forgery was a capital offence, though the Banks and the City generally—the chief losers by the crime—opposed the death penalty, and when they did have to prosecute tried to avoid bloodshed. Still, Wainewright must have known the risk he was running—the really terrible risk in that property-worshipping age; but it is impossible to say whether his action was due to that still unexplained nervous disease "on the verge of insanity" which affected him as a young man, or to his "giddy, flighty disposition", or to an unfounded belief that he was astute enough not to be detected.

Here is what happened. By his will Ralph Griffiths left his nephew only the income on £5,000 Navy Five Per Cents, which were deposited with the Bank of England and vested in three trustees, Robert Wainewright (uncle) and (cousins) Edward Smith Foss and Edward Foss. Using his skill as an artist, Wainewright forged their names, ordering the transfer of the funds into £5,250 of New Four Per Cents. The object of this, of course, was to make the additional £250 in capital. Then, on July 15th, 1822, Wainewright produced a forged power of attorney from the trustees which put him in possession of £2,250, but of course reduced his income to £120. Less than two years later, on May 17th, 1824, he got hold of the remaining £3,000; and of course his income then disappeared entirely. Wainewright afterwards argued that, all said and done, the money was really his, and he only took an irregular way of getting hold of it; but, in law, it was so little his that when the fraud was discovered the Bank had to restore the original investment, the income on which event-

ually went to Eliza Wainewright and her son after the
forger's death in Tasmania. There seems to have been slack-
ness in both the trustees and the Bank, since the former
apparently never bothered to verify accounts and must have
allowed the income to be paid direct to Wainewright, while,
as the judge at one of the trials pointed out, the Bank made
this transfer without taking the trouble to get into touch with
the trustees. Consequently, amazing as it seems, years
elapsed before the affair was discovered!

Obviously, if this had been the full extent of Wainewright's
transgression everyone's feelings about him would be far
more sympathetic, especially in view of the dreadful
brutalities he must have endured in his first eighteen months
as a convict. In a great financial and mercantile centre such
as London in the 1820s already was, forgery was clearly
much more dangerous to society than it had been in the
Middle Ages; and the ferocity of the legislature had done the
rest. All sorts of excuses might be thought up for Wainewright merely as the man who had technically broken the
law to get hold of his own money, ranging from "the artistic
temperament" to the illness which Havelock Ellis seriously
thought might have predisposed the man to crime. Unluckily, all this is wiped out by the dreadful fact that for the
sake of money Wainewright was certainly guilty of the
murder of one near relative and most probably of two others.

Between July 1822 and September 1827, Wainewright had
got his hands on sums amounting to between £5,000 and
£6,000, in addition to anything he may have made as a
secret art-dealer. It is perhaps worth noting that after he
discovered this illegal way of making money he wrote only
two more articles for *The London Magazine*, and dropped it
after January 1823. Yet in spite of what were quite considerable sums even in so wealthy a city, the Wainewrights in the
autumn of 1827 were in such straits that they were very glad
to abandon their luxurious London rooms to go to live with

George Griffiths at Linden House. Mrs. Wainewright was then pregnant; and the great financial crash of 1825–26 must have virtually put an end for the time to any profitable trading in bibelots. And one can scarcely count as a financial asset Wainewright's last literary publication in 1825, *Some Passages in the Life &c of Egomet Bonmot, Esq., edited by Mr. Mwaughmaim, and now first published by ME;* a small book of forty-five pages published at two shillings. Wainewright's last recorded exhibition at the Royal Academy was also in 1825.

George Griffiths had sold *The Monthly Review* in 1825, and in 1827 was an old man. Since Wainewright's creditors were becoming more and more urgent, there were from his point of view equally urgent reasons for the speedy demise of his uncle; who, in fact, did die on February 5th, 1828, in great agony and convulsions, with symptoms now thought to show that he had been poisoned by strychnine, then comparatively little known. Did Wainewright poison his uncle to get his money sooner? The evidence is weak, apart from the fact that in the next two years two other relatives, from whom he hoped to profit financially at their death, both perished of identical symptoms; which, on the third occasion, was loudly commented on by the old family nurse, and strangely ignored by the doctor.

If Wainewright did poison his uncle, and there seems little reason to doubt it, then he must have followed rather closely the progress of toxicology, for strychnine was not discovered until 1818. Nux vomica, which he is also supposed to have used later, is a very closely allied drug. In any event Wainewright found to his consternation that his inheritance was far less than he had expected, amounting to £5,000 and Linden House. Most probably Griffiths had lost money in the 1825–26 crash, and it is said that under him the review had greatly declined. Yet if the house came to him unencumbered Wainewright had here a chance to retrieve his fortunes by using a little common sense and self-control of his propensity to show off at all costs. Linden House was said to be worth about £12,000, could have been rented for £400 a year, but cost nearly £1,000 a year to keep up. Now, in 1830, after murdering his mother-in-law, Wainewright also poisoned Helen Abercromby (his wife's half-sister) in the hopes of collecting £16,000 insurance money which he never got. Yet in 1828 if he had instantly sold Linden House for a good price, he would with the inherited cash have had just about that amount of capital. But no! he preferred to keep on this large mansion with no means to maintain it, running heavily into debt with the local tradesmen to entertain such guests as Lamb and Cary, Procter, and a Royal Academician, Richard Westall. To speak of this conduct as 'light-hearted' is surely too kind. It is more like insanity or the determination to try and make a living by poisoning, for he cannot have hoped to keep going for more than a few months, or a year. The birth of a son not long after the death of Uncle Griffiths did not deter Wainewright from pursuing his career as poisoner, and there is reason to think that his wife became his active accomplice.

Why did Wainewright poison his mother-in-law, Mrs. Abercromby? She and her two daughters by her second husband, Madeleine and Helen, had gone to live at Linden House because they were almost destitute. When Mrs. Abercromby made her will in August 1830, she owned £100 and a little house property, all bequeathed to her eldest daughter, Mrs. Wainewright. This seems curious, since after all Eliza was a married woman, and the two girls had nothing but a pension of £10 a year each from the Ordnance Office, in which their father had been employed. It seems like insanity for a man to poison another human being, his own wife's mother, for so little; yet the fact is that six days after she made her will Mrs. Abercromby died with exactly the same dreadful pain and convulsions as marked the other two deaths attributed to him. The main reason must be that he had

already begun to insure Helen Abercromby's life with
various companies for a period of only three years. Whether
Mrs. Abercromby suspected anything or not, the fact is she
opposed these insurances on the obvious ground that to
insure the life of a young, healthy girl for so short a period
was sheer waste of money. She was therefore an obstacle to
Wainewright's planned *coup* of making £16,000 out of
Helen's death; and she had to go.

English law does not allow anyone to insure another
person's life unless he has some monetary interest in it, but it
does not forbid making over a policy for a real or nominal
sum of money. The details of the insurance of Helen Abercromby are complicated and tedious. The main fact is that,
accompanied by Mrs. Wainewright, she called on various
companies and tried to insure her life for two or three years
for various sums. One or two companies refused, all naturally
asked questions, and at least two mistakes were made—
different stories were told, and the fact that other policies
had been taken out was concealed. Between March and
October 1830 Helen Abercromby's life was insured, mostly
for a period of only two years, with several companies for
amounts totalling £16,000.

But why did Helen consent to all this? Did she want to be
poisoned? A double explanation is given. She was a simple-
minded girl only just of age and did what her half-sister and
brother-in-law suggested; and then they had partly revealed
the plot to her, with the important difference that they were
all to go abroad and Helen was to pretend to die until the
money was collected. This seems taking a great risk with a
simple-minded girl, but then wasn't the whole scheme
extremely risky?

Meanwhile, Wainewright's financial affairs and creditors
had become desperately pressing, and to save him the girl
had to die before the end of December 1830. And die she
did. The whole family moved to London, with two servants,

including the old nurse who had already seen two suspicious
deaths. After a visit to the theatre Helen was supposed to
have caught cold with wet feet and to have been made ill by
oysters and beer. The night before, she had been given
lobster and beer. A doctor was called in, failed to diagnose
the symptoms of poisoning, and among other prescriptions
actually gave the girl tartar emetic, which made her very ill,
for it was akin to the poison (antimony) Wainewright was
giving her. On Tuesday, December 21st, the patient seemed
much better; but before going for a walk with her husband
Mrs. Wainewright gave the girl a jelly with powder in it,
supposed to be medicine. Helen died in agony before they
returned, although the doctor had been called, and had gone
away, thinking she had recovered from a convulsion! It is
recorded that she told the doctor she felt she was dying. The
servant, Harriet, remarked aloud that Mrs. Abercromby had
died in the same way, and Helen exclaimed: "Yes, my poor
mother—oh, my poor mother!" The doctor paid no attention
to all this. The excuse he afterwards gave was that strychnine
was then a new poison, and he did not know the symptoms.
Apparently Wainewright had used antimony to begin with,
but death was caused by strychnine given her in the jelly by
her half-sister. If Mrs. Wainewright was not an accomplice,
she must have been of a very unenquiring turn of mind and a
singularly lax conscience, since she did not demand to know
why Helen had died so soon after the alleged medicine
powder. According to Mr. Curling's careful and detailed
study, Wainewright first weakened the girl's resistance with
antimony, the symptoms of which may easily be mistaken for
a gastric chill, and then finished her with the strychnine
given by Mrs. Wainewright, who, in spite of G. A. Allen's
defence, he thinks must have been guilty.

Here was a ghastly set of achievements—within three
years the dandy-æsthete had poisoned three of his relatives
for money and had made his wife a murderess! Yet despite

his affected sensibility he could later on make the cynical jest that he murdered Helen "because she had such thick ankles", so doubtless he was not much troubled by qualms of conscience. Indeed that snake-like face probably bore an expression of extreme satisfaction for the few days when he believed he would be able to collect the criminal £16,000 without difficulty. But this satisfaction lasted but a very short time. Almost at once things began to go wrong for him, and continued to go wrong until the end. The last fifteen or sixteen years of his life were one continual punishment; but in this case nemesis had a comparatively easy task, for Wainewright himself prepared most of the traps which caught him. That he was never indicted for murder is true enough, but that was due to the incompetence of the original medical evidence, which was afterwards persisted in probably from professional *amour-propre*.

The delusion lasted exactly fifteen days. Helen Abercromby died in agony on December 21st, 1830; and on January 4th, 1831, the insurance companies involved had a meeting and decided to refuse payment on the policies, the premiums on which had cost Wainewright over £200. This did not now deter him, for he made up his mind to sue, and even found a solicitor to take up his case and to lend him £1,000 on the strength of the policy taken out with the Eagle Insurance Co. With this money Wainewright contrived to stave off the most pressing of his creditors (he owed over £600 to a money-lender with the appropriate name of Sharpus), but in those days Chancery proceedings were very slow, though Eldon's reign was over. Other creditors urged him, and in May 1831 the one-time dandy abandoned wife and child, and took refuge in Boulogne.

Practically nothing is known about Wainewright's life during the six years he was in France. The story that he persuaded a friend, "a Norfolk gentleman", to take out a policy for £3,000 with the Pelican Co., and then poisoned him "to be revenged on the company" was conclusively disproved by G. A. Allen. According to Wilde, after the poisoning Wainewright "went for a sketching tour through the most picturesque parts of Brittany", which has no greater basis than the fact that he did visit Brittany. In 1832 a lawyer's clerk saw him on business at St. Omer when he was living with a Frenchman, supposedly wealthy. At any rate he was poor enough when Procter came upon him in Paris in 1833, for he then asked for "a very small loan or gift of money", and Procter goes on to state:

"When he had to tell of his wretched state, his tone deepened. 'Sir, I starve,' he said, adding that he had been obliged to pawn his only shirt, in order to enable him to pay the postage on his letter."

Apart from a rumour that he was imprisoned for registering with the French police under a false name, that seems to be all. And then in January 1835 the Bank of England at last discovered the forgeries of 1822 and 1824, and a warrant was issued for his arrest, with no more immediate result than the visit of two Bow Street runners, named Forrester, to Boulogne, where all they could do was to find him and note his appearance. In that same eventful year nemesis came nearer. The suit against the insurance companies was heard in June, and the jury disagreed. It came up again in December, and this time the jury found for the companies. That was the end of the financial hopes for which Wainewright had played so foully. It does not appear that he was made a bankrupt, but Linden House was sold (and presumably any other property he still had), for the benefit of the creditors, who of course now included the solicitor who had lent money and incurred law costs.

Then comes another blank of seventeen months, followed by an unsolved mystery. Knowing that a warrant was out against him, that he was guilty, and that Bow Street runners

F

had his 'likeness', what made Wainewright return to London in May 1837? Was it the 'Weathercock' again, the "giddy, flighty disposition", or was he really sometimes insane? Or had he grown so desperate in his destitution that he came to London in the wild hope of getting some help? The romantic story that "some strange mad fascination" made him follow a "woman whom he loved" seems to have no firmer basis than the fact that one of the newspaper reports of his arrest says that he was talking to a woman "near a lamp, in Howland Street, Fitzroy Square" when he was recognised and arrested. So romantic and unprofitable a motive seems unlikely in one who for years had been tasting the strychnine-like bitterness of near destitution. Another story is that he was hiding in a hotel in Covent Garden, lifted the blind to see what was causing some noise in the street, and was recognised and arrested by one of the Forresters, who happened to be passing.

How on earth Wainewright came to return voluntarily to London with a warrant out against him for so serious an offence is a mystery. The romantic story of a woman is surely nonsense? Might it not be that he fell into complete destitution, was taken up as a vagabond by the French police, and expelled in consequence? When the Duke of Wellington was Ambassador in Paris such a case was referred to him by the French authorities, and he told them to throw the man out. More mysterious is the complete discrepancy between Wainewright's stunned and dejected attitude before the magistrate and after his trial, and the defiant attitude and perky anecdotes told of him while he was under remand. Are not these anecdotes another example of the "psychology of dupes", seeing and hearing what they wanted to see and not what was really there?

When, after the arrest, the Lord Mayor's deputy at the Mansion House asked Wainewright what he was, he replied:

"I am nothing. I have been an independent gentleman, and had considerable property, and I was originally an officer in the 16th Foot."

Less than three weeks afterwards, when Wainewright was in Newgate prison, he was seen by Dickens, Hablot Brown, Forster and Macready; and Forster says the "shabby genteel creature with sandy disordered hair and dirty moustache" looked at them "with a defiant stare" and seemed "at once mean and fierce, and quite capable of the cowardly murders he had committed." Macready on the other hand more prosaically says he looked through an eyelet-hole in one of the cells and recognised Wainewright. Still more dramatic is the account of an anonymous interviewer who is said to have asked, rather superfluously, if Wainewright did not see "the folly of his proceedings." Here is the alleged answer:

"Not a bit. I have always been a gentleman, have always lived like a gentleman, and I am a gentleman still. Yes, sir, even in Newgate I am a gentleman. The prison regulations are that we should each in turn sweep the yard. There are a baker and a sweep here beside myself. They sweep the yard; but, sir, they have never offered me the broom."

But a gentleman would have taken it.

At the trial Wainewright was persuaded to plead guilty to two minor charges of the indictment, not involving capital punishment, and was sentenced to transportation for life. In the melodramatic words he used in his (unsuccessful) attempt to get a ticket-of-leave:

"He pleaded guilty, and was forthwith hurried, stunned with such ruthless perfidy, to the hulks at Portsmouth, and thence in *five days* aboard the *Susan*, sentenced to Life in a land (to him) a moral sepulchre."

'Moral' is good. But when we read these self-pitying words we remember his snake-life ruthlessness to his victims. He would have been hanged if he had been convicted of murder or forgery, and the hell he did suffer was inflicted

legally for two comparatively minor offences. It might have
been better for Wainewright to hang than to endure the hell
of the crowded convict ship which took him to Tasmania,
and the worse hell of the Rocky Hills Probation Station,
about which Mr. Curling has published such appalling
revelations. And we learn with amazement that this pre-
view of Buchenwald in the Antipodes was, for part of the
time when Wainewright served his term, under Mr. Gladstone at the Colonial Office!

All the same Wainewright was favoured, for he spent only a
year in a hell where three convicts would draw lots. The
longest straw was the luckiest—he was murdered; the
second was the murderer, and he was the next luckiest, for he
was hanged; but the unlucky witness might not be hanged.

Wainewright was sent to Hobart, where he worked as
orderly (on "third-class wages") in the hospital, and was
allowed to make paintings and drawings. He became an
opium-eater, and for two and a half years was a patient in the
hospital. His application for a ticket-of-leave was refused, as
already noted; at last in November 1846 he was recommended for pardon; but before the confirmation came from
London he died of apoplexy in August 1847. His widow
eventually was allowed to receive the £5,250 three and a half
per cent annuities which the Bank had supplied in place of
the securities Wainewright had illegally secured for himself.
It is the final irony in this fantastic tale, for though the
woman was destitute, she was the murderess of her half-
sister. The Law is certainly a strange affair. In this complicated network of cruelty and crime, it failed utterly to
protect the innocent, punished one of the guilty murderers
for minor offences, and rewarded the other with money
replaced by the Bank for what had been stolen by her
husband.

FOUR

Roger Tichborne or Arthur Orton?

I

Wise after the event, and fortified by the verdicts of two juries against the claimant who was sent to prison for perjury, we naturally say: "How can there be any question about it? Of course the claimant was Arthur Orton and not Roger Tichborne." A perusal of the eight folio volumes of law reports on the 188 days' trial for perjury (fascinating reading!) carries complete conviction in spite of the frenzied annotations by the claimant's counsel, Dr. E. V. Kenealy, Q.C. Nobody but an eccentric would now try to prove that the claimant was Tichborne, and he could no more get round the evidence than Kenealy could. But we must remember that this was far indeed from being the case during the years 1866–1874, when English public opinion was as over-excited and bitterly divided over "the Tichborne claimant" as that of France over the Dreyfus affair. The cunning, unscrupulous impostor collected a huge body of supporters from all classes of society, and even succeeded—for reasons which will be explained—in imposing on the real Roger's mother, who was thus mainly responsible for the success of the fraud. Seldom has the psychology of dupes been more strikingly illustrated—what won't people believe so long as it is absurd! If it had come to a national referendum at any time between 1867 and January 1872, there is not much doubt that the claimant would probably have received a majority of votes. We must remember the complexity of the evidence and the difficulties of collecting and verifying it, the cunning skill with which the claimant ceaselessly picked up facts about the real Roger and, though he frequently bungled from ignorance, managed to remember so much. For years people hadn't the facts, and indeed not until the speech of the Solicitor-General (Sir J. Coleridge) in the ejectment case before the Court of Common Pleas were the complex facts convincingly revealed. That speech really convicted Orton; yet another two years were needed to get him behind bars, and even after he was in prison a huge body of dupes still believed in him. A petition to Parliament for a Royal Commission to review the trial is said to have carried 200,000 signatures. Ten years after the sentence, when the impostor was about to emerge from prison a thinner though probably not a wiser man, Parliamentary candidates were amazed to find themselves still heckled on their attitude to the "Tichborne case".

Roger Charles Doughty Tichborne was born on January 5th, 1829, in the Rue de la Ferme des Mathurins, Paris. He was descended from the very ancient Roman Catholic family of Tichbornes, and through his father James (afterwards 10th baronet) was heir to the Tichborne and Doughty estates; and if Roger had lived he, and not his younger brother Alfred, would have been the 11th baronet. Sir James seems to have been a good-natured, dull English country gentleman, very much dominated by his wife, Henriette Félicité, with whom he was continually quarrelling and to whom he continually succumbed under what appears to have been the influence of genuine affection. She is an important person in the drama. She was a natural daughter of Henry Seymour of Knoyle and of a Princesse de Bourbon-Conti, from whose family she inherited 450,000 gold francs. She was a 'spoiled beauty', a capricious, possessive, jealous woman, exorbitant in demanding the whole affection and interest of her husband and sons, hating England and her English relatives—especially those most devoted to her husband—and determined to bring Roger and his brother up as Frenchmen. In some cases there is a good deal to be said for a foreign education provided the mother tongue is not lost, but in this family French and not English was spoken, and Roger's education was shamefully neglected to please his mother's whims. Up to sixteen he had no proper schooling, only a series of tutors, good and bad and all subservient to the mother's will and caprices, so that at sixteen he could not correctly spell the French which was his maternal tongue, while the future head of an English county family at that age knew practically nothing of England and could not speak English! Among the other misfortunes inflicted on Roger by her whims was a medical fad of the time, the artificial creation of a running sore on the arm, either a 'seton', made by a thread pulled to and fro in the flesh, or an 'issue' which was a sore kept open with a dried pea. Roger's was an 'issue'. It was only closed by the interference of his English aunt, Lady Doughty, and is important as an identification mark, since the scar never disappears. The claimant had marks like a 'seton' but no 'issue'.

Poor Sir James Tichborne seems to have been usually subservient to his wife's will and terrified of her bad temper, about which he complained in his letters to her English half-brothers, Henry Danby Seymour and Alfred Seymour, although the relationship was never openly acknowledged, and Roger never called old Mr. Seymour 'grandfather' or used the word 'uncle' to the sons. At all events, Sir James did not dare take Roger from his mother and put him in an English school without a strategem, and that not until the boy was sixteen and a half. Sir James took advantage of his brother's funeral to bring Roger to England and to place him at Stonyhurst College, where he remained from July 1st,

1845, until August 1st, 1848. Roger's knowledge of English was so slight that he was intentionally paired off with an English-speaking French lad in order to learn his own tongue! Up till the time of his disappearance in 1854 he always spoke English with a French accent, and though his letter-writing greatly improved he always made little mistakes in spelling and idiom such as a Frenchman would make.

For the next twelve months Roger prepared himself to enter the Army, to the fury of his mother, who would have allowed him to enter any Army but the British! Roger had a good deal of his mother's obstinate will, and never yielded to her or his father after he came of age if he thought there were good reasons for not doing so.

Mention of the Army and of his determined resistance to what he thought unreasonable demands by his parents does not mean that Roger Tichborne possessed either a robust physique or an impressive personality. He was light-weight (between eight and nine stone in one record), medium height (five feet eight and a half inches), with very thin legs, a quick, awkward gait, champagne shoulders, a long bony hand and narrow hips. Someone who knew them both said he was "an ugly version of his mother", who was a very thin woman. Roger had a long sallow face, blue-grey eyes with long black lashes, lank dark hair which fell over his face before he had the Army hair-cut, and ears and lobes attached to the cheek. He had a melancholy expression, and often sat with his head drooping to one side. He was gentle and very good-natured, but awkward and shy, and though women sometimes liked him he was certainly the butt of the officers' mess and subjected constantly to crude and even brutal ragging.

The next twelve months (August 1848 to August 1849), which were spent in preparing for the very easy Army examination of that epoch, were passed mostly at Tichborne

Portrait of George Psalmanazar

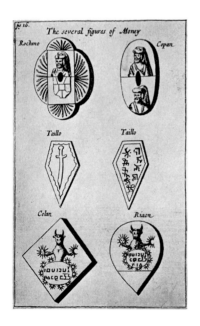

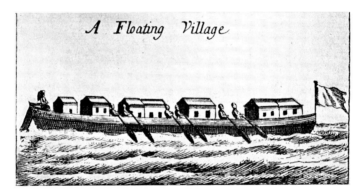

Three illustrations from Psalmanazar's *Description of Formosa*

(By permission of J. Curling, author of Janus Weathercock)

Self-portrait of Thomas Griffiths Wainewright

(*Picture Post*)

A photograph of Arthur Orton, the Tichborne claimant

(*Picture Post*)

An idealised contemporary engraving of the Tichborne
claimant

"The Claimant's Farewell". A contemporary engraving
showing Dr. Kenealy shaking hands with Orton at the end of
the trial

A contemporary engraving of Graham's "Celestial Bed with
the Rosy Goddess of Health reposing thereon".

Maundy Gregory, a year before his death

with his paternal uncle, Sir Edward Doughty, who had changed his name from Tichborne on inheriting the Doughty estates. His aunt, Lady Doughty, was fond of Roger, corresponded regularly with him in his absences, and indeed was far more of a mother to him than Henriette Tichborne. At this period Roger developed close relations with two persons, who long afterwards became key witnesses in the "Tichborne case". One was Vincent Gosford, the land agent of the Tichborne estate, Roger's intimate friend and confidant, who fortunately preserved many of his letters and whose evidence was of the first importance in baffling the impostor. It is not too much to say that if Gosford had betrayed his trust, as others fortunately less informed did, he could have given the impostor so much important and intimate knowledge that justice and the Tichborne trustees might well have been baffled. The other person involved was Catherine Doughty, the still almost schoolgirl daughter of Sir Edward and Lady Doughty, with whom Roger Tichborne fell in love with some reason to think his suit was not hopeless.

About this time and at various dates afterwards before he left for South America in 1853, a curious little fact was noticed. Roger Tichborne had on his left arm a tattoo mark in blue of a cross, a heart and an anchor, with his initials underneath. The symbolical design had been made (according to Roger) by a Breton sailor, and the initials were added later by a fellow pupil at Stonyhurst. The reader will see at once the importance of such an indelible mark in a question of disputed identity, and the claimant had no such tattoo mark.

Roger passed the (then very easy) Army examination in every subject but arithmetic, and was gazetted to the 6th Dragoons on condition that he earned certificates for competence in mathematics. It is some indication of his genuine desire to qualify for his profession—which for a man of his wealth was merely a public duty, not a source of income—

that he gave up the society of his English relatives at Upton
and Tichborne to live solitary in London and near his tutor
in mathematics.

Yet even when he joined his regiment in Ireland the
disadvantages of his foreign upbringing and his awkward
physique reduced him to the condition of a butt. A so-called
practical joke robbed him of a five-pound note for transport
by boat when none was necessary, and left him to flounder
deep in mud. Having no available change of clothes, he
arrived in such a state at the orderly room that the colonel
was about to send him to the cookhouse when he presented a
letter from Lord Fitzroy Somerset at the Horse Guards.
Roger tried hard to be an efficient officer, but although he
learned his drill in theory he could never remember it on
parade; though a very good rider to hounds, he never
learned the cavalry seat or how to manage his horse at drills;
and even if he gave the right word of command his French
accent made the men laugh at him. They called him
'Frenchie' and the officers 'Teesh'. As already noted, he was
brutally ragged by his brother officers even to the extent of
such witty jokes as introducing street women to his bed,
varied by an occasional donkey.

Meanwhile there was this passion for his cousin, Catherine
Doughty, which he had confided to her mother and his aunt,
Lady Doughty. There were difficulties. They were very
young, and then they were first cousins, which is a pro-
hibited degree for marriage in the Church of Rome. True,
dispensations were sometimes granted, but this kinship was a
serious obstacle to Lady Doughty and still more to her
husband, Sir Edward. Moreover, however fond of Roger she
was—and that seems to have been a very genuine affection—
Lady Doughty was disturbed by his excessive smoking, a
tendency to drink, and a liking for uninhibited French novels
which alarmed her prudery. On the other hand Roger was
heir to an estate of £20,000 to £25,000 a year, and his wife

would be the female head of the whole family. It was a dilemma, and the good lady tried to deal with it in a manner which was not very fair to her nephew. Shorn of all *politesses* and euphemisms, what she proposed was this one-sided arrangement: until she came of age Catherine Doughty was in no way to be bound to him but to be allowed freely to choose any other eligible husband, while Roger was to consider himself bound to her. It was very much a "heads I win, tails you lose" arrangement; and though he certainly was deeply in love, the young man showed his spirit by rejecting it, or at least not agreeing to it.

Roger had joined the Army entirely against his mother's wish, though his father encouraged it. She had flown into one of her violent tempers over it, so violent that Roger described it in a letter as "the great blow up", and she had prophesied that he would at once be sent to India, there to perish from disease or violence. Roger himself wanted to go to India, but from the time he joined his regiment in October 1849 until the middle of 1852 he was stationed in Ireland and then moved to Canterbury. At the time of this move the 6th Dragoons were under orders for India, but at the last minute, after they had made all preparations, the order was cancelled. After vainly trying to transfer to an Indian regiment, Roger in some disgust sent in his papers and left the Army in December 1852, having determined to go abroad for a long tour of South America and Mexico. One little episode of Roger's rather unsuccessful Army career must be mentioned. He seems to have suffered from asthma, and on one occasion was so near suffocation that the surgeon decided to bleed him, but as the usual incisions had no effect he opened the saphena vein in the ankles. The scars left by the lancet usually remain for life.

Roger last saw his cousin, Catherine Doughty, at Tichborne on June 22nd, 1852, and in saying farewell he gave her a paper containing a vow to build a church to the Holy

Virgin at Tichborne if he married her "before three years are over at the latest". He told her that earlier in the year he had given a copy of this vow to his most intimate friend, Vincent Gosford, but Gosford did not know that a copy had been given to Miss Doughty.

Before leaving England, Roger made a will, and in so doing showed a knowledge of the Tichborne and Doughty estates and of the various legal settlements involved which "in a cavalry officer" greatly surprised the Chancery expert who helped Mr. Slaughter, the attorney, to draw up the document.

On March 1st, 1853, Roger Tichborne sailed from Le Havre on the French ship *La Pauline*, was storm-bound in Falmouth until the 12th, and reached Valparaiso on June 19th. On June 29th he received there a letter from Lady Doughty telling him Sir Edward was dead. This made Roger's father Sir James Tichborne, made Roger himself the immediate heir to title and estate, and raised his income from £500 to £1,000 a year. He travelled in Chile, and then crossed the Cordilleras and the Pampas to Buenos Aires, arriving at Rio after various wanderings in April 1854. After writing for money to be sent him to Kingston, Jamaica (he had spent all he had) he said he planned to return to England by way of Mexico, and asked to be put up for the Travellers Club. He sailed from Rio on April 20th in the *Bella*, which disappeared and was never heard of again, though the long-boat with the *Bella*'s name on it and other wreckage were found floating in the sea four days later.

Thus suddenly and calamitously ended the brief and rather frustrated life of Roger Tichborne, a life of no particular interest, which would have been forgotten except by a few relatives but for the extraordinary events of the years 1866–74 when a person stating he was Roger Tichborne (mysteriously saved from the wreck) turned up in Australia and came to England "to claim his rights". In the ensuing law suits, documents were brought out, family history revealed, old letters scanned with legal minuteness, and hundreds of witnesses examined and cross-examined, so that after his death the most minute circumstances of this insignificant life became known to hundreds of thousands, if not millions, of people who had never heard of Roger in his lifetime. The legal battles fought over the claimant must be among the bitterest and certainly the longest in our history. This claimant, who for years posed as Sir Roger Tichborne, Bart., who counted his followers and supporters by thousands and was lent large sums of money by enthusiastic dupes for his legal defence and extravagant living, was eventually proved to be Arthur Orton, the son of a Wapping butcher.

It is anticipating, but since a short study cannot possibly give more than a fraction of the detailed evidence convicting Orton, this is the obvious moment to mention the main reasons for the impostor's long success. Most important were the selfishness, obstinacy, folly and delusion of the Dowager Lady Tichborne (Roger's mother) in maintaining (to the intense distress of her husband up till his death in 1862) that Roger was not drowned, that he had been saved, and would turn up some day. Any beery sailor who came to Tichborne and told the tale of how the *Bella*'s crew had been saved was certain of money from her. Sir James had servants posted to keep off these veracious sons of Odysseus. (After the Tichborne case, one sees how wise Penelope was to insist on real proof of the identity of her claimant!) Some cynic who knew her remarked of Lady Tichborne that she was so determined to have Roger back that she would have identified as her son an Egyptian mummy if some old salt swore it was Roger. Her folly in continuing to advertise for news of her son was only exceeded by the silliness with which she gave the impostor vital information and 'recognised' him on no proof at all! But the once spoiled beauty had always had her own way, and she was determined to have it here—not reflecting that she was disinheriting her grandson, impoverishing her daughter-in-law, and bringing a cuckoo into the Tichborne-Doughty nest! It is unfortunate for the cause of truth that she died before she could be put in the witness-box. She could never have stood up to the cross-examination of Coleridge and Hawkins.

Next in importance must be ranked Orton's effrontery, unscrupulousness and East End cunning, his remarkable skill in pumping people for information and the amazing memory which enabled him to cover up much of his ignorance and seem to correct mistakes, a superficial "Tichborne look" in his face, a rough sort of eloquence and coarse geniality which won over many of the vulgar, joined with a native aptitude for imitation and acting which deceived some of the upper classes into thinking he might have been a gentleman— though how anyone could have thought that after comparing the first (and un-coached) letters of the claimant with the last Roger Tichborne letters is a mystery. But what will people not believe if they want to believe? Among the large numbers of absurdities and improbabilities adduced by the claimant's counsel, E. V. Kenealy, Q.C., LL.D., is the statement that the claimant's manners were as fine as George IV.'s (they both weighed over 300 pounds), while in another panegyric by Kenealy "Sir Roger", after courteously taking off his glove to shake hands, then points to somebody "with his delicately gloved hand"! It is amazing that the finest intellects in the Courts at that time—Coleridge, Cockburn, Hawkins—had to exert all their powers to unmask this fraud.

On top of all this must be added the fact that very important evidence came from Australia and South America, where witnesses could not be subpœnaed, and the payment of expenses and compensation by the Crown was instantly denounced by Dr. Kenealy as 'bribery', in spite of the fact that his client most assuredly had practised direct and indirect bribery.

What more? The gullibility, the credulity, of our species, the habit of forming an opinion on some slight or uncritical basis and clinging to it with all the passion we feel for our prejudices! Contemporaries state that not until the great speech of Sir John Coleridge in the Court of Common Pleas (nearly six years after the fraud had started!) did educated persons realise for the first time the extent of the fraud and the overwhelming weight of evidence against the impostor, who thereafter was supported mainly by the rabble and by those, like Kenealy, Onslow and Whalley, who came under the Lord Chief Justice's (Cockburn) definition of "fanatics and fools". But by that time "the Claimant" had become "a Cause", linked with No-Popery, Down-with-the-Aristocrats and so forth; and it is not only among the Jesuits that the end is held to justify the means. If I had not read them myself I should not have believed that even an Irishman could have made the vindictive and fatuous assertions made by Kenealy in his periodical *The Englishman*. It is a poor cause which has to be supported wholly by abuse, misrepresentation, and quibbling. It is astonishing to see how much irrelevant and improbable 'evidence' be brought forward to confuse clear issues.

And so we come to Arthur Orton.

He was the youngest of twelve children of George Orton, a Wapping butcher who kept a shop and also supplied meat to ships. Arthur was born on March 20th, 1834, and was therefore rather more than five years younger than Roger Tichborne. He received some schooling, but at the age of nine he was terrified by a fire close to his home, and was in consequence afflicted with twitchings of his face and limbs known as St. Vitus's Dance. With a view to curing this, Arthur was apprenticed as a seaman and received, as was then the custom though it has long been abolished, a 'ticket'

of identification numbered 393,710, and sailed for Valparaiso, where he arrived in June 1849, and deserted his ship
on the 25th. He made his way to a small town called
Melipilla, where he told a pathetic story of ill-treatment by
the captain of his ship, and later put out various tales of his
importance, such as that his father had been the Queen's
butcher (or Chancellor) and that he (Arthur) had played
with the Queen's children. There is other evidence of
Orton's habit of telling highly embellished tales about
himself, and on the last day of the trial the Lord Chief
Justice made some cogent remarks on liars. Taking up the
statement of Dr. Kenealy that the claimant had "a habit" of
telling untruths, the Chief Justice said:

"I quite agree with the learned Counsel that there are men
who are habitual liars. And it may be that, in addition to
those who do not scruple to have recourse to falsehood, in
order to work iniquity, or to satisfy the base and sordid
desire of gain, or to gratify the dark and detestable passions
of hatred and revenge, men have been known who, labour-
ing under some mental disorder, have mistaken the creations
of their diseased imaginations for reality and fact. Some men
are said to lie from a morbid pleasure in lying, or in mystify-
ing others or making fools of them. Some men lie from
inherent love of mischief."

It is perhaps worth noting that long after his release from
prison Arthur Orton sold his confession to a Sunday newspaper (which in the usual manner of popular journalism
made a hash of it) and stated that he began his impersonation
merely as "a lark", a hoax. A hoax! It is as much the
habitual plea of the impostor as that of the fraudulent
cashier is that he had merely temporarily borrowed the
money and meant to repay it. The question is: when does a
'hoax' become criminal? Is it only when it is used to obtain
money? Might the criminality not be extended to an un-
deserved reputation? However that may be, the fact is that
the tales told to the simple people of Melipilla by the deserter,

Arthur Orton, were believed by them and helped him to free food and lodging, the loan of a horse and gun (he had learned to ride Shetland ponies in Wapping, where one of his brothers dealt in them) and eventually a purse to enable him to return to England.

While he was in Melipilla, two episodes happened. They are unimportant in themselves, like the marks on Roger Tichborne, but extremely valuable later as evidence. A motherly woman cut off and kept a lock of Orton's hair. And to curry favour with the Catholic population Orton was received into the Catholic Church and re-baptised. Now, one of his closest friends and benefactors in Melipilla was José Maria Toro, and when Orton shipped for England he gave his name, not as Arthur Orton, but as Joseph M. Orton. He disguised the 'Maria' because he knew the English sailors would jeer at it.

Arthur Orton landed in England on June 11th, 1851, and swaggered about Wapping in the clothes and cap of an officer of the merchant marine, doubtless telling tall stories of the innocent 'hoax' type, until economics forced him to resume work as a butcher in his father's business. While in London he made love to a girl called Mary Ann Loader, and when he left for Australia in November 1852 it was with the understanding that when he made good in that distant land she was to follow and to marry him. His 393,710 'ticket' was renewed, thereby identifying Joseph M. Orton and Arthur Orton as the same person, and he sailed from Wapping for Hobart in the *Middleton* on November 29th-30th, 1852, taking with him a couple of Shetland ponies for the owner of the vessel, who lived at Hobart, where the ship arrived in May of 1853.

Now, since the claimant denied that he was Arthur Orton, and Arthur Orton had completely disappeared from Australia, a good deal of detective work was necessary to trace his movements there before he disappeared and the

G

claimant, who had been living under the name of Tom
Castro, came forward and said he was Roger Tichborne.
Perhaps it should be said here that the claimant explained his
knowledge of Orton and the Orton family on the grounds
that as Tom Castro he had known Arthur well for years, and
Dr. Kenealy, unable to deny this, made the absurd suggestion
that Castro-Tichborne had lived so much under the sway of
Orton's stronger personality that he had come to believe that
Orton's experiences were his!

There is no need to go into the details and chronology of
Orton's life in Australia as gradually re-constructed, but one
or two points are worth noting. Arthur Orton worked in
Hobart as a butcher's assistant, and in 1855 borrowed £14
(he got £18 by mistake) from a distant relation by marriage,
a Mrs. Jury (ominous name!), who went to reclaim her
money in August 1855 and found Orton had disappeared.
He was traced at various times in Gippsland and New South
Wales, working as a stock-driver and butcher, and apparently at less reputable activities. It was stated, though, I
think, not definitely proved, that Tom Castro was not heard
of in Australia until Arthur Orton was indicted for stealing a
horse, disappeared, and was recognised later under the name
of Tom Castro by one of his former mates. Again it was not
proved, but there were strong rumours that Orton spent the
period between the disappearance of Orton and the emer-
gence of Castro with bushrangers; and it is certainly sug-
gestive that he refused under oath to give an account of that
epoch on the grounds that it might incriminate him.
Eventually (Orton having disappeared) "Tom Castro"
turned up at Wagga-Wagga, where he was employed as
slaughterman by a Mr. Higgins, then set up on his own as a
butcher, failed, and went back to work for Mr. Higgins. And
it was at Wagga-Wagga in 1865 that Thomas Castro did not
so much come forward as cunningly arrange that others
first began to suspect, and then by his carefully planned hints

came to believe, that here was the long-lost Tichborne heir, miraculously discovered eleven years after the total loss of the *Bella* in the person of a bankrupt cockney slaughterman in Australia.

As I have already pointed out, this could not possibly have happened but for the Dowager Lady Tichborne's obstinate self-delusion and "spoiled beauty" selfishness. Her husband was dead; her younger son, Sir Alfred, a desperate spend-thrift whose excesses were hurrying him to an early death. She was alone in the world, for she seems to have disliked all her Tichborne, Doughty and even Seymour relatives. Roger had been her favourite, though one of his last letters to his friend Gosford had insisted that some provision should be made for her at his father's death, since he (Roger) was determined not to live with her and endure her fits of bad temper. Roger had disappeared in the sinking of the *Bella*, but she had always refused to believe he had been drowned, simply because she did not want him to be drowned. She had tortured Sir James by references to Roger as still alive 'somewhere' for years after the wreck, when Sir James and everyone else knew Roger was dead; and, as I have already mentioned, she had to be protected against the vagabonds who abused her credulity with wild tales. She more than ever wanted Roger back now that she was solitary; she had always had her own way; and therefore Roger must be found. Soon after her husband's death the Dowager began advertising in English, French and Spanish, offering a reward for information leading to the discovery of her son. Just how competent this old lady was to investigate the matter and to baffle impostors may be judged by the fact that even in one of her advertisements (the Spanish one) she gave away information instead of requiring it, and continued to do so in her letters to Australia and afterwards to the claimant in person. Moreover, she was so ignorant that she supposed New Zealand was part of Australia, and seems to have had a hazy notion that both were somewhere in South America. A more obvious and willing prey for an impudent impostor could scarcely be imagined. Orton of course did not know this until after they had met, when she, without the slightest investigation or even question, had 'recognised' him.

It was never exactly determined at what date the claimant determined to try his luck in this (one would have thought) palpable fraud. The Chief Justice seems to place it between the claimant's marriage in January 1865 and the writing of a certain letter in April of that year. From the outset the difficulties in the claimant's story were so numerous and his explanations of them (or the explanations invented by Kenealy for him) were often so fantastic and absurd that the marvel is that anyone believed in him.

There was so much that needed explaining. Setting aside for the moment the story of his rescue from the wreck of the *Bella* and landing in Australia, consider the claimant's life there. Why, for example, should Roger Tichborne, who loved writing and getting letters, especially to and from his family, and Gosford, never write for years? "Oh," says his learned Counsel, "he was disgusted with his family, particularly his father, and his former life, and wanted the free adventurous life of Australia. He had determined not to come home until his father was dead." But when his father died in 1862 he made no sign; and what was there so adventurous in ten years of stock-riding, horse-dealing and butchering to tempt the Tichborne heir? If the claimant had been really Roger Tichborne, he was entitled to £1,000 a year from the day he landed, and to about £20,000 a year after the death of Sir James. Why, with all that money at his disposal, did he spend his life at uninteresting jobs for about twenty-five shillings a week? The learned Counsel replied to this by citing the story of St. Alexis, who abandoned his wealth, family and wife on his wedding night, and after a long pilgrimage ended his days a beggar at his own door—a

picturesque legend, but was it evidence? Then came the
query, why, if the claimant was Sir Roger Tichborne, did he
spend so much of his life at Arthur Orton's job of butchering,
which was hardly likely to be an accomplishment of a
baronet, an officer in the 6th Dragoons, whose main re-
laxations were smoking, drinking and fox-hunting. The
learned Counsel said this skill in butchering—for which
"Tom Castro" was more than once commended in Wagga-
Wagga—was easily explained in Sir Roger because he had
dissected cats when at Stonyhurst. There was no evidence
that Roger had ever dissected cats at Stonyhurst or that
dissecting cats makes a skilled Wapping butcher; and it is
not surprising that the Chief Justice told an enquiring jury-
man that he thought the argument not worth dissection.

Probably the claimant's biggest blunder in trying to
account for Tichborne-Castro's Australian years was in
linking himself beyond possibility of equivocation with
Orton as a stockman on the Foster stations of Boisdale and
Dargo in 1857-8. Now, in those days in Australia the
remoter stations sold to their employees clothes and other
necessaries, to avoid the necessity for very long rides to the
nearest settlement. This meant that the station had to keep
separate accounts for every employee, debiting his purchases
against his wages. It so happened that the Boisdale accounts
were made up very carefully, and the books themselves had
been preserved by Foster's widow. From these she was able
to prove in court that no Tom Castro had been employed at
Boisdale, but that Arthur Orton had. Documentary proof
like that naturally impressed both judges and jury. Evidently
the claimant's imagination had failed him and he had
credited his fictitious life as Tichborne-Castro with his real
life as Orton, probably not knowing in his ignorance that
account books had been kept, or perhaps never thinking that
so close an investigation would be made. Kenealy tried to
discredit this by a gratuitous charge that Foster's widow had

been bribed, since she had been given a compensation of £1,000 to bring herself and family to England to give evidence. Unfortunately for this story, the lady was in no need of money, and she had produced the books and given her evidence in Australia long before there was any question of bringing her to England for the perjury trial.

The claimant's marriage with Ann Bryant, a totally illiterate domestic servant who already had a child, has been held to show that in January 1866 he can hardly have decided then to claim the Tichborne title and estates. But, though "Lady Tichborne her mark" would unquestionably have startled the county families, after all, other aristocrats have made *mésalliances*. But what are we to think of the fact that he declared himself as Thomas Castro, a Chilean, native of Chile, and that the ceremony was performed by a Dissenting minister, although a Catholic priest was available? This was surely remarkable in the representative of so staunch and ancient a Catholic family, even though Roger was far from being a fanatic? The claimant's answers are a good example of his cunning in wriggling out of difficulties. First, he said he was on bad terms with the priest. Then, when it was shown that this was no obstacle, he said that in the obligatory confession he would have been compelled to reveal his true name—though in the circumstances it is by no means certain this was true. But is it not strange that Castro-Tichborne gave the exact age of Arthur Orton, thirty; whereas Roger Tichborne would then have been thirty-six? How did it happen that "Sir Roger" mistook his age by five years?

A more dangerous link with Orton was the Richardson letter. Ten or twelve years had passed since Arthur Orton had communicated with his family in England, and if the claimant was Orton and not Tichborne, he would have to find out at once what had happened to the members of the Orton family. If he was Arthur Orton and wrote personally, they would recognise his handwriting, and in any case he had to find some excuse for writing to England. He went to a Wagga-Wagga schoolmaster and persuaded him to write a letter and to sign it "Tom Castro" asking for information about Orton and his family and "his son Arthur", with whom the claimant said he was trying to get into touch, as he thought earlier letters had been destroyed by bushrangers! This letter was not addressed to Arthur Orton care of his family, or to any member of the family, but to an old friend of theirs, James Richardson, 72 High Street, Wapping. The production of this letter, which the claimant no doubt hoped had been destroyed, raised some awkward questions. Why was Sir Roger Tichborne so interested in the whereabouts of the Ortons? How did he know Richardson's name and address? Well, there were the usual glib excuses: Orton had been an old friend in the bush, the claimant had failed to get in touch with him, Orton had given him the Richardson address. But why—since it turned out that Arthur Orton had no more kept in touch with him than with any other person in England? And once more, why would Sir Roger Tichborne be so much interested in the Orton family, to whom the claimant bore such a resemblance?

The actual 'discovery' in Australia that Tom Castro was Tichborne was cunningly arranged. The claimant, being about to file a petition in bankruptcy, 'confessed' to his solicitor that he had property in England. Then he hinted that he had been shipwrecked, and the solicitor, who had seen the advertisements for Roger Tichborne, began to prick up his ears, especially as his wife was much interested, and as the claimant carved the initials 'R.C.T.' on trees and posts and eventually on his pipe. Mr. Gibbes, the Wagga-Wagga solicitor, who had read the "missing heir" advertisements put in the Australian newspapers on behalf of the Dowager, got highly excited, and said: "You are Roger Tichborne!" This is exactly what Orton had played for, but he pretended to be highly displeased. However, he allowed himself to be

mollified, and began borrowing money from Gibbes. Mr.
Gibbes was not dishonest, he was merely credulous, but not
averse from earning the "large reward" offered for the
discovery of Roger Tichborne. How Gibbes and Cubitt, the
Sydney agent for finding "missing friends", could have
believed in Orton staggers comprehension.

Passing over many damning details, we can now see how
Orton gave himself away continually, and yet saved himself,
partly by his cunning, effrontery and remarkable memory,
but mainly because Australia and England were then so far
apart and without telegraphic communication. The difficulty
—which Orton exploited so shrewdly—was that in Australia
and South America they did not know what was known in
England, and vice versa. How could a solicitor in Wagga-
Wagga know the facts about Roger Tichborne and Orton?
For instance, it occurred to him that the claimant's Wapping
mangling of the Queen's English was hardly creditable or
credible in the heir to a baronetcy and a large income. The
claimant explained that his education had been wholly
neglected because as a child he had suffered severely from St.
Vitus's dance. Well, that sounded a good explanation,
particularly since the claimant suffered from occasional
twitchings. How could Mr. Gibbes know that Roger Tichborne never had St. Vitus's dance, and Arthur Orton had?
That was one of the innumerable little points against the
claimant which could not be known in England until, after
years of legal delay, Mr. Gibbes was persuaded to come over
from Australia and to give evidence on oath. And by that
time the "fools and fanatics" (as the Chief Justice rightly
called them) on Orton's side had reached such a pitch of
folly and fanaticism that any evidence against him was
treated by them and their mob supporters as perjury or
prejudice.

There came a moment when the claimant in Wagga-
Wagga could no longer evade writing a letter to his 'mother',

the Dowager Lady Tichborne, in France. Obviously, this was a serious test in many ways. Without reproduction in facsimile of the originals I cannot show the immense difference between the handwriting of the undoubted Roger and the handwriting of the claimant, nor how closely the claimant's resembled Orton's. But we can compare the style and spelling of one of the undoubted Roger's last letters to his mother with the first from the claimant. It must be understood that Roger's upbringing in France and the neglect by his parents of his education until he went to Stonyhurst resulted in spelling mistakes and the use of French idioms in translation. Here is the letter from the undoubted Roger:

"Buenos Ayres, March 1st (1854)

"My Dear Mother,

"It is certainly strange that every one of your letters as far back as I can remember have always been and are still now always on the same subjects, without the least variation. Those subjects are invariably the duties of a Son towards his Mother which fills up as a matter of course at least the first two pages. The other two pages are generally filled up with all kinds of imaginary fears, and a list of accidents, the illness and sickness of every description which are quite unknown to anybody but yourself. It must be certainly the work of your imagination, which makes you think of so many things. Another thing also, where I don't think you don't at all treat me fairly; you treat me in your letters exactly like if I was twelve or thirteen years of age, and moreover as if I was quite incapable of taking the least care of myself. I beg to say that I am quite old enough to take care of myself, and that I act as circumstances require it. Afterwards if you are always determined to think that I am ill or sick or anything else, when I tell you in my letters that I am very well, it is perfectly useless for me to write to you to let you know how I am, as you don't appear to believe what I say in my letters. I shall not in future wait for your letters to write as they don't contain any news from you or my Father, or any kind of news which require an answer. I shall therefore write to you from the principal towns at which I shall stop, without waiting

any more for your letters. . . . It is quite impossible for me
to fix in any kind of way the time of my return to England.
The life which I am following suits my taste too well for me to
leave it in a hurry, especially as my health is remarkably
good, and promising to keep so for a long while to come.
. . . When you answer this letter direct yours Post Office,
Kingston, Jamaica, West Indies, where I shall only call to
get my letters on my way to Mexico, where I expect to be in
about 3 month and a half. I have not time to now to send
you an extract of my daily journal to-day but I shall write it
out for you as soon as I shall have time."

The only vulgarism there is 'month' for 'months', but
there are several translated French idioms, such as "the life
which I am following" (*la vie que je suive*) when we say "the
life I am leading"; and "as soon as I shall have time " (*dès que
j'aurai le temps*) when we say "as soon as I have time". And so
on. The contents of the letter let one see why he pitied his
father for having to live with his mother, and why he insisted
that after his father's death he would never live with her.

When Mr. Gibbes (on January 17th, 1866) insisted that the
claimant should write to his mother, he began drafting a
letter which was so lawyer-like that the claimant saw at once
it was absurd as from a long-lost son to his doting mother,
and he produced the following original contribution:

"Wagga-Wagga, January 17th, 1866
"My dear Mother,
"The delay which has taken place since my last Letter,
Dated 22nd April, 54 Makes it very difficult to Commence
this Letter. I deeply regret the truble and anxsity I must
have cause you by not writing before. But they are known to
my attorney and the more private details I will keep for your
own ear. Of one thing rest assured that although I have
been in A humble condition of Life I have never let any act
disgrace you or my family I have been A poor Man and
nothing worse. Mr. Gibbes suggest to me as essential That I
should recall to your Memory things which can only be
known to you and me to convince you of my Identity. I

don't think it needful My Dear Mother. Although I send them. Mamely, the Brown Mark on my side. And the Card Case at Brighton. I can assure you My Dear Mother I have kept your promise ever since. In writing to me please enclose your letter to Mr. Gibbes to prevent unnesersery enquiry as I do not wish any person to know me in this Country. When I take my proper prosition and title. Having therefore made up my mind to return and face the Sea once more I must request to send me the Means of doing so paying a fue outstanding debts. I would return by the Overland Mail. The passage Money and other expences would be over two Hundred pound. for I propose sailing from Victoria not this Colonly And to Sail from Melbourne in my own Name. Now to annable me to do this my dear Mother you must send me . . ."

The second sheet of this letter is lost, but contained a request for four hundred pounds; which is obviously the kind of demand an impostor out for money would make. Illiterate as that letter is, it was either corrected by Gibbes as he stood by or has not been reprinted exactly, for the Chief Justice not only says that the claimant used none but a full-stop, he says that the claimant almost always used 'i' for 'I'. Even if the spelling of the letter has been improved, the contrast with that of the undoubted Roger is startling. The blunders are always cockney vulgarisms and never the translated French idioms of the undoubted Roger. Here is an extract from another letter (dated January 26th, 1866) from the claimant to Cubitt, the agent for "missing friends":

". . . Mr. Cubitt Sir Mr Gibbes has shown me a letter in which you state you have received. News. of great imporance from my Mother. I requested Mr. Gibbes to write to you. to know if the News you allude to is merely my whereabouts. Or anythink connected with the Estates. I believe He has receved an answer from you. But has not sort proper to let me know your answer. Mr Gibbes has no doubt made it known to you that I have wrote to my Mother though him. I wish you to let me know What power my

Mother has envested you with. or weather you have receved any advances from her If you have not. let me know what your charges are for advertisements and cr are That I may settle them before leaving colonoly. Has most likely on recept of answer to my letter I may proceed to England via Melbourne . . ."

Making all allowances for the fact that Cubitt knew nothing whatever about the undoubted Roger and in his searches for "missing friends" doubtless had to deal with some pretty rough nuggets from the gold diggings, one cannot help being surprised that he accepted such a letter as the probable or even possible work of the missing heir. But of course the real significance of these letters only became apparent years later when they were put in as evidence and could be carefully studied and compared by Counsel, judge and jury. There is a great mass remaining of Australian evidence, most of it showing that the claimant was not Tichborne, much of it connecting him with Orton, and some of it showing how this wily impostor picked up Tichborne information from more or less guileless persons who thought they were testing him when he was in fact picking their brains. Thus, by the time he arrived in England he had already got hold of enough genuine Tichborne information to correct some of his early blunders in Australia, and most cunningly used what knowledge he had got to collect more.

In June 1866 the claimant, in the name of Roger Tichborne, made a will at Wagga-Wagga. He did so because it was one of the demands made by the bank before they would advance money for him to go to England. The Dowager had not then sent the £400 he had asked for, and his financial position was so desperate he was reduced to begging constantly for advances of a pound or two from Gibbes. At that time the claimant almost certainly thought that if he was 'recognised' by the Dowager he could at once enter into possession of the Tichborne estates, repay the bank and make another will, whereupon the one he was about to make would disappear or could be destroyed. He was in such straits anyway that his only hope was to get away from Australia, and he certainly did not realise what damning evidence he was leaving against himself. Omitting minor or purely legal points (which the real Roger, however, would have known), he gave his 'mother's' Christian names (which he only knew to the extent that she had signed letters "H. F. Tichborne") as Hannah Frances when she was Henriette Félicité. He left his 'mother' his property in Cowes, where the Tichbornes and Doughtys had none. He bequeathed non-existent 'estates' at Ryde and 'Wymmering' and a Hermitage estate. Curiously enough there was a farm called 'Hermitage' in the genuine Tichborne property, but this was in no sense an 'estate' and anyway was bought after the real Roger left England. It was noted in the trial that in Wapping there is or was a Hermitage Wharf and a Hermitage Street. Still more damning is the fact that he appointed as executor and guardian of his children respectively "John Jarvis of Bridport" and "Henry Angel of Dorset" and in case of their failure "Sir John Bird of Hertfordshire". These characters remind one of "little John Doit of Staffordshire, and black George Barnes, and Francis Pickbone, and Will Squele a Cotswold man" though in fact only "Sir John Bird of Hertfordshire" was a figment of the claimant's imagination. Jarvis and Angel existed, and—fatal circumstance—were old friends of the Orton family, while by no possibility could they have been known to Roger Tichborne! And if the maker of the will was really Roger Tichborne, why did he not give the names of his former executors, Gosford and Slaughter?

In June 1866 the claimant moved to Sydney, and not long afterwards there arrived a letter from the Dowager to Mr. Gibbes which greatly disturbed him and the Wagga-Wagga banker, who had advanced money on their faith in the claimant's statements. And well it might, for it contained a number of highly important facts in the life of the undoubted Roger which the claimant had either denied or evaded. For the first time the Australian banker and lawyer learned that Roger spoke French better than English. Gibbes, trying to find what the claimant's education was, had tested him in languages and had found that he spoke a little colloquial South American Spanish, but not a word of French. Was it possible that the real Roger could have totally forgotten his mother tongue, and yet remember the Spanish he had picked up on his travels? Then they learned that, far from having been only scrappily educated by a Christian Brother because he had St. Vitus's dance, as the claimant alleged, Roger had never had St. Vitus's dance, and had spent three years at Stonyhurst. And there were other disturbing revelations.

Accordingly one or both of them telegraphed some questions from Wagga-Wagga to the claimant in Sydney. He was asked where he was educated and replied "High School, Southampton," which of course was quite untrue. He later denied that he had ever been at Stonyhurst. He was asked the name of his brother's school and replied "Winchester College, Yorkshire," which never existed, and Alfred Tichborne had been to school at Prior Park. He was asked the name of his father's agent, and said "Hallin of Bridport." He did not know the name of the agent for Tichborne Park, though in fact it was Roger's old and most intimate friend, Vincent Gosford. He was asked what regiment he had been in and replied "The 66th." Later he said that he had not been an officer, had been a private for only thirteen days and then been "bought out" by his father (this to excuse his total ignorance of drill) and stated that the "66th" was a cavalry regiment and known as "the Blues". He added that his father had kept him strictly at home after that until he sailed from England in November 1852. It was Orton who sailed on that date. Roger Tichborne sailed in March 1853.

Here comes another strange fact. Apparently it was in Sydney that the claimant learned that Roger Tichborne was a Catholic. Orton, as I have mentioned, was converted in Melipilla and baptised as "Joseph Maria". Now, the claimant at first had intended to leave his wife in Australia, but after the birth of his child he decided to take them with him, and he and his wife were re-married by a Catholic priest. The claimant specially returned for this ceremony from Sydney to Goulburn, where he had left his family. He evidently did not know the Tichbornes were Catholics until he got to Sydney, and he learned the fact either from a letter of the Dowager to Cubitt or from a 'Baronetage', which he certainly consulted there.

Now here comes another accidental intervention in the claimant's favour, as unpredictable by anyone as the Dowager's determination to recognise almost anybody as her son, and the strange fact that there seems to have been some slight resemblance to Roger in the upper part of Orton's face. It seems probable that, after the revelations just described of the claimant's ignorance of Roger's life, the Sydney bank would not have advanced the money he was trying so hard to get. Among the officials at Government House was a Mr. Turville, who had known Sir James and Lady Tichborne in Paris though he had never met Roger, and therefore could hardly be considered qualified to swear to the identity of the claimant. However, he was brought in, and proceeded to put three test questions. "Was your mother stout or thin?" was the first, and the claimant said she resembled a tall, burly woman in Sydney called Butts, though in fact Lady Tichborne was not very tall and so thin that she was almost emaciated. On this the amazing Mr. Turville commented that it was not quite so, but doubtless that could be explained. He then asked where the claimant and his parents were in May 1852, and after much thought the claimant said his parents were in Paris and he (Roger)

was in Dorset. Of course by then the claimant had learned
that Roger's parents were nearly always in Paris until Sir
James inherited, but in fact Roger was not then in Dorset,
but with his regiment in Dublin. In a later attempt to
wriggle out of this he suggested that the year named by Mr.
Turville was really 1853, but that didn't help because Roger
was then at sea on his way to Valparaiso. What the third
question was nobody could remember. On the strength of
these answers Mr. Turville 'recognised' the claimant, shook
hands, and said he looked like his father "especially about the
mouth", whereas most of Roger's relatives and near friends
insisted that he was "an ugly version of his mother". But of
course a recognition from someone at Government House
turned the scales, and the claimant was eventually able to
raise from the bank and elsewhere about £20,000, of which
£10,000 were spent on buying a hotel which the claimant
bragged that he would make the finest in Australia when he
returned. Mr. Turville certainly has a good deal of mischief
to answer for, as without his foolish interference the claimant
might never have been able to get to England and do all the
damage and cause all the trouble which he did cause.

Before leaving Australia and these rather detailed pieces of
evidence (which must convince anyone today that the
claimant was not Roger but a liar and impostor and plainly
Arthur Orton) we must look for a moment at something most
characteristic of the claimant's technique of imposture. In
one of her letters the Dowager had foolishly announced that
Bogle, a negro family servant, was living in Sydney, and that
Guilfoyle, formerly a gardener at Tichborne, was living near
at hand. Guilfoyle could not be induced to come to England
for the perjury trial, but from his letters it is plain that he saw
the claimant, who from Guilfoyle's unskilful questions then
learned for the first time that his (the claimant's) most intimate
friend in England was Vincent Gosford. What else he learned
there can only be inferred from the fact that later he was able

to tell things to Bogle which that simpleton thought only Sir Roger could have known. The claimant wrote his 'mother' that Guilfoyle had 'recognised' him as Sir Roger, whereas Guilfoyle wrote that he had done no such thing, and did not think the claimant was Sir Roger. It seems obvious, however, that he unwittingly—like so many others—let slip valuable information without intending to do so. At the trials the lawyers naturally showed impatience at the way various friends or dependants of Roger gave away information of priceless value to the claimant, but after all they were average, well-meaning, more or less honest persons who had never met a cunning impostor any more than they had learned how to conduct a cross-examination without giving away some or most of the answers in the questions. A lawyer would ask: "Will you tell us the name of your best friend in England?" which of course would baffle the impostor completely. But apparently (we haven't the evidence) Guilfoyle must have asked: "Surely you must remember your best friend, Vincent Gosford?" And the impostor, who had never heard the name before, of course would answer: "Why, yes, what was I thinking of? Dear old Vinny." And give himself away again to a trained legal mind, because Roger never used the nickname 'Vinny'. . . . Of course I don't give this as evidence, but merely as a conjectural example.

Now it seems very likely that the claimant made use of what he managed to pump from Guilfoyle in order to impress the simple-minded Bogle with his knowledge of Tichborne, and thereby acquired a most valuable source of future information, which he made certain by taking the old man into his service although he was too old for work. Although the claimant subsequently swore that he did not know Bogle was in Sydney, a letter of his to the Dowager (which he had evidently forgotten) was found and put into court which showed that he did know. Hearing that Roger Tichborne

H

had been miraculously saved from drowning and restored to the world after twelve years, Bogle went up to the hotel, and sat down to wait for him. Presently, the claimant came in with another man, and as he passed said: "Hullo, Bogle, is that you?" And later Bogle was taken into the hotel, and more or less won over. Now, if the claimant had not known that his uncle's old servant was in Sydney and had recognised him at once, that would be a point in his favour. But as the claimant had learned from Lady Tichborne's letter that Bogle was in Sydney and who he was and that he was old, there was nothing very strange in his making the guess when he saw a white-haired negro waiting at the hotel. There can't have been many in Sydney, if there was one beside this old valet. And the knowledge of his sons' names, which so much impressed Bogle and won him over, had almost certainly been incautiously dropped by Guilfoyle. That was the technique the claimant used all along: pick up some fact or facts from some dependant or friend of the Tichbornes, and use them to create a feeling of confidence in the next person met, who would thus be all the more likely to let out more valuable information. I don't recollect if it was mentioned in court—it must have been, for there was very little the Chief Justice missed in his summing up—but on more than one occasion when the claimant gave wrong information and stuck to it, the cross-examination of Bogle subsequently showed that the original mistake was his.

Now of course none of this was known to any members of the Tichborne and Doughty and Seymour families when the claimant arrived in England and went about gathering information and adherents. One sees the immense difficulty they had in defending the lawful heir, the infant son of Alfred Tichborne. The only member of the family who knew a little of what had gone on was the Dowager, and there were many things she never knew until the day of her death in 1868. In any event she had formed and acted on the (to her) convenient theory that "poor Roger" was "living in a dream", which is a most fanciful and sentimental description of the astute and unscrupulous rogue who stopped at no trickery, no perjury, no baseness in trying to steal her grandson's inheritance. Whenever she was given proof that her newly-found 'son' had made some completely untrue statement she threw it off by saying that "poor Roger" had suffered so much from his shipwreck and from his hard life in Australia that his memory was seriously affected, and that it was her duty and everyone else's to re-build his memory by telling him what the real facts were! Why she foisted this gigantic cuckoo—he eventually came to weigh twenty-six stone whereas the real Roger seemingly was only about ten—into the Tichborne nest I have already tried to explain. She intended to have her son back, and no absurdity was too fantastic to disturb her. But I cannot help thinking there may have been some deep grudge against her English "in-laws" which, consciously or unconsciously, fortified her obstinacy. The judges and the prosecuting lawyers were careful not to make any such charge, which obviously couldn't be proved; but her dislike, if not hatred, of these (to her) foreign relatives was certainly intense, and it is a fact that she warned the returning 'Roger' not to see any of his English relatives until he had seen her. Did she mean to coach him? Who can say? But on the basis of the undoubted Roger's letters it seems clear that at any rate Lady Radcliffe, Lady Doughty and Gosford meant more to him than the mother he had so emphatically asserted he would never share a house with.

2

On September 6th, 1866, the claimant sailed from Sydney on board the *Rachaia*, unconsciously leaving behind him in Australia evidence (of which I have given the most important) which even if it had not been confirmed and extended in other parts of the world would alone have sufficed to convict him of imposture and perjury. In face of that it must seem inexplicable that Orton was able to make the enormous impression he did, but one cannot stress too often that years were to elapse before all the evidence was made public, and by that time the claimant had collected such a retinue of accomplices and dupes of all ranks that men's minds in England had got beyond the point where they will attend to reason and fact, and were capable only of the angry defence of rival prejudices.

The claimant was accompanied by his wife and their baby daughter, by a natural child of his wife's, by a 'secretary' called Butts, and by Bogle. Now as Bogle had been in the service of the Tichborne family since he was twelve and was, moreover, a guileless old man, we can guess—though we can never know—how much priceless information the claimant must have got from him on that long voyage. Here is one little example, from which the rest may be inferred. Just before they left Sydney, Bogle had brought the claimant an old print of the Doughty mansion at Upton, and long afterwards told the court that when the claimant saw it he said: "Ah, there is old Upton." Now for the claimant to recognise at once and unaided a print of what had been almost a home to Roger and certainly a house of which he was very fond looks like striking evidence in his favour. But under questioning the naïve Bogle revealed that on bringing the print he had said first: "There is a likeness of Upton," whereupon the claimant then remarked: "Yes, there is old Upton": a very different thing! That is a small but definite example of the claimant being accidentally given a piece of knowledge he certainly hadn't had before, used by his noisy followers and even his counsel as 'proof' that he must be Roger Tichborne.

From Panama the party sailed to New York, and thence

by a ship called the *Cella*, which arrived in London on
Christmas Day, 1866. Evidence was brought later that on
both these ships the claimant's uncouthness and low-class
English with all its misplaced aspirates caused much surprise
and amusement as coming from an English baronet. It was
also a curious thing that the claimant took a slow boat to
London instead of a fast boat to France, as the Dowager had
asked him, at the same time warning him to come direct to
her in Paris before seeing any of his other relatives. Why this
change of plan? We shall see. Meanwhile, as the *Cella* came
slowly up the Thames estuary, the claimant, who always
liked to show off, made the curious mistake of asking the pilot
if he knew one of the Dundee pilots named John Ferguson.
It turned out later that this man could not have been known
to Roger Tichborne, while he was well known to Arthur
Orton since he acted as pilot to ships which brought in
Shetland ponies!

As the party landed, Bogle once more proved his value.
"Bogle," said Butts on behalf of the claimant, "what hotel
had we better go to?" "Oh," said Bogle, "we had better go
to Ford's Hotel, Manchester Square; that's where the family
always went." How curious that Sir Roger Tichborne
should have to ask his late uncle's valet which hotel the
family stayed at! How very narrow sometimes is the gap
between a dupe and an accomplice!

Almost as soon as he was installed in his West End hotel,
the claimant did a very curious thing, almost inexplicable if
he were Roger Tichborne, but only too understandable if he
were Arthur Orton. He had just come off a long sea voyage,
and although it was Christmas Day and bitterly cold, he left
his wife and comfortable hotel immediately after dinner, and
took a long cold cab drive across London to Wapping!
Arrived there, he went to the Globe public-house, which (as it
was Christmas) was empty except for the landlady, Mrs.
Jackson, and her mother, Mrs. Fairhead, also a publican in

Wapping. Their account of what happened, which there is
no reason to doubt in spite of Kenealy's assertions that they
had been bribed to perjure themselves, is another instance of
the claimant's mixture of effrontery and cunning and
excellent memory with ignorance, carelessness and love of
showing off which caused him to leave clues to his real
identity which years later inevitably led him to prison.

Over sherry and a cigar he told the women that he had just
been to the Ortons' house in High Street and had found it
shut—what had happened to them? He was told that both
the old people were dead. "Where is Mary Ann Orton?" he
asked, and was told she had married a Mr. Tredgett but was
recently a widow, and that her address could be got from
Charles Orton, who was living in that very street. The
claimant said he wanted nothing to do with Charles Orton,
and Mrs. Fairhead offered to get the address from a servant.
He then asked after a number of persons who had lived in
that small area of Wapping, most of them small shop-
keepers whom he mentioned by name—the Cronins,
Schottlers, Gosheron, John Warwick, the Wrights—whose
occupations and former addresses he knew. He then walked
up the passage to the bar parlour and back, and remarked
that the house had not changed a bit. Whereupon Mrs.
Fairhead remarked that he must be one of the Ortons, since
he looked so much like the old man and knew so much about
Wapping. He denied this, and said he was a friend come to
assist the family, but Mrs. Fairhead insisted he must be an
Orton, the son "who left twelve or fourteen years ago". He
denied this again, and went off to find Mrs. Tredgett (Mary
Ann Orton), who was away.

That was not the end. Next day (December 26th, 1866),
the claimant again went to Mrs. Tredgett's house, and found
she was still away for her Christmas holiday. He then sent in
a card (on which was written "William H. Stephens,
Australia") to her sister-in-law, Mrs. Pardon, and said he

wanted to ask some questions about the Ortons. Whereupon she instantly said: "Are you an Orton? You look so like old George Orton?" He denied that, but said he was a great friend of Arthur Orton, one of the wealthiest men in Australia(!), whom he had promised to assist the Ortons; and went on to tell Mrs. Pardon that he was an Australian reporter on his way to Ireland to investigate the Fenians. He then gave her a letter for Mrs. Tredgett, and went away. Mrs. Tredgett returned later that day and opened the letter in the presence of her sister-in-law and read:

"Wagga-Wagga New South Wales June 3'd. /66. My Dear and Beloved sister It many years now since i heard from any of you. I have never heard a word from any one I knew since 1854. But my friend Mr. Stephens is about starting for England. And he has promised to find you all out. and write and let me know all about you. I do not intend to say much because he can tell you all about me. Hoping my dear sister he will make you welcome has he is a dear friend of mine so good bye Arthur Orton."

The signature was followed by a hieroglyph peculiar to Arthur Orton, which he had picked up from the Chileans in Melipilla, where everyone had his own special mark of the kind. The letter was unquestionably in the handwriting of Arthur Orton, and equally unquestionably was written by the claimant! The name "William H. Stephens" was not that of an Australian but of an American journalist going to Ireland, whose acquaintance the claimant had made on board the *Cella* coming from New York. This was a fatal blunder, for how could Arthur Orton in Wagga-Wagga in June know an American who had never been in Australia, but had casually met the claimant in December? Moreover the word 'Australia' on Mr. Stephens's card was written in the claimant's handwriting.

There is no need to point out how impossible it was that the genuine Sir Roger Tichborne could have behaved in this

way, or that his very first care on arriving in England could
have been to visit—not his own family—but those who could
tell him about the Orton family! The claimant explained
this at first on the grounds that he had promised "to assist"
the Ortons; and, forgetting this later in his ever-increasing
labyrinth of lies, he said he wanted to find out if his friend
Orton had reached England. But if the claimant was Orton
he had a very powerful motive for finding out about the
family, whose members he must somehow induce to keep
silent about his real identity. And this must have been
impressed on him the more since three people in Wapping
who had never before set eyes on him asked if he was "an
Orton" simply because he so much resembled "the old
people" now dead.

The calculations underlying this Christmas Day trip to
Wapping were only revealed much later, but the revelation
is instructive. Although the reason for hurrying down to
Wapping on the day he arrived was stated by the claimant to
be his eagerness to 'assist' the relatives of his old friend
Arthur Orton, he in fact did nothing about them for nearly a
year. By giving the name 'Stephens' and the address Poste
Restante, Liverpool, he easily baffled any effort of poor
people like the Ortons to follow him up. But in October
1867 the claimant found out that the Tichbornes were at last
aware of the Arthur Orton clue and were following it up.
Then, and seemingly not till then, the claimant began sending
them money surreptitiously, obviously to induce them to
keep quiet—and they took the money and did keep quiet—
until the money ceased, whereupon Charles Orton in great
indignation went over to the other side! This seems to
indicate the level of Orton morality. I have mentioned the
claimant's irresistible urge to show off, instanced in the life of
Arthur Orton by his telling the Chileans that as a child he
had played with the Queen's children! In a petty way he did
the same sort of thing on the Wapping visit. He could not

refrain from trying to astonish the two landladies by showing his detailed knowledge of Wapping characters and the interior of their own public-house; thereby, of course, arousing their suspicions, and leaving evidence against himself. Though he was playing at being Tichborne (or in this case "Stephens of Australia") he had to show off Orton's knowledge. Similarly, he told Mrs. Pardon that Arthur Orton, his friend, was one of the richest men in Australia. The strangest and most complicated example is that he also showed her with pride a portrait of his own wife and child as those of Arthur Orton—which indeed they were, but he was supposed to be "Mr. Stephens"!

We have now traced the course by which Arthur Orton, the Wapping butcher of Wagga-Wagga, evolved into "Sir Roger Tichborne, Bart.", the claimant to the name, title and estates of an ancient and wealthy family. In so doing we have again and again had to note facts and episodes which show him to be a liar and a gross impostor. How then did it happen that when he finally appeared in England he managed to collect so many supporters and to divide the whole nation into bitter factions opposing each other with a fierceness which had not been seen in England since the American War of Secession had split the country in two? The answer is, as we have seen, that when at the end of December 1866 "Sir Roger Tichborne" presented himself at Alresford (the nearest town to Tichborne) not one of these damning facts was known. The only person who might have known some of them if she had chosen was the Dowager Lady Tichborne, and she didn't choose to know or at any rate to draw the natural inference. After Mr. Turville in Australia, she is primarily responsible for the bolstering of a fraud so preposterous it now seems incredible that anyone should have been taken in.

We must always remember in defence of the adherents that they did not know the truth until it was too late for their factious partisanship to recognise the truth. Moreover, the impostor had amazing luck. He had found Cubitt, the advertiser, to discover him; Gibbes, the solicitor, to give him money; Turville, the Government House jackass, to 'recognise' him; and then he had found Bogle. Through them, he was to find more dupes in England, all of whom supplied him with "Tichborne facts" which enabled him to convince others. And so the snowball grew, in the way that such delusions do grow.

On December 28th, 1866, the claimant, who had moved his family to Gravesend (to avoid arrest for the bills drawn in Sydney), while leaving Bogle and Butts at the West End hotel to mislead people, set off 'incognito' for Alresford, where he put up at the Angel Inn under the name 'Taylor'. Why had he gone there? Obviously, before he met his 'mother' he must learn something of the "dear old home" he had never seen. His first experience at and near Tichborne Park was a rebuff. He met the village blacksmith (who had known Roger well), gave him sixpence to buy beer, and after some talk asked if he thought the person speaking to him was Roger. The answer he got must have staggered him a bit: "No, I'm damned if you are. If you are, you've turned from a racehorse to a carthorse."

This must have been what Euphues calls "a cooling card", but of course so impudent a charlatan would not be in the least abashed, especially since he had found a much more useful person who seemed likely to become an ally. By a stroke of luck, the landlord of the Angel Inn at Alresford, where the "Mr. Taylor of London" was staying, was a Mr. Rous, who had been clerk to the solicitors for the Tichborne and Doughty properties, Dunn and Hopkins. Think what valuable information he could give! How Rous was won over we don't know, but he was, and on Monday, December 30th (1866), he drove the claimant over to see his paternal mansion for the first time. Next day the claimant wired for

Bogle to come down, and spread the news so cleverly that more than three hundred people turned out to welcome the old negro, whom they all knew and liked. Of course, the moment Bogle arrived, "Mr. Taylor" became "Sir Roger Tichborne"; and Bogle, the old family servant, announced his belief. One of the purposes for which Bogle was employed at that moment was to get into the Tichborne mansion and report on the pictures there. 'Roger' would have to remind his 'mother' of the pictures in the "dear old home" of the Wapping butcher!

Hopkins, the retired solicitor of the Tichborne estate, and Baigent the antiquary, who both became strong adherents and helpers with information, apparently did not speak to the claimant on this occasion, though he passed them in the street, but without recognising them. Before leaving for London he was interviewed by Bowker (Lady Tichborne's solicitor), who formed a very unfavourable opinion and left with the conviction that the man was an impostor. And strangely enough the claimant went to Paris without attempting to see Mrs. Greenwood (formerly Katherine Tichborne), who had been on the most friendly terms with Roger. And after he got back to Gravesend he was seen by Roger's greatest friend, Gosford, who behaved indiscreetly indeed, but very soon saw that the claimant knew nothing about Roger's intimate life. As Gosford became a key witness in the subsequent legal proceedings, and was publicly thanked by the judges for his evidence, while Kenealy and the claimant did all they could to blacken his character, something must be said about him. For many years he had been the Tichborne land agent, at what seems a rather inadequate salary, and had involved himself in a land improvement scheme of his own, in which he sank a lot of money. Unluckily for him, before this venture became paying, the trustees had to demand payment of rents he had received. Still more unluckily, he had paid them into his own account, and could not refund. He gave up everything he had, but was left owing £9,000. In addition, he had an overdraft of more than £500 with the local banker, Bulpett. Clearly, with his intimate knowledge of the estates and the complicated settlements, his long friendship with Roger and possession of many letters and documents, his confidential knowledge of the Catherine Doughty secret, his recognition of the claimant would have been decisive, and moreover entirely in his interests, since 'Roger' would not press for payments which the trustees, though friends, were forced to do. His probity in sticking to the truth is therefore clear. Yet Bulpett not only betrayed to the claimant confidential facts which Gosford had told him to prove the claimant a fraud, he went further and when Gosford proved incorruptible insisted on repayment of the overdraft. Kenealy in court asserted that the Tichbornes had compounded a felony for Gosford, and the judge had to intervene sternly and peremptorily to deny it.

A fortnight after his arrival, the claimant had still not seen any member of his family nor visited his long-lost mother, who was eagerly and peevishly awaiting him in Paris. And instead of asking his closest friend, Gosford, to find him a solicitor, he chose a man named Holmes who was recommended to him by a chance hotel acquaintance and a brewer's agent named Leete, both of whom he took with him when he left for Paris on the 10th. Bowker, the Dowager's solicitor, had been vainly trying to get in touch with the claimant, and had been put off and sent on fool's errands by false information from Butts. He got to Paris a day before the claimant. It is some indication of the Dowager's state of mind and pre-determination to 'recognise', that Bowker found her in a great rage with Gosford for saying that the claimant (whom she had not yet seen!) was an impostor, and that when she found Bowker still advising caution, she instantly dismissed him.

The 'recognition' by the mother in Paris was more absurd than the most fanciful 'agnition' in a late Greek novel. Instead of going at once to see his mother, the claimant pretended he was ill, took to his bed, and refused to see her except in the presence of his solicitor and Leete. His illness, however, had not been so serious as to prevent his making a hearty breakfast. When, after an exchange of messages and orders, the Dowager found the claimant would not come to her, she went to him and found him lying fully dressed on his bed with his face turned to the wall. The Dowager came in, and without asking a question or even looking at him closely, bent over and kissed him, saying that he looked like his father and his ears were like his uncle's! All this in the presence of Holmes and Leete, and a servant of Lady Tichborne's, named Coyne. The claimant, to excuse his lying down in a darkened room, muffled up and turned to the wall, said he was ill—a misfortune which frequently occurred to him in situations which made it awkward for him to be out and about. The Dowager instantly sent for a Doctor Shrimpton and then Sir Joseph Oliffe, who was physician to the British Embassy, and in their presence stated that the claimant was her son. Later, Holmes wrote a letter to *The Times* saying that the Dowager had recognised her son; and she announced that she meant to live in England with him, and until he got his estates back she would give him the £1,000 a year she had been allowing her daughter-in-law.

There had been some newspaper mention of the return of the "missing Tichborne heir" and considerable local excitement in and about Alresford after the arrival of Bogle, but it is safe to say that the great Tichborne case and controversy dated from the publication of the Holmes letter. Now that the affair is virtually forgotten it is hard for us to realise the bitterness of controversy which ensued, that, as I have already indicated, "personal bias ran so high that parents and children were estranged for ever, life-long friendships made and severed, political factions and commercial and social alliances sealed and sundered, feuds of every magnitude bred and fostered." Obviously Mr. Turville and the Dowager had a serious responsibility. Just how determined she was to accept him at any cost is shown by her conduct all along, especially by her getting rid of her solicitor, Bowker.

A striking instance during these first days in Paris was the Chatillon episode. He had been one of Roger's early tutors and had kept in touch with him up to the last day Roger was in Paris. The Dowager went to Chatillon and told him she wanted him "to recognise" Roger. He asked permission to have his breakfast first, but in her domineering way she insisted on taking him off at once, repeating in the carriage that she hoped he would 'recognise' her "dear Roger". On arrival, he suggested that his name should not be announced, an excellent test, for how could the real Roger fail to recognise his old tutor? But the moment they got into the room she gave the game away by saying: "Sir Roger, here is Monsieur Chatillon!" When Chatillon refused to 'recognise' and told her "This is not your son", she simply got rid of him as she had got rid of Bowker.

Excuses can be made for a lonely ageing woman who was on bad terms with all her relatives, and wanted some sort of companionship at almost any cost. But Hopkins, the Alresford solicitor, behaved in much the same way and was obviously just as determined to allow nothing to alter his preconceived opinion. Henry Seymour (the Dowager's halfbrother and therefore Roger's uncle) came to see the claimant and Hopkins, bringing with him a former valet of Sir James Tichborne's, who had become a Customs officer and was unknown to Hopkins. As soon as he saw Seymour, Hopkins said: "Sir Roger Tichborne—Mr. Henry Seymour", surely an unnecessary introduction? Seymour asked the claimant if he recognised the friend he had brought, and after a considerable hesitation the claimant said it was his "Uncle Nangle", a man who was then over seventy, while the claimant obviously didn't recognise his father's former valet. At the same interview, after the claimant had hopelessly failed to answer Seymour's questions, the ex-valet produced an envelope and asked the claimant if he recognised the handwriting. The claimant said: "No." Mr. Hopkins gave one glance at it, and said: "Good God! It's your own father's handwriting!" The retired solicitor knew it at once, but not the writer's own son! Yet Hopkins continued to support him.

The finishing touch so far as the English relatives were concerned was provided by a letter to Mrs. Greenwood (formerly Miss Katherine Tichborne and Roger's first cousin) which one would think would convince anybody that the writer could not possibly be an Anglo-French gentleman and must be a vulgar impostor. The letter was written as an excuse for not seeing Mrs. Greenwood and was dated February 3rd, 1867, after the claimant had returned from Paris:

"My dear Cousing Kate I am very sorry i am not able to come and see you before i go, my head is so bad that i am not fit to come. Mr Baigent is very much annoyed about it, but i am coming here to spend a fue day at the end of the week. and i shall then have the pleasure of meeting you again. You will excuse me for not coming has it will only be a fue day before i am with you. I have an invitasion from Mr Hopkins to spend a fue day with him so i shall be down about Thursday. Give my regard to cousing William and G. I shall soon be down again and have the pleasure of a hunt with my old friend George. With my best regards my dear Cousin to you and your family I remain your affectionate cousin R. C. Tichborne. I have to meet Mamma to morrow at Dover and our address will be Essex lodge thornton heath Croydon."

After that one is not surprised that the claimant failed to recognise his other "Cousing Kate", i.e. Lady Radcliffe, with whom the undoubted Roger had been so much in love.

Little setbacks of this kind did not discourage "Sir Roger". He discovered and took into his service one of the undoubted Roger's batmen named Carter, and another old trooper called M'Cann. He also procured somehow from the Horse Guards the official register of the regiment's movements; and he who in Australia had only served thirteen days in the 66th Cavalry ("the Blues"!) now remembered that he had been three years a subaltern in the 6th Dragoons and re-collected many little episodes of his service. Thus he went on playing the game of using what he picked up from one person to impose on another and so pick up more. Amazing to relate, he was not only 'recognised' by many of the rank and file, but even by some of the officers. He was invited to Alresford by Hopkins and his wife as their guest, and presented as the "undoubted Sir Roger" (who didn't know his own father's handwriting!) to Colonel Lushington, the tenant of Tichborne Park. He was asked to stay there, and came with Baigent to prompt him, astonishing the Colonel by his knowledge of the family pictures. He was presented to a number of Hampshire gentlemen, whom he converted, among them a violently Protestant M.P., Guildford Onslow. His ignorance was excused on the grounds of defective education, and the vulgarities of his speech and manners attributed to his years of roughing it in Australia. Anybody who 'recognised' the claimant as Roger Tichborne was asked to give his evidence in the form of an affidavit. These were taken down by Rous or Baigent, who touched them up, while others were still further improved by legal experts. Free drinks were served out to all 'recognising' locals and soldiers who would testify, and all these affidavits were printed and used to stimulate the production of others and to influence public opinion. A Chancery lawyer, Mr. Locock Webb, had a hand in polishing some of these documents; and it is said that for years afterwards touching up a legal document was known among lawyers as "Locock Webbing" it!

Proceedings were started in Chancery on behalf of the claimant on June 27th, 1867, to demand possession of the very valuable property which would have been Roger Tichborne's if he had lived. The trustees for the infant heir determined to resist, and obtained permission for the cross-examination of the claimant on July 30th. This lasted three days, and each day the claimant entered with his 'mother', and dutifully handed her to her carriage when the court rose.

On August 2nd the claimant produced the dirtiest of all his many dirty lies. On the 1st, Gosford under oath had to admit that he had destroyed the secret paper left him by Roger (the vow to build a church if he married his cousin) and apparently he did not know that Roger had given a copy of it to the girl on the last day he saw her. Hitherto the claimant had denied (and Bulpett the banker knew he had denied) all knowledge of what was in the paper. Now in the presence of Bulpett and Holmes, the solicitor, the claimant said that among other things it was a direction to Gosford:

". . . to show great kindness to my cousin Kate, and let her have anythink she requires my cousin give me to understand that she was enciente and press me very hand to marry her before I left. I did not believe such was the case nor have I since heard it was so. allways believed it was said for to get me to marry her at once to this my father tried to persuade me . . . Gosford was also to make arrangements for Kate to leave England if such was true. Both Gosford and wife pressed me very hard to marry her ar once other matters of no consequence. I don't think Mrs Gosford knew about Kate. R. C. Tichborne."

These Chancery proceedings were not reported, but of course a charge like that was soon buzzed round, and there was no way in which Lady Radcliffe could crush it for nearly

I

seven years. But while the Chancery proceedings dragged
on, the claimant had troubles of his own. Lady Tichborne
soon had enough of life with her 'son', and left Croydon in
April, saying it was "too noisy". She spent much of her time
in Paris, but was furious when the claimant proposed to take
a house in the country, and he then discovered what his
"dear Mamma" could be when in a temper. She still gave
him £20 a week, but he was harried by money-lenders, and
in March 1868 fled to Boulogne to avoid arrest. On the 12th
of that month she was found dead in a London hotel, and
with her death went the claimant's £1,000 a year and his
most useful and influential supporter. He hurried back for
her funeral, and behaved abominably to his 'uncle' (her halfbrother Alfred Seymour), thrusting him from his place beside
her coffin and saying: "I know you, Alfred Seymour; you
are a damned backguard, who is trying to keep me out of my
rights." A horribly vulgar scene such as this, coming on top
of the charge against Lady Radcliffe, makes it incredible that
so many people continued to support the claimant. And
they had to do so in another sense, for the claimant and his
family would have been destitute in the streets but for money
subscribed for him. In the end he was issuing "Tichborne
Bonds" to be repaid at some very large premium after he
"recovered his estates". Amazing to relate, there were many
speculators, and once again it was proved how dearly the
English love a fraud.

Meanwhile the lawsuits dragged on. It is certainly true
that in the end the mills of Law ground the claimant "exceeding small", but so complicated did the case become, while
evidence had to be collected from such distant places
(Australia and South America), that they ground exceeding
slow. In this brief and necessarily over-condensed review of
the famous case I have mainly limited myself to the Orton-
into-Tichborne aspect, which indeed is the essence of it. If
the claimant were Arthur Orton, and legally proved so, he

couldn't be Sir Roger Tichborne. But other aspects had to be investigated in court with minute accuracy—the undoubted Roger's life in Paris, at Stonyhurst, in the Army, in South America, the loss of the *Bella*, the claimant's story of his alleged rescue by the *Osprey*, the settlements of the estates, Roger's will, his friendship with Gosford, his relations with the cousin he had hoped to marry; and so forth. Why not prove just one of these, and let the rest go? Because the claimant's lawyers would instantly have said that the other side were afraid to tackle the other issues, and the jury might have believed them. Everything had to be investigated down to the colour of Roger's hair, the size of his boots, how many novels of Paul de Kock he read, and whether he ever played cards for money.

The guardians of the infant heir scored a preliminary success in June 1868 when they managed to get the case transferred to the Court of Common Pleas. This meant trial before a jury with witnesses, not just a conflict of affidavits—and we have seen how dubious some of the claimant's were. Then he started a friendly ejectment suit against the tenant of Tichborne Park, Colonel Lushington (a heavy subscriber to the defence funds), to establish his right as landlord. The Tichborne lawyers demanded a commission to collect evidence abroad, which was of course opposed by the claimant; but, as was only just, the demand was granted. Obviously it was essential that the claimant should accompany the commission, confront the witnesses abroad, and establish his identity as Roger Tichborne. He dodged that with typical effrontery. Instead of going round to Valparaiso by boat, he got off at Buenos Aires, saying he preferred to travel overland, went as far as Cordoba, and then returned to England without facing witnesses, on the pretext that he felt ill, as he always did feel ill at awkward moments.

Meanwhile, in October 1868, Charles Orton, having

received no money of late, turned up ready to swear that the claimant was his brother Arthur. This was a shock to Holmes, the claimant's solicitor, followed by the further shock of learning that the witness, who was supposed to have known both Castro and Orton together in Wagga-Wagga, now denied it. On top came the news from Melipilla that no Roger Tichborne had ever been known there, but Arthur Orton had, and so the lock of hair—part of which had been sent to the claimant from Melipilla while the rest remained there—which he had sworn was his turned out to be Arthur Orton's! And then, in the middle of January 1869, Holmes learned that his client had dodged the South American test. Though Holmes had advanced £5,000 he decided at once to throw up the case, and this defection in turn produced others when a meeting of country gentlemen was held on the claimant's return, when Holmes showed the "Mr. Stephens" letters and some of the damaging Melipilla evidence was read. The claimant (of course!) said the Stephens letters were forgeries, but most of these upper-class supporters now abandoned him. Bulpett, Onslow M.P., and a few others persisted, but the main body of respectable dupes was now lost. Soon after, the claimant quarrelled with Rous (the ex-clerk of Hopkins), who, like Holmes, possessed very damaging letters to give the Tichborne lawyers.

You would think that such important defections would have influenced the mass of the claimant's supporters, and even have discouraged his vulgar effrontery from persisting in his fraudulent claims. But not at all. Since the case was pending, the newspapers (under pain of contempt of court) could not publish the evidence produced at the meeting. They could only record that these defections had occurred, and these were easily explained away by the claimant as due to the 'tricks' of his 'enemies' and to bribery and pressure from the Tichbornes. (As a matter of fact, the bribery in the case which I find proved is that of the claimant—of his

family, of old Tichborne servants and of the cohorts of
thirsty ex-cavalrymen.) He must have been shrewd enough
to know the game was up, but what was he to do? He was
deep in the clutches of money-lenders, and at the same time
he was still finding dupes who would pay for his upkeep, his
cigars and brandy, and so forth. If he bolted, where was he
to bolt, and how was he to live? The only thing was to go on.
Apparently he was a good shot (Roger, his brother officers
and sportsmen said, was a "shocking bad" one) and the
claimant made a practice of attending the infamous pigeon-
shooting massacres then tolerated, and cultivating popularity
by condescending to the riff-raff which hang about 'sport-
ing' events. He would get up and make them speeches on
how he was defrauded of his rights, and the very vulgarity
which was one of the many pieces of evidence against his
claim here stood him in good stead. And his enormous size
struck these very numerous supporters as evidence in his
favour—a man of 350 pounds must be John Bull in person.
Class hatred came into it, and the mob supported his claim
that he was a gentleman because they instinctively knew he
wasn't a gentleman. Without formulating it, they wanted to
get back at the 'aristocrats' they hated with the frightening
hatred of the British proletariat, by foisting on them this
obvious impostor. After the sentence, when comment was
possible, *Punch* put the position in a nutshell. A rather
intoxicated Tichborne fan at a meeting says to his friend:
"I don't care whether he's Cashtro or Orton or Tishborne—
I don't like to see poor man kep' out of his estates."
"Thash what I say," says the other. *Bos locutus est.* Stealing
the property of the upper classes is not stealing—which
we might almost say has become a fiscal maxim of
democracy.

The trial was just ready to start when the siege of Paris in
the Franco-Prussian War delayed it, because essential witnesses were in the beleaguered capital. Years later Kenealy

asked why they could not come out by balloon, like Gambetta! The man who could make such a remark must have been either dishonest or a fool. At all events, the Common Pleas trial did not start until May 1871, so the impostor had already lived for nearly four and half years in luxury on the contributions of his dupes and accomplices. Then was it seen how the mild but incorruptible justice of England was within the reach of the poorest and humblest of Her Majesty's subjects. For the claimant—still the plaintiff, not yet defendant—appeared Mr. Sergeant Ballantine, Mr. Giffard, Q.C. (later Lord Halsbury), Mr. Pollard, Mr. Jeune and Mr. Rose. For the defendants, the champions of the infant Tichborne, appeared the Solicitor-General, Sir J. Coleridge, Mr. Hawkins, Q.C., Sir George Honeywood, Q.C., Mr. Chapman Barber and Mr. Charles Bowen. All these disinterested gentlemen, having been 'briefed', needed to be 'refreshed' daily, while watching briefs (also 'refreshed') were held by Mr. Henry Matthews, Q.C., and Mr. H. F. Purcell. How natural that the British legal system, so simple, so uncostly, should be the envy and admiration of the world!

Thirteen days were spent in hearing the opinions of witnesses, when an impatient jury demanded that the claimant and Bogle should go into the box. The interminable fencing and evasions of the claimant are of no interest now, but for all his dodging he was not allowed to evade stating on oath what he had declared in the Court of Chancery to be the contents of the secret letter left with Gosford:

The Solicitor-General: I repeat the question again. What is the event you hoped had not happened?
Plaintiff: The confinement of my cousin.
Solicitor-General: Do you mean to swear before the Judge and jury that you seduced this lady? (She and her husband were in court.)
Plaintiff: I most solemnly to my God swear that I did.

Instantly he was shown, and the jury were shown, the duplicate of the "secret letter" given to Miss Doughty, as she then was, on June 22nd, 1852, with the vow about building the church, and a letter to himself which Gosford had found from Roger about his will, saying that he would not mention the church in his will since "I will only build under the circumstances I have left you in writing."

That must have cooked the plaintiff's goose with any but the numerous class-hating or Jesuit-hating morons supporting him. Nevertheless, he stood in the box from May 30th until July 7th, when—speed being so valuable in justice—the case was adjourned to November 7th, for the legal gentlemen to refresh and repose themselves. The case went on with more and more evidence of witnesses, until at last on January 15th, 1872, the Solicitor-General began that masterly speech already referred to, which lasted until February 21st. A whole book would be needed to record and illustrate this remarkable speech. I can only quote the opinion of a lawyer that its effect was "to roll away the web of mystery and imposture which for five years had shrouded the Tichborne case". He then began calling his witnesses. On the one hundred and second day of the trial, the foreman of the jury stood up and informed the court that the jury required to hear no further evidence. After a delay, Mr. Sergeant Ballantine rose and said that his client "elected to be non-suited". But he didn't get away with it as easily as that, for the Chief Justice stated that in his opinion the plaintiff had been "guilty of wilful and corrupt perjury". He ordered him to be imprisoned until his trial unless he found bail for £10,000. The Chief Justice made a point of clearing Lady Radcliffe.

The claimant had not been able to face the ordeal of sitting in court, where the case was so obviously going against him, and was arrested by the police at the Waterloo Hotel in Jermyn Street, where he was reposing with brandy and cigars, and taken to Newgate. From that moment the claimant was virtually a condemned man, in spite of the fact that during the period of nearly a year which elapsed before the criminal trial opened he and his friends by their pigeon-shooting matches and "Tichborne Defence Fund" meetings contrived to arouse class and sectarian prejudices and hatreds to a really dangerous extent. The rabid Protestants heard that there was a Jesuit plot against the claimant, while the Radicals and lower classes in general were told that the money and political influence of the 'aristocrats' had been mobilised in some mysterious way against "Sir Roger", whose own appearance and manners ought to have shown them he was not the 'aristocrat' he claimed to be.

The trial at Bar on the perjury charges did not open until April 23rd, 1873. This long delay of a year was mainly due to the fact that the evidence taken on commission overseas could not be admitted in a criminal trial, so that witnesses from Australia and South America had to be cajoled and paid to come to England. Inevitably the proceedings had to cover the same ground as the action in the Common Pleas, and there was naturally a feeling of weariness and exasperation engendered, which latter was particularly shown by the claimant's leading counsel, Dr. Kenealy. Towards the end of the trial two new witnesses for the defence caused much excitement and did the claimant considerable harm. Among the many weaknesses in his story was his account of the sinking of the *Bella* and his rescue by the *Osprey*. There now arrived a "Captain Brown", who told a story of the *Bella* sailing with everyone drunk on board. Maritime records showed no trace of an *Osprey* arriving at Melbourne at the period stated by the claimant, but Brown swore he knew an *Osprey* of Baltimore and, what was more, a sailor named Luie who had helped rescue the claimant. 'Luie' was produced triumphantly by Dr. Kenealy, and told a long and fantastic story which included such veracious details as that he had treated the claimant's sun-stroke by keeping him continually drunk on rum! Eventually the Crown was able to prove that 'Luie' was an ex-convict and a bigamist, and that his evidence was a mass of lies. Both Brown and 'Luie' were eventually found guilty of perjury, and sentenced to penal servitude. They were not a very good omen for the claimant, and this episode surely shows up the credulity and prejudice of his friends and ranting counsel, who could produce two such 'witnesses' without apparently any enquiry into their antecedents.

In the lurid comments on the case published after it was over by Dr. Kenealy in his *The Englishman*, he constantly complains that the result of the perjury trial was a "foregone conclusion", for which he blames the bias and unfairness of both the judges and the jury. The first part of the statement is in a sense true. The reason was that the claimant's real trial was before the Court of Common Pleas, where he had had the immense advantage of being the plaintiff. He had given his evidence, all his witnesses had been heard; but after hearing only seventeen of about 280 witnesses for the defence, the jury had stopped the case and had given a verdict against him. Chief Justice Bovill had thereupon ordered the claimant to be committed for trial on charges of perjury. But the alleged bias and unfairness were absolutely mythical. I have just re-read the whole of the verbatim report of the perjury trial, as published by Kenealy with his comments, and I fail to see any unfairness. Indeed, the judges were very patient indeed, for they saw how tragically their friend and colleague was throwing away his whole career. This trial at Bar was more the tragedy of Dr. Kenealy than of Orton, whose fate had been sealed long before, and anyway deserves no sympathy.

Edward Vaughan Kenealy was born in Cork on July 2nd, 1819, educated as a Roman Catholic, read widely at Trinity, took a degree as LL.D., and was called to the Irish and then

the English bar. He left his Church, and tried to work out a
private religion of his own from studies in Oriental religions.
In 1850 he was sentenced to a month's imprisonment for
cruelty to his natural son, Edward Hyde. Some say the
Bench treated him harshly, and certainly his devotion to his
numerous legitimate children was deep and warm. His
daughter, Arabella, evidently loved him, and revered his
memory. He was a personal friend of Disraeli, and, strange
to say, one of his closest friends was Chief Justice Cockburn,
who presided over the perjury trial, with whom Kenealy
bickered so fiercely and indecorously, and whom he attacked
afterwards in *The Englishman* so indecently. Kenealy's
position at the English bar just before the "Tichborne trial"
was distinguished, and if he had not allowed himself to be
dragged into that squalid intrigue he might most reasonably
have expected the honours of elevation to the Queen's
Bench. He was leader of the Oxford Circuit, a Q.C., and
Bencher of Gray's Inn—legal honours which surely are not
easily won, and are seldom wrongly awarded. Barristers
indeed are open to the charge that they are a small and
highly-favoured profession, but that very fact means that
they know each other thoroughly and are the less likely to
support and promote the unworthy.

Kenealy, unluckily for him, had too many literary and
reforming and sectarian interests to maintain the cynical
aloofnesss of the good advocate. He was inclined to believe in
the guilt or innocence of his clients, and even spat in his own
soup by doubting the perfection of British justice:

"January 23rd, 1856. The scenes of perjury, robbery, and
falsehood which I see in these Courts absolutely appal me.
We seem to be as bad as was Rome in its worst days."

That is an extract from his diary. If he believed that,
why did he go on practising? But there was a fine side to
him, as may be inferred from this entry in March 1858:

"The men who struggle with the evil, the deceit and rascality they encounter every day, and strive to overcome it, are true knights-errant and deserve honour even although they are conquered."

How did it happen that such a man converted himself to the belief that such an obvious fraud as Arthur Orton was Sir Roger Tichborne? It is a problem. He certainly seems to have felt dislike for old colleagues who had been promoted. In his diary I find this remark about Chief Justice Bovill, who presided over the "Tichborne case" in the Common Pleas, under the date November 2nd, 1872, before Kenealy was briefed for the perjury case:

"Dined at Gray's Inn, talked of Bovill. He does not appear to have left a friend or one who speaks otherwise of him than as a bad prejudiced Judge who delighted in inflicting pain on all who came before him."

Strange to relate, the last part of that sentence applies to Kenealy as advocate, for he certainly displayed a malicious and most unpleasant joy in taunting the witnesses against Orton with their failings. There was really something vile in the gloating way he forced Lord Bellew to admit his liaison with a married woman—and, for heaven's sake, what had that to do with the case? He was even worse in his ferocious attempts to discredit Gosford, whom he knew to be the key witness, by representing his financial misfortunes as felony. There has seldom been a worse exemplification of the old maxim: "When you have a hopelessly bad case, take refuge in calumny and misrepresentation". The severity of the Chief Justice's condemnation of Kenealy is all the more striking since up till that time they had been close and even intimate friends. And when Mr. Justice Mellor sentenced the impostor—as we may now call him—to fourteen years penal servitude, he also passed sentence on Kenealy. Mr.

Justice Mellor's words include sentences which are the epitome of all frauds and impostures:

"The marvellous growth and development of your knowledge as to the circumstances connected with the history of Roger Tichborne, and with the circumstances connected with his military life, leave it uncertain whether your original design was not enlarged by reason of the ease with which you found people ready to become your dupes, and, I fear, in some instances your accomplices."

Was Kenealy a dupe or an accomplice? It seems equally difficult to believe either of a senior Q.C. and a Bencher of Gray's Inn. Of course there are cases when an advocate gets carried away by his own eloquence, but as a rule a word from the Bench brings him up sharp. Not so with Kenealy. He went out of his way to scatter accusations of bribery, perjury and collusion, and pressed the charge against Lady Radcliffe with lurid details and unnecessary vindictiveness. Indeed, he made every effort to vilify every member of the Tichborne, Doughty and Seymour families except the Dowager and one or two rather distant connections who had 'recognised' the claimant. When one or other of the judges called him to order, he wrangled disrespectfully, made allusions to Scroggs and Jeffreys, and made disparaging remarks in tones loud enough to be heard by the reporters but not by the Bench and jury. According to him, foreign witnesses were not to be believed because they were foreigners and Roman Catholic witnesses because they were Roman Catholics. In his violent disparagement of the Tichbornes he even included Sir James and the undoubted Roger, though according to him they were the youthful days and the father of his client! When sentence had been passed on the claimant in terms of unusual severity, Kenealy shook hands with him and said: "Well, good-bye, Sir Roger, I am sorry for you." Which surely was equivalent to saying openly in court that he thought the verdict wrong and the sentence unjust?

In any event, Kenealy continued his agitation for the 'cause' of the now convicted claimant in his *The Englishman*, though he tried to deny his editorship. The periodical was full of political and sectarian hatred, which leads one to infer that Kenealy was in the main the victim of his own political and religious fanaticism. In his favour it must be remembered that he had far too little time to study a most complicated case, that he was suffering from diabetes, and after the trial had a complete breakdown. In spite of that breakdown, however, he found strength and energy to conduct *The Englishman* with scurrilous personal abuse of his former friend, Chief Justice Cockburn, and indeed almost everybody who did not accept his view of the case. As a sample of the frenzied if impotent hatred developed by *The Englishman* I will quote part of a letter which it printed in 1878. I should premise that the "Wardour Castle" party was an alleged jollification of the Tichborne family over the result of the trial, and that some of the persons named were concerned in it. Here is the extract:

"The miserable creatures who assembled at Wardour Castle to celebrate the verdict, saw two of their number blown to pieces by the explosion of a cannon.

"Colonel George Greenwood was found, smothered in his own blood.

"Mr. Henry Danby Seymour was cut off, almost in an instant, after enduring two years of horrible agonies.

"Mrs. Childers died by poison, and was found lifeless by her husband's side in bed.

"Lady Coleridge was carried off, after two days' fearful suffering; and the wife of Dickins, the Foreman, died of a most horrible disease, howling in agony for the part she had taken.

"Bovill was killed by the evidence of Luie, which all men thought, at the time, was true; and Judge Archibald, who framed the indictment, perished in the prime of life by a painful disease.

"Etheredge, the blacksmith, is paralysed.

"Ballantine, the traitor, I hear, is almost begging.

"The detectives are in jail; Bellew's son blew his brains out; Lush's son flung himself into the ocean in a fit of *delirium tremens*; and Gibbes, the Australian lawyer, was also carried off. Mina Jury is again a convict; Lady Radcliffe has taken to drink; and Joyce Q.C., one of the Gray's Inn Benchers, dropped dead soon after they expelled the Doctor. Now the three Spenders are swallowed up. Who next?"

What next indeed! Only that this insane effusion of vindictive hate is headed "The Vengeance of God" and signed "A Believer in God"! Nobody can say whether it was or was not written by Kenealy, though as editor he was certainly responsible for it. Amazing to relate, there was such appetite for rabid ravings of this sort that printings of 100,000 were insufficient to meet the demand for *The Englishman*, and its editor was elected Member for Stoke-on-Trent by a large majority. He had vainly tried to persuade the Courts to order a re-trial; and in Parliament on April 23rd, 1875 he made a speech of three hours on a "motion to refer the conduct of the trial and the guilt or innocence of the prisoner to a Royal Commission". On division, the result was: For the motion 1; against 433. Majority against 432.

Meanwhile his punishment by his own profession had been severe, too severe some may think. He was expelled from the barristers' mess of the Oxford Circuit, not unanimously but by a majority. His patent as a Q.C. was revoked, and he was disbenched and disbarred by Gray's Inn. Such extreme measures against a brother barrister are very rare, and indicate how deeply members of the Bar had resented Kenealy's conduct of the case and his really outrageous insults to the judges. *The Englishman* and the election to Parliament were a courageous attempt to fight back, but after that crushing vote in the Commons, what hope was there? *The Englishman* ended up by printing the kind of frenzied nonsense I have quoted; in the general election of 1880, Dr.

Kenealy was bottom of the poll, and died a few days later. He had used his talents and position at the bar to bolster with every kind of unscrupulous and unfair argument the claims of a most obvious and odious impostor. *The Englishman*'s mixture of minute quibbling over side-issues and frantic abuse is after all characteristic of charlatans trying to defend a fraud. But Kenealy carried the system to a point where it became almost maniacal, and inevitably led to his disgrace, ruin, and death from a broken heart. Yet his undaunted courage makes one sorry for him.

As for Orton, in prison he suffered much from insufficient nourishment for his twenty-six stone of weight, and was allowed extra rations by the prison doctor. How characteristic that he kept up his bluff, and apparently studied French in order to supply that defect in his impersonation of Roger Tichborne. How much he had become a politico-religious 'cause' rather than a human being may be guessed by the conduct of his 'friends' who visited him at Dartmoor Prison. Instead of bringing him what little comfort and affection might alleviate his hard lot, they came armed with a schedule of questions to be used in their "Tichborne case" propaganda! Could the inhumanity of lovers of humanity go further?

Not much is recorded about the life of Orton after he was released. He addressed public meetings, trying vainly to kindle a spark of the old flame of popular hate by stirring the ashes, but in vain. He made a little money by appearing as a music hall turn. When the public wearied even of that poor show, he worked in a pub and then in a tobacconist's. Driven by poverty he sold his 'confession' to the *People*, for £3,000 it is said. If the confession was authentic, the re-write man on the *People* made a sad hash of it, for the thing is full of blunders and mis-statements. Perhaps Orton gave them so, to allow a loophole for the subsequent recantation. Yet there is truth in the statement that he had always had a habit of bragging and "trying to lead people into the belief that he was of good family and would eventually come into money". If he had not tried to get possession of other people's estates and money, and had limited his braggings to more or less imaginary heroic feats as a bushranger, he might now be a hero of Anglo-Australian mythology. He died in April 1898, and was buried as "Sir Roger Tichborne".

But the last word cannot be left to the impostor and to his brave but misguided counsel. There is a little document which closes this strange eventful history:

"Telegram. Her Majesty the Queen to Lady Radcliffe. The Queen sends her assurance of sympathy and congratulates Lady Radcliffe on the result of the Trial."

FIVE

'Dr.' Graham and his Celestial Bed

WITH OTHER MEDICAL FRAUDS

The topic of medical fraud is immense and coeval with human history and proto-history; and it is also a subject where the layman is at a disadvantage and must be wary of rash assertions. Yet it is safe to say that in few human activities, if any, have hard-won knowledge, probity and skill been forced to so prolonged a battle with ignorance, superstition and fraud. It is not so easy to decide the point where genuine error becomes fraud. When diseases were thought to be 'caused' by the 'possession' of evil spirits, it was natural to try to keep them away with amulets and charms; and, after they had effected an entry, to try to drive them out with spells, orders to depart based on an appeal to divine aid, vile suffumigations and unpleasant decoctions. We smile at the ancient Egyptians for their fantastic magical prescriptions, and certainly there is something disconcerting about a pharmacopœia which included not only such comparatively harmless though not particularly indicated drugs such as wine, beer, vinegar, oil, but the milk of a mother with a boy baby, lizard's blood, lion's dung, papyrus boiled in oil, the brain of a tortoise, and human urine and excrement. The idea was to annoy the devils, but the patient had to suffer the internal battle. Luckily the Egyptians made free use of castor oil, which—let us hope—

K

helped to neutralise the rest of the 'cure'. The amulets, spells, charms and exorcisms can have done no harm, and may have done some good to suggestible patients. They may even have put an end to some maladies of nervous origin.

The *Golden Ass* of Apuleius gives a striking view of the infinite superstitions which flourished in the Eastern parts of the Roman Empire, and the Romans themselves were not much better, especially in borrowing or inventing ridiculous medical prescriptions. The seeds of wild cucumber were supposed to cure lumbago, and when snuffed up in the form of powder cured jaundice and asthma. The pulp of colocynth mixed with salt and wormwood cured toothache, and mixed with vinegar made loose teeth healthy again. Its seeds sewed in clothes reduced fevers. It was also supposed to deal with ear-ache, corns, inflammation of the eyes, wounds, gout, erysipelas and stomach-ulcer. Most of us have been taking such homely productions as turnips and radishes all our lives without knowing that they are also valuable medicines. In Roman superstition hot mashed turnips cured chilblains, and when cold "every kind of disease of the feet". (There must be some sympathetic magic here, but the connection between turnips and feet escapes me; I should have thought them more appropriate for diseases of the head.) Even more surprisingly, turnip seeds in wine are an antidote for poison, including snake bites. Radishes in various forms are diuretic, dissolve gall stones, cure snake bites, kill scorpions, are an antidote to mushroom poisoning and that comparatively rare affliction, mistletoe poisoning. Taken with mustard they are recommended in cases of epilepsy and dropsy; with honey they eliminate worms; with wine they heal intestinal hernia; and with mud internal ulcers.

Touching for the king's evil, scrofula, continued until the time of Queen Anne—Dr. Johnson had a dim memory of undergoing the cure (unsuccessfully) in his early childhood.

The Romans were equally practical. With a trowel or fork made of gold you had to dig up the roots of marshmallow exactly at sunrise, wrap them in the undyed wool of a ewe with a ewe lamb, and lay the whole on the afflicted parts. The same prescription frightened away snakes and healed bee-stings.

Still more extraordinary and universal are the healing powers of cabbage, wild cabbage, and Brussels sprouts, which we ignorantly use merely as vegetables, while they were employed medicinally by both Romans and Greeks. The list of ailments they were prescribed for would arouse the wistful envy of any seller of patent medicines. They include headache, dim eyes, spleen and stomach troubles, gout, rheumatism, wounds, sprains, fistula, tumours, insomnia, dysentery, deafness, impetigo, drunkenness, paralysis, palsy, diseases of the kidney, mushroom poisoning, tetanus, epilepsy, jaundice, hoarseness, hiccups, flatulence, snake bite, bruises, baldness, convulsions, sciatica, rupture. Brussels sprouts are a good depilatory. A smelling-bottle of powdered wild cabbage will cure all diseases of the nose, including, one supposes, the sense of smell. It was also a cure for hydrophobia. The root of asparagus boiled in vinegar was recommended in cases of elephantiasis. Basil was prescribed for consumption and ear troubles in babies, also for removing warts.

There are innumerable such receipts from antiquity, but these should suffice.

Yet we can hardly afford to jeer. Our own Saxon ancestors were thriftily inclined to the use of charms and spells, at any rate in minor ailments, while in the Middle Ages what little medical science remained from the tradition of Hippocrates and Galen was mainly derived from Arabs and Jews, and misunderstood at that. Even after the Renaissance the fashion for strange prescriptions still remained, as witness the once famous Dr. Andrew Boorde, half genuine, half charlatan, who treated gout with a mixture of saffron, bread-crumbs, oil of roses, cow's milk and egg yolks, to be applied externally, not internally. Melancholy Burton had more sense, for he says somewhere that a few herb remedies properly understood and prepared are much better than the fanciful and elaborate concoctions sold by the apothecaries. Clearly one reason why complicated and, to our way of thinking, ridiculous recipes were liked by the apothecaries was because they were expensive and profitable to the compounder.

It is difficult to say when conscious fraud and charlatanism came into medicine, for obviously in many, if not in most, cases these fantastic treatments were rather an affair of traditional superstition and ignorance than of wilful cheating for gain or power. Doubtless the wise woman and the white wizard in some form or other existed always alongside the supposedly regular practitioners, but it was a dangerous occupation or hobby, especially after the Inquisition had to find occupation for its zeal. When medicine itself was so much infected with superstition, white magic, and traditional absurdities of all kinds, the difficulty of drawing the distinction is extreme. Clearly in many cases before the revival of science the 'regular' practitioner was as much a fraud as the mountebank or white wizard, but then he may not have known it. Only with the revival of science and the gradual progress of genuine medicine did the distinction between the real doctor and the charlatan become clear. And even the charlatan had his excuse. Whenever he had some medical instruction, as was often the case, he must have known he was cheating, but then his patients in a sense asked to be cheated—they preferred the age-old superstitious remedies and treatment to the methods of the Faculty, which, if we may believe Molière, were often as bad as the charlatan's.

Still, by the eighteenth century at latest medical science had so far advanced that there could be little difficulty in distinguishing between the genuine leech and the medical exploiter of the credulous. It is to that epoch that we must assign one of the most impudent medical frauds in our history, practised not on poor people in remote parts of the country but on the wealthy and supposedly educated in the centre of fashionable London. Indeed, the whole episode is so curious one might suspect that it never happened but that the accounts of it derive from a satirical farce which Colman mentions in his *Random Records* as having been staged to make fun of 'Dr.' Graham and his 'medical' establishment; but the fact is described by the German traveller, Archenholz. I put the 'Dr.' in quotation marks because it seems improbable that such a fraud can have been qualified; yet he may have been if it is true that he was a brother-in-law of Mrs. Macaulay the historian.

It is unlucky that the notices we have of Graham are so scrappy and that, slight as they are, they are not wholly in agreement. All we are told of Graham's antecedents is that he was a Scotsman, which might easily have been inferred from his name. His once notorious "Temple of Health" is placed by one person in the Adelphi and by another in Pall Mall; but since the establishment was kept up during four or five years it may well have been moved from one address to another. All accounts agree that it was founded in 1780 and lasted until March 1784. 'Dr.' Graham had two footmen or hall-porters at the door, dressed in handsome livery and gold-laced cocked hats, distributing advertising leaflets to people passing by. "The Temple of Health" was furnished with a luxury which seems to have been more extravagant than in good taste. The rooms were lighted through stained glass, were decorated with coloured glass globes, satin sofas on glass legs and white marble statues. There were "figures of dragons", whatever that may mean, and a large "medico-electrical apparatus". The trophies of cures were displayed in the shape of crutches and ear-trumpets and similar supposedly discarded aids no longer needed. Perfumes and incense were burned to the sound of music, and a "goddess of health" sang exciting or soothing melodies to the patients. One account states that this beautiful goddess and songstress was Lady Hamilton in the days when she was still only Emma Lyon, but this seems rather improbable.

The health devices sold in this temple were certainly strange. The many-coloured glasses and perfumes were presumably free like the singing, and the rooms were flooded with artificial moonlight also without fee. But the *Treatise on Health* cost half a guinea a copy, the "earth-baths" were a guinea a time, and the "divine balm" was sold at the same price. These were the merest *hors d'œuvres* to the "magneto-electric beds", with electricity and perfumes laid on, which cost fifty pounds a night to sleep in, presumably for the purpose of acquiring or regaining virility. In what was named by the 'doctor' his "Holy of Holies" was a more splendid electro-magnetic bed on which he claimed he had spent sixty thousand pounds. It is said to have stood on six heavy glass legs, with heavily-perfumed purple and blue curtains, and of course electricity. To sleep in this "Celestial Bed", as he called it, 'Dr.' Graham made the modest charge of one hundred pounds a night, for he promised that the result would be a beautiful child. This was an ingenious idea, and after it the "elixir of life" sounds rather common-place, though he is said to have charged as much as a thousand pounds for a supply sufficient to ensure im-mortality, one assumes, or perhaps merely potency.

Who were the 'doctor's' patrons? Where did he find persons willing to pay such sums for so obviously silly a fraud, which could have appealed only to these of a like silliness? "Half the English nobility," says one irascible commentator, who later specifies as the chief customers "captains of privateers, nabobs, spendthrifts and old noble-men." What we are not told is whether 'patients' slept alone or accompanied, or how "the self-playing organ" was worked. If the beds were jointly occupied it is difficult to see how the 'doctor' escaped indictment for keeping a disorderly house, unless indeed he bribed and had influential protection. If the "self-playing organ" was worked by electricity, as seems possible in that highly electrified establishment, the 'doctor' might have done better by selling his invention than by swindling old nabobs and sea captains. One thing is certain. In the end the fraud, like most frauds, was found out. The treatise and the earth-baths and the divine balm did not procure health as promised, and though the "Celestial Bed" and its humbler imitations doubtless produced offspring, they were probably no more beautiful than their parents. The elixir of life, of course, had not been given a fair trial; but possibly a confiding purchaser died soon after taking it. At all events, the dupes dwindled in number and finally ceased to come at all, and the Temple of Health with all its fittings was sold at a public auction. It is safe to say that the "Celestial Bed" did not make anything distantly approaching sixty thousand pounds. We are not told what happened to 'Dr.' Graham, but presumably he was not prosecuted or we should hear of it. The eighteenth-century law, which would hang a poor girl for stealing a bit of finery or a desperate man out of work for snatching food for his starving children, had a fellow-feeling for rogues of the Graham class. They worked on similar lines.

Norman Douglas used to say that the name 'Geoffrey' always made him think of a low blackguard—I paraphrase for obvious reasons. In the same way the name 'Graham', particularly when it is a Christian name, always suggests to me a foolish and pretentious hypocrite. The feeling, which is undeniable, is probably based on some forgotten association of ideas. In Norman's case it may have been with Judge Jeffreys, but naturally I have quite forgotten my 'Graham', no doubt some insignificant person. This 'Dr.' Graham certainly justified my intuitive mistrust of his name. He must have been a hypocrite to pretend that his quackeries had any medical value, and his methods of salesmanship were certainly pretentious. Moreover, he was a fool to imagine that the public would not in time find him out for the fraud he was. It is hard to find something to say in his defence. Still, it is a fair inference from the scanty notices one can collect and the self-conscious tone of the writers that the main ailment 'Dr.' Graham proposed to treat was impotence. This may seem strange in the supposedly hearty days of the eighteenth century when the Public School system had not been fully developed, but doubtless there were contributory causes in the strenuous lives of nabobs and legalised pirates. In such cases suggestion may be of great value, and there is much to be said no doubt for a treatment which included electricity, perfumes, a more than imperial bed, songs from a Queen of Health and Beauty and a self-playing organ.

It is a truism to say that all who have practised fraudulent healing have always adapted their methods to the prejudices of their victims, and have varied their appeal and nostrums according to whether they hoped to cheat the rich or the poor. What is impossible to determine is how far in earlier times the treatments which all educated persons now know were absurd or futile were due to genuine error and how far to conscious fraud. Setting aside the medical school of Cos associated with the name of Hippocrates and the Græco-Roman school of Galen, most medical treatment for many centuries must have been either crudely empirical or merely superstitious. But that does not make the practitioners frauds. When the medicine-man of our Saxon ancestors recited a charm to remove a wen, ordering it to become smaller than the hip-bone of a worm, he was obviously an imbecile from the point of view of modern medicine, but he was not necessarily or even probably defrauding his patients knowingly, as 'Dr.' Graham must have done. Whether his "elixir of life" was supposed to be an aphrodisiac or a means of prolonging existence, he must have known it was a cheat. His main attraction was of course the electric current, which would certainly be mysterious to sea captains and nabobs. It is perhaps worth noting that in 1775, five years before Graham opened up his Temple of Health, Volta had invented an apparatus for generating electricity, which he called an 'electrophorus'. The writers who describe so censoriously the luxury of the Temple have not deigned to give us any account of the "immense electrical machine" that was sold up with the other assets. It is possible that electrical treatment might have benefited some of the victims at the shrine, and it is just possible that Graham was an enthusiast for the medical use of electricity. But the prices he charged show that he had no intention of benefiting humanity at large, and the whole method of presentation betrays the fraudulent charlatan. A genuine investigator with a genuine discovery would have taken it to the Royal Society, not to the limping debauchees of the West End.

Graham's commercialised quackery was adapted to the social conditions of the 1780s by appealing to the ignorant rich, and doubtless that system was continued so long as there were any rich left to exploit. But a century or so after Graham's time the discovery was made that the comparatively poor with only a few shillings to spend had become so numerous and were so credulous that they formed a most tempting body of dupes for easy and lucrative exploitation, though some of the wealthy were also taken in by the alluring promises of the numerous patent medicines on the market around the year 1900. A careful analysis of the so-called "secret remedies" and of the methods used to foist them on the public was made and published by the British Medical Association, and it is significant that none of the charlatans exposed dared to go into court although they used every method of abuse and misrepresentation in attempts to hide the truth. I have a copy of this report by the B.M.A., published in 1909, by which date over 100,000 copies of the book had been sold. Those interested in concealing the truth must have pursued an artful policy of sending out agents secretly to buy up all copies which came on the second-hand book market. Obviously it would not pay to buy them first-hand, for the B.M.A. would have continued to issue new impressions at the expense of the buyers. So successful has this suppression been that one of the most able and experienced London book-buyers assures me that this copy is the only one he has ever come on in thirty years—and that period shows that the scarcity is not due to the war-time destruction of books for news-print. The same method is followed in other fields of charlatanry: the newspapers are utilised to keep down the original sale by misrepresentation, and after a suitable interval the book or books which have exposed a profitable fraud are quietly bought up and destroyed.

The types of fraud revealed by these analyses vary. We have first the very serious illness, such as cancer or consumption, treated with useless drugs and resulting in unnecessary suffering. Then a malady may have been treated with the appropriate drug (this is rare) but without the necessary adjustment of dosage to the individual case. Comparatively minor ailments were given either harmless drugs which had no effect, or some very simple remedy far short of the extravagant claims made for it. Then again, some ordinary illness would be met by a drug which might in many cases be effective but also in some might be very dangerous. All these drugs were sold at an enormous profit over their prime cost, since the main expenses of the "secret remedy" quacks were advertising, taxes to the Inland Revenue, packing and distribution. Some idea of the money involved may be obtained from the figures published by the B.M.A. They estimate that in the financial year ending

March 31st, 1908, the public spent on these nostrums over two million four hundred thousand pounds gold, or well over ten million of our currency. The tax paid to the Government, which preferred to exploit rather than fight this unscrupulous defrauding of the public, amounted to £266,403 gold in 1899. By 1908 the sum paid in taxation had risen to £334,141 gold, but whether from increase of sales or from a raising of the duty payable is not stated.

A distinction must be made between those 'firms' which supplied 'medicines' supposed to effect a cure of such a condition as baldness—doing no good indeed, but no particular harm except cheating the purchaser out of his money—and those who really did harm by pretending to cure serious ailments. Again, a comparatively harmless aperient in pill form would arouse no particular moral indignation if sold only for the purpose of stimulating a sluggish liver, but does become pernicious when advertised as a cure for about thirty different diseases, including venereal disease.

One of the most wicked of these impostures was known as "Stevens' Consumption Cure", obviously sold to persons who were too poor to spend the winter at Davos Platz or on the Nile. It was introduced by the usual mendacious palaver, which in this case is particularly impudent, since it denounces "American quacks" and "Polish or German Jews" who are alleged to sell fraudulent cures. Mr. Stevens possessed "African herbs" unknown to any doctor, and made the frank offer: "I will guarantee to cure you if you are consumptive, or return your money in full." However, as the B.M.A. sarcastically points out, his Guarantee Bonds were limited by such conditions that "it appears unlikely that Mr. Stevens is ever troubled with applications for return of money under one of his 'Bonds'." Moreover, "Stevens' Consumption Cure" was also vaunted as something of a cure-all, since it is "fatal to all disease germ growths". He even professed to give the formula: 80 grains of Umckaloabo root and thirteen and one third grains of Chijitse to every ounce. It may be surmised that he didn't give away much, since a chemical analysis revealed the following composition:

Rectified spirit of wine   23.7 parts by measure
Glycerine   1.8 parts.
Decoction of krameria (1 in 3) to 100 parts by measure.

'Krameria' is a root also known as 'rhatany', and comes from South America. It is astringent, and is or was used for intestinal hæmorrhage, also for a relaxed throat; but it could have had no effect on the lungs. The B.M.A. estimates that two and a quarter fluid ounces of this preparation would cost about three halfpence, and a bottle containing exactly that amount was sold for five shillings! Mr. Stevens had the 'honour' to appear in the *Truth* Cautionary List for 1908; but apparently continued his career unchecked for several years. Certainly the only persons who benefited by his 'cure' were the advertising media, the retailers, the Inland Revenue and himself.

An equally impudent fraud was that of an American company which charged £2 10s. for two bottles of their 'Tuberculozyne' "for a month's treatment", but patients were exhorted to 'persevere' even if improvement was "not at once pronounced". Analysis of bottle one gave the following:

Potassium bromide . . . .   3.4 parts
Glycerine   12.0
Oil of cassia   0.1 part
Tincture of capsicum   0.17
Cochineal colouring   q.s.
Caustic soda   0.06
Water to   100 fluid parts.

Bottle two:

Glycerine	18 parts
Essential oil of almond	0.1 part
Burnt sugar	q.s.
Water to	100 fluid parts.

The cost of the ingredients in the two bottles sold at two pounds ten was estimated at about twopence halfpenny!

The section on cancer is too painful for quotation, and there is a doctor's report, on the case of a woman who had been 'treated' by one of these quack remedies almost until death, which is so appalling its memory haunts one. It is very disquieting that the British Government allowed this sort of thing to go on, while taking money from it in taxation and merely disclaiming responsibility by printing on the Inland Revenue Tax stamp the words "This stamp implies no Government guarantee". Or, as Clough put it:

> "Thou shalt not kill, but need'st not strive
> Officiously to keep alive."

Apropos 'Dr.' Graham and his "electric beds", we may note that as recently as the beginning of this century the word 'electric' still struck the public with mystic awe, much as the misused word 'atomic' does now. The B.M.A. points out that one of the 'cures' for cancer, extensively boomed by an unnamed journalist-editor, was marketed as 'electric fluid' or 'electricity' at several shillings the fluid ounce. Chemical analysis showed it was ordinary water! Although the fraud had been exposed publicly, it was still on sale in 1908. Another of these cancer 'cures' turned out to be nothing but "diluted and slightly impure alcohol".

The chapter on the fraudulent remedies for diabetes was of course written before treatment by insulin became possible, so that in those days diabetes was as incurable as consumption and cancer. One of these quackeries came to us from France in the form of a medicated wine sold at eight shillings for twenty-four fluid ounces. The wine was alleged to have been strengthened by the addition of pepsin and azotate of uranium, though analysis showed no trace of unchanged pepsin and the uranium amounted to 0.02 of a part. Another "Diabetic Mixture" came from Manchester and was advertised as "the only known remedy for this deadly disease". It came in two-ounce bottles, sold three at a time, and the purchaser was firmly told that "the remedy, it is needless to say, will have to be persevered with", i.e. he or she would have to go on buying these bottled triplets at eight shillings and threepence. Chemical analysis revealed the following formula:

Sodium bicarbonate	7.4 parts
Extract of hydrastis	1.5
Resin, resinoid & other extractive	2.2
Alcohol	35
Water to	100

Hydrastine (and berberine, also detected) are derived from the roots of the plant golden-seal (*Hydrastis candensis*) and are used in medicine as an "internal styptic". There was also a little caulophyllin. At the very outside the B.M.A. thought that elevenpence was the total cost of the six fluid ounces. The chapter ends with a warning against some of the advertised "Diabetic Foods" then sold as supposedly free from starch, whereas they were found to be made of "practically ordinary wheaten flour".

A rather different form of fraud is revealed by the analysis of the nostrums sold for epilepsy. In every case but one it was found that the high-priced "secret remedy" consisted mainly of bromide salts, "a drug which is described and discussed in every medical work dealing with the disease." This is obviously less reprehensible than selling some completely useless or even harmful concoction as a 'cure' for a serious or incurable disease. The wrong here consisted in selling at an outrageously high price a drug which might well have been prescribed by a doctor. Thus a 'remedy' called 'Ozerine', which came from Ireland and had no medicine stamp, contained a mixture of potassium bromide and two or three other ingredients which cost less than fourpence and was sold for four and sixpence. Another which cost the sellers a penny was boomed as "W. and J. Taylor's Celebrated Anti-Epileptic Medicine", was priced at two shillings and ninepence, and consisted of bromide salts and water. "Osbourne's Mixture for Epilepsy", containing much the same formula, sold threepence-worth of the drugs for two shillings and ninepence. Another Irish one, "Trench's Remedy for Epilepsy and Fits", sold about one pennyworth of the drugs for three shillings. "Professor O. Phelps Brown's Vervain Restorative As-similant" was composed of a decoction of vervain, a little port, and rectified spirit and water, cost about fivepence, and was sold for two shillings and ninepence. Vervain was one of the old superstitious 'Druid' nostrums, and it is curious to find it still being sold medicinally in this century.

The most obvious case of a rather dangerous drug being sold as a "secret remedy" was acetanilide, which does indeed remove the symptom of a headache, though without attacking its cause, but may have very disagreeable effects on some people. As its name implies, acetanilide is formed by the interaction of glacial acetic acid and aniline, and a quite independent reference book consulted says that "it removes symptoms of headache but has a depressant action on the muscle of the heart". Obviously if taken by persons with weak hearts an overdose would have unpleasant and possibly fatal consequences. The six patent remedies listed, including one with the seductive name of "Bell's Fairy Cure", all contained acetanilide, in one case without anything added, in the other five there was either phenacetin, or phenacetin

and caffeine, or ferric oxide or cocoa. Three of them were
sold in packets at one shilling and three-halfpence, and the
cost of the ingredients is given respectively as nine-tenths of a
penny, just under a penny, and one farthing. The two
others sold at sevenpence-halfpenny, and the cost of the
ingredients was one farthing, and one-eighth of a penny,
respectively. There were also "large numbers of headache
powders" sold singly wrapped in a folded paper for a penny.
Apart from the risk already mentioned, this seems modest
until we learn that one pennyworth of acetanilide is sufficient
to fill thirty-six such packets. Apparently no advertising was
needed and as the drug was unmixed no Stamp Duty was
payable; so that the profit both wholesale and retail must
have been relatively enormous.

In the matter of charging high prices for cheap drugs or no
drugs at all the various American nostrums sold in England
for "kidney and liver troubles" seem to be the most impudent in their extortion. Thus "Munyon's Kidney Cure"
(manufactured in U.S.) was sold with the inscription:

"Cures Bright's disease, gravel, all urinary troubles, and
pain in the back or groin from kidney disease".

The purchaser was ordered to take "four pellets every
hour", and a supply of 132, enough for thirty-three hours,
was sold for the modest sum of one shilling. The amazed
analyst discovered that they were made up of one hundred
per cent ordinary white sugar; and the price does not seem so
modest when you reflect that at the time the ingredients of
four hundred and twenty shilling bottles could have been
bought for one shilling. The fact that the pills or pellets had
absolutely no medicinal value whatsoever may perhaps be
extenuated by the argument that if the sugar was clean it
probably did no harm. But it may be questioned whether
this was what the sufferers paid for, and it would have been
interesting to know what they would have thought and
said if they had known they were virtually making a free

gift of their money to the ingenious swindler and his agents.

Another American company advertised "Dodd's Kidney Pills" which were "a positive cure" for all kidney diseases, rheumatism, Bright's disease, diabetes, backache, female weakness, dropsy and "any form of heart disease"—obviously a benefactor of humanity. The puff (I nearly wrote "the blurb") confidently states that the pills "consist of the active principles of vegetable substances which have been carefully studied by the discoverer of the remedy", although *a priori* one would say that the main "vegetable substances" studied by this projector must have been the wooden heads of the credulous public. The B.M.A. analyst, who by this time was evidently becoming rather cynical, says that in spite of the statement about the pills consisting of vegetable substances "it was no surprise to find that the principal ingredient was potassium nitrate". Here is the full analysis:

Extract of cascarilla (alcoholic)	0.15 grain
Jalap resin	0.3
Hard soap	1.0
Potassium nitrate	1.0
Sodium bicarbonate	0.85
Hard paraffin	0.5
Turmeric	0.3
Wheat flour	0.8

Thirty-five of these pills were sold for two shillings and ninepence and cost the 'Company' one penny. Two other American products are listed. One of them offered forty kidney pills and four liver pills for what was evidently then the 'popular' price of two shillings and ninepence, which was modest, since the estimated cost of the ingredients was as high as one halfpenny. The other supplied three farthings-worth of useless ingredients for one shilling and three halfpence.

Our own countrymen did pretty well too in the kidney line. "Fitch's Kidney and Liver Cooler" consisted of nothing but a solution of potassium nitrate in water, and two shillings would buy what cost one-eighth of a penny. The style of advertisement of this product is as crisp as Mr. Jingle:

"Oh my back, how it aches! Why? Fitch's Kidney and Liver Cooler. Trade mark. Sluggish liver. Inactive kidneys. Over-heated blood. Bad urine. Acts chemically by absorption."

Very.

As the B.M.A. analyst points out, the full iniquity and absurdity of these frauds can only be appreciated by comparing their extravagant claims with the results of chemical analysis. Unluckily, few of them indeed emulate the snappy brevity of Fitch's Kidney and Liver Cooler, and long before we come to the end of their grandiloquent assertions Nature asserts herself and we turn the page. I find a certain bizarre interest in the claims made for "The antigouty powders of the R.R. Benedictine Mothers of Pistoia for the treatment of a gouty source." (If only I had known about these while Pino Orioli was alive we could have investigated the R.R. Mothers in Pistoia together, though it is possible that they do not exist.) They are earnest to warn us of counterfeits:

"Having known that in some towns of Italy, and even in Pistoia, some antigouty drug circulates under the name of 'Vegetal Antigouty Powders of the Cloister' or under other names alike, making every body trust that they come from our Monastery, we think ourselves, in duty bound, to remember to our Customers that no deposit of our Antigouty Powders is to be found neither in Pistoia nor in other towns or places in Italy or abroad, and that we have accorded to nobody the faculty of preparing or selling them."

'Outis' or nobody was a pseudonym of the wily Odysseus, and a proper person to compound these Antigouty Powders and to pen the puff. It states definitely that the powders contain no "colchicum, belladonna, or any other poisonous substances . . ." I fear I had become infected with the cynicism of the B.M.A. analyst, for on looking at the formula he gave from the analysis of some French doctors it was "without surprise" that I read the first item:

"Colchicum corm   10 parts . . ."

I will not dwell further on these veracious and modest claims, but merely suggest that if the reader can only find a copy of *Secret Remedies* he has plenty of entertainment for the next rainy afternoon. But I must be allowed one more quotation, this time from the high-toned publicity of another American company which sold a cure for obesity, about seventy-five per cent of which was made of powdered sea-weed and its extractive, with a little dried thyroid. Fourpence-worth of ingredients was sold for half a crown. And here is the opening of the sales talk:

Is Fatness a Social Offence?

" 'The female form, being capable of expressing a high degree of grace, should be an inspiration in our daily lives and lead up to higher ideals of beauty,' said an art lecturer lately. Therefore the fat woman is an enemy to the artistic uplift, for she is entirely too heavy for the wings of fancy to raise. A woman may take but little exercise and enjoy the best of food, and still preserve a beautiful figure. She has at hand a simple fat-reducer that takes the place of starving and gymnastics. It consists of a dessertspoonful after meals and at bedtime of this simple mixture . . ."

As advertising copy that is hopelessly dated by its lack of snappy flavour and its misguided appeal to the lost prestige of Art—what woman in her senses would want to look like one

of Picasso's adipose giantesses or the calamitously bulging
'sculptures' by artists whose names I have forgotten? The
appeal today would perhaps have to be based on social and
religious grounds, though the line about the 'uplift' of a good
figure might well be retained. It would be excellent practice
for the young aspirant to advertising fame and fortune to re-
write that old-time screed in the peppy, tangy phrases of our
contemporary masters of ballyhoo.

Who were the dupes of all this fraud and its eloquent
propagandists? The natural inference from the crudity of the
publicity and the obviously ineffective nature of most of the
ingredients so grossly over-priced is that the purchasers must
have come from the working-class. Very likely in the main
this was so, but the B.M.A. writer is definite that the poor and
ignorant were not the only dupes. He says:

"The well-to-do and the highly-placed will often, when
not very ill, take a curious pleasure in experimenting with
mysterious compounds. In them it is perhaps to be traced to
a hankering to break safely with orthodoxy; they scrupulously
obey the law and the Church and Mrs Grundy, but will have
their fling against medicine. Usually, however, people of
these classes take to some system. It used to be electricity or
hypnotism or some eccentricity of diet; nowadays it is more
often Christian Science."

The writer does not say how he obtained this information,
but one can to some extent confirm from personal experience that a similar state of affairs still exists. One
obvious reason for the popularity of Christian Science
among the wealthy is that, unlike more austere philosophies
and religions, it openly and not merely secretly makes a
moral merit of possessing wealth. This is at any rate a
welcome change from the religions which profess to scorn
wealth and in fact obsequiously court it. The reference to
electricity is interesting, in view of 'Dr.' Graham's exploiting

of this upper-class fad over a century earlier. Eccentricities of diet are still with us, though probably less often and less snobbishly since war-time rationing was strictly enforced for so long. The essence of all snobberies, including the dietetic, is exclusiveness; and you cannot be very exclusive on a weekly two ounces of margarine, one shilling and three halfpence-worth of meat, and a biannual tin of sardines.

It is worth noting that the writer qualifies these statements about the rich by saying they do these things "when not very ill". Perhaps from that we may infer that they did not purchase quack remedies for such grave disorders as cancer, tuberculosis, diabetes, and Bright's disease. Perhaps gout should be included, since in many cases "luxurious living" is said to be one of its main causes. So if the B.M.A. writer is correct, we may assume that the rich used nostrums chiefly for minor ailments and such symptoms as headache, while the poor used them for everything. Twenty or thirty years ago many of the poor in country districts at least (and it was probably even truer of towns) were highly suspicious of doctors. Being entirely materialist in outlook, they grudged paying a fee for mere advice based on years of study and experience, and insisted on being given some tangible return for their money in the shape of a bottle of medicine, even when none was indicated. Thus the country doctor sometimes was forced to give a harmless but useless potion for psychological reasons. Moreover, the village malcontents professed even if they did not really believe that entry into a hospital was invariably fatal, since poor patients were supposed to be used only for purposes of experiment with hazardous operations and dangerous drugs, so that if any were by chance successful they might be utilised afterwards for the exclusive benefit of the rich. Discussion, evidence and argument were entirely useless, as they always are against *parti pris* and groundless prejudices. It was useless, for example, to point out that the main reason why so many rural patients died in hospital was simply because their loving relatives only sent them there to avoid the upset and inconvenience and bad luck of a death in the house.

People of this sort, in whatever class of society, are much more responsive to the quack's impudently positive promises of certain cure than to the more cautious reserves of the man of science. They distrust and dislike all knowledge they can label 'theory', by which they mean knowledge which does not provide them with some immediate material profit, and they despise all apparently unremunerative study. There is a short story by the Provençal poet, Joseph Roumanille, about a young village doctor who could get no practice at all because he always read a book on his daily walk. Since he studied every day, the peasants argued, it must be because he was ignorant, and what use is an ignorant doctor? But the doctor also was of the Midi, and triumphantly restored his prestige and practice by tricking them into thinking he could raise the dead. The appeal is to the human craving for the supernatural, the marvellous, the wonderful. Yeats used to say reprovingly: "We have lost the sense of wonder." I don't think we have, we have merely shifted it from poetry to pseudo-science and charlatanism. And would it be such a loss?

Although I have cited experiences of anti-medical prejudices in country people, it is clear that the great vogue for patent medicines developed with the industrial system, and it is a fair inference that the bulk of the nostrums went to the towns. But the industrial population were mainly country people or their descendants, who emigrated to the towns, allured by economic quacks who gave them higher money wages and far less for them. These people took with them and handed on to their descendants a belief in various herbs and cures which probably derived from a greater antiquity than one might suppose. D. H. Lawrence has recorded that his coalminer father used to gather herbs and plants in the fields, and brew himself concoctions from them which he claimed were of great benefit. As the towns grew, it became impossible to grow or gather any such herbs and plants, and the patent medicines took their place. It is noteworthy that the Continental equivalents often claimed the prestige of some religious person or body, such as the picturesque Benedictine nuns of Pistoia, or in France some equally imaginary Abbé. This is complicated by the fact that in a more distant past simple remedies may indeed have been given to the peasants by monks or nuns, themselves no great friends to scientific medicine. In the English industrial towns the memory of the traditional home treatment was flattered by such advertising phrases as "Balsamic Elixir", "African herbs . . . never used by any white doctor or chemist", ". . . contain the best properties of Sarsaparilla, Dandelion, Burdock, and Quinine", ". . . a purely vegetable compound", "contains . . . the active principles of seaweed", "contains those substances which Nature intended for the use of man", "a Concentrated extract of Herbs", and so forth. No doubt vaguely and confusedly the victim got the impression that these must be the very herb remedies which grandfather swore by.

It is a curious chapter in social history, but has the end of the chapter been written? Look at the advertisements.

SIX

Maundy Gregory

AND HONOURS EASY

"I could not love thee, dear, so much,
Loved I not money more."

If any satirical novelist of the period long ago nicknamed
"the Long Armistice" had invented the character and career
of Maundy Gregory, he would unquestionably have been
journalistically howled down as an impossible libeller. "It
can't happen here." Yet it did happen, and thanks to the
investigations of Mr. Gerald Macmillan we have at least the
main outlines of an episode in high life which illustrates
wonderfully the politicians' and other non-combatants'
statements about the spiritual and moral regeneration
achieved by War. The nature of the case put great difficulties
in the way of his biographer. Gregory was a braggart and an
exhibitionist who could not help exaggerating in a manner
most flattering to himself everything about him; if he was not
actually a liar, his "tales arrived full-blown", and one can
sympathise with Mr. Macmillan's struggles to disentangle the
facts from the tales. Probably the task was impossible, and
even Gregory himself subjected to the test of the alleged
truth-compelling drug could scarcely have unravelled so
tortuous a skein. Moreover, the very nature of Gregory's
financial arrangements and of his long career as the Sir

Pandarus of National Honours exacted secrecy, and the
camouflage of a self-created character-part as the very
wealthy and influential man about town. Except in one or
two cases, Gregory's dupes or accomplices have naturally
kept silence from fear of ridicule or worse.

The overworked and smug slogan "Crime does not pay"
is at best a debatable proposition, but in Gregory's case
there can be little doubt that a mixture of bluff, bounce,
snob appeal and lack of scruple *do* pay, or did for a considerable number of years, and that very highly indeed. It is
true that at the age of fifty-six Gregory was compelled to pass
several weeks in the uncongenial but not very onerous post of
librarian to Wormwood Scrubbs and even paid in addition a
fine of fifty pounds, though that cannot be considered
excessive for a man who, it is said, habitually had on hand
about £5,000 in Bank of England notes. And it is also true
that after he ceased to be an unwilling and incarcerated
librarian he hastened to Paris, and remained in France until
he died in a German concentration camp during the war.
But then exile was no great hardship, and a man of Gregory's
tastes and habits might well prefer Paris to London, while his
exile was soothed by a pension (not of course a Civil List
pension or anything official) said to have been £2,000 a year
tax-free, which is certainly far higher than any official
pension to a person of mere artistic, literary or scientific
merit. Moreover, in those last years in France he was able to
do what he had never been able to do in England, namely, to
be accepted as Sir Arthur Gregory on the strength of a
(purchased) Papal order. It was surely dulcet and decorous
that the great broker of titles should himself be titled, though
not from the Fountain of Honour whose cordial and reviving
waters he had so often been the means of bestowing on those
who had so richly deserved them.

Gregory has another distinction, unique, I should imagine,
even in a recorded legal history so long as that of England.

While it cannot be claimed that the Honours (Prevention of Abuses Act) of 1925 was passed especially to catch him, the fact is that so far Gregory is the only person who has ever been prosecuted and punished under that Act.

Maundy Gregory was the elder of two sons of a Hampshire clergyman, and born in 1877. He was educated at a small private school and passed over three years at Oxford, which he left without taking a degree early in 1899. This last fact, which was followed by the death of his father, by his mother's going to live in what was really a home for indigent widows of clergymen, and Gregory's employment as assistant master at a small school, goes to support Mr. Macmillan's inference that the family was poor. Here we touch the drab tragedy of many of the really poor clergy. Theoretically it is an excellent idea that each community or section of a town should have one educated man and his family devoting themselves to other than purely commercial interests. But in the days of Gregory's youth they were expected to keep up the standards of 'gentry' on quite inadequate incomes, while they naturally tried to educate their children as 'gentry', which too often meant fitting them to spend while unfitting them to earn. However, too much must not be made of this to excuse Gregory's faults and deplorable end. His brother, who obviously was brought up in the same environment, became a distinguished officer in the Army of one of the great Dominions. It is equally tempting to attribute some at least of his more flamboyant and ostentatious flourishes to the fact that he was a homosexual, but this again may be delusive, though it might help to explain his great interest in such personalities as 'Baron' Corvo and T. E. Lawrence.

Unfortunately, in spite of all Mr. Macmillan's researches, there are important episodes and transitions in the life of Gregory which are not fully known. For instance, it is not clear how Gregory managed to escape from his confined life as a very minor schoolmaster to the wider, freer life of the stage. From the fact that a cousin and his wife had been on the stage Mr. Macmillan plausibly infers that Gregory may have been influenced by them, but nothing certain is known. At all events, after a considerable period of what must have been near penury, he began to get engagements as an actor and then as general manager. As Mr. Macmillan points out, the fact that he held that position for three years under Sir Frank Benson is good evidence of his competence. Unluckily, he set up as theatrical manager on his own, and at first had some success; but failed disastrously in February 1909, after eight or nine years of stage work. His failure seems to have been due not to lack of ability but to lack of capital, and to the intransigence of the musicians in his employ, who walked out of what seems to have been a quite successful show because he could not immediately pay up a few days' arrears of salary.

This stage career, as Mr. Macmillan relates it, is perfectly honourable, if not particularly distinguished. The little newspaper puffs and embellished advertisements Gregory put out about his productions and himself are an understood part of the trade, little more than euphemisms to catch custom, much as when out of a job he would inevitably have described himself genteelly as 'resting'. The interest of this stage career lies in its obvious appropriateness as training for his future 'dedicated' life-work as (apparently) the most successful and highly paid honours tout in English history. Nature, when preparing one of her human masterpieces, works slowly, obscurely, inflicts harsh lessons, insists on what seem like irrevelant experiences, and then, when the moment arrives, sends out her favourite equipped for the arduous trek to the constellations she has been grooming him for all along.

An actor! Of course, Gregory had to have experience as an actor and, above all, as a stage manager and general theatrical manager, to fulfil his destiny. However much he may have forgotten the instruction he received in youth, it is safe to say that he always understood the necessity for serious purpose in life and the paramount importance of keeping up appearances. Whatever faults may be alleged against him— and let him that is without honours among you cast the first stone—his genial nature is attested by many acts of kindness and lavish gifts chosen always with care if not with taste; and Gregory was never corroded by the evil influences of modern scepticism. Indeed, like so many of his kind, he eventually became a convert to Roman Catholicism. From Oxford, along with other tastes, he naturally derived the speech and manners of a gentleman, so important in modern salesman-ship, especially of a kind requiring delicate handling.

Almost literally, Gregory's life as an honours salesman became that of a man playing a part in a drama of his own devising with a stage setting which did him every credit as a manager. Dealing mainly with the snob public, which he must have studied with the subtle cynicism of a popular actor gauging his 'public', Gregory soon realised that, given sufficient effrontery and cool assumption, he could make them believe almost anything he wanted. Provided it was carried off with an air, hardly any device was too gross for their credulity. Sometimes the over-scrupulous realism of the artist led him to make unnecessary concessions in his stage settings. Thus, he went to very great trouble to find a private house which suited him and was in the right neighbourhood and bore the number 'ten'. On his instructions, when he was engaged in his office with some social climber who needed to be impressed with Gregory's importance and lofty contacts, he was rung up from this residence, and the message was brought that he was "wanted by number ten". With a significant look, Gregory would apologise for the interruption and engage in a fictitious conversation with somebody whom the dupe instantly inferred was the denizen of 10 Downing Street. But why go to the trouble of actually owning or renting a "number ten"? Surely it would have been sufficient for the message to be brought, and for Gregory to talk impressively into a disconnected telephone? Perhaps he thought that the secretary who gave the message had to be duped too, but the actual house at "number ten" was an extravagant piece of stage setting. But then Gregory was extravagant; it was part of his daily make-up, and one of the most successful tricks in catching his moneyed flat-fish.

Unfortunately there is a gap of about a decade between Gregory's failure as an actor-manager in 1909 and his début on a wider and loftier stage as a high-class intermediary for the lucrative disposal of new titles in 1919. What was he doing in the meantime? How did he live? What did he do in the Great War? And how above all did the penniless and presumably rather friendless stage failure find the capital to set himself up in the honours business and thus be accepted by the great, good and wealthy?

No satisfactory answer can be made to these questions, except that a little is recorded of his war service. In 1914 Gregory was thirty-seven, too old, especially after a sedentary life, to face the exacting hardships of active service. He was in fact not called up until July 1917, and was demobilised in February 1919 after what seems to have been a period of home service only. Of course, as usual, Gregory had his own highly embellished or wholly invented story of the important work he had done for his country at that time. It seems almost superfluous to specify that this work was for the Secret Service section of Military Intelligence. In the mythology of popular heroes, interesting for its unintentional revelation of popular psychology, no hero is complete unless he has spent at least part of his life as a spy. What is new about this is the moral attitude implied. Other epochs have had their spies, have recognised the utility of the dirty work and the qualities and courage involved, but at most have apologised for them as necessary, and then hurried them out of sight. It was reserved for the twentieth century to elevate to the level of heroism the deceit, the treachery, the lying and the under-hand procedure of espionage. Gregory did not hesitate to claim for himself the prestige of these chivalrous enterprises, but the supporting evidence seems rather flimsy. If he had really been a war-time spy in Germany it seems unlikely that a German reporter would have come over specially for Gregory's trial, saying that he was well-known in Germany. And the apparently verified facts that after the war he acted as factotum for various dethroned and exiled monarchs, and even possessed gold cigarette-cases inscribed and presented to him by the ex-King of Greece and a member of our own Royal Family, may be explained on other grounds than as rewards for successful military espionage. The last gift was unquestionably in acknowledgement solely of Gregory's aid in raising funds for some charity—which perhaps goes to show what a multitude of sins Charity still covers.

But how did it happen that in little more than a decade the penniless actor-manager had reached a position of osten-tatious opulence from which he was able to patronise monarchs? All we get by way of answer are two tantalising hints. At some unspecified time, but apparently between the collapse of Gregory's stage career and August 1914, he astonished one of his friends by taking a taxi to drive a distance of nine miles to see her; and, on her expressing surprise, Gregory implied that money was now no object with him. At the same or perhaps another time he accounted for this sudden and unexpected affluence by a vague reference to his intimacy with a newspaper proprietor. *A priori*, there seems nothing in the least improbable that Gregory should have been connected, and successfully, with popular journalism, particularly in what used to be called "Society news". One of the reasons for his success as an honours tout was his sincere and naïve snobbery, his unfeigned rejoicing over the attractions of 'blood' and titles. Even if he could have bought an English title, which no doubt he could easily

have done in the days of his splendour, Gregory could not
have used it, for obvious business reasons. So he went in for
'blood'. By a series of genealogical switches from male to
female ancestors Gregory contrived to trace his descent from
Edward III (as indeed a good many people still do) in a
pedigree which must have infuriated the College of Heralds.

Add that to Gregory's capacity for romancing himself and
others and his undoubted gift of the gab, and we can easily
see how useful he could have been to the editor or indeed the
proprietor of 'Society' journals. Even in a humbler situation
on a daily he could have gratified the tastes of himself and his
readers by composing such head-lines as "Viscount's Niece
Weds Ex-Burglar Bookie" or "Peer's Cousin Injured in Car
Smash" and the like tributes of class-love. We can point to
the fact that in the days of his glory Gregory himself owned,
edited and partly wrote a 'Society' periodical called *The
Whitehall Gazette and St. James's Review*, which ran from
August 1919 until December 1932. True, it was mostly
given away gratis though priced at half a crown, but then it
was sent mainly to clubs and Government departments, and
apparently more than covered its cost by publishing
illustrated articles on aspirants to titles, for which they paid
heavily.

Unluckily 'Society' journalism, however obsequious and
oleaginous, was never very profitable to those who wrote it,
so that the conclusion can hardly be avoided that Gregory
must have found some other way to dignity and emolument
through this vaguely discerned figure of a friendly "newspaper magnate". One cannot help feeling, in spite of the
total lack of evidence, that Gregory during the period 1910–
1919 may have had useful work to do for his country in
company promoting. It is among the most highly remuner-
ated activities, and therefore presumably of the greatest
national importance, and so likely to attract the interest of an
ambitious and fastidious man like Gregory, keenly on the

look-out for anything where money was to be made. It was, after all, the period of Horatio Bottomley's greatest triumphs in the combined worlds of pelf and patriotism, and if ever there was a time when easy money was to be made it was in the Lloyd George epoch.

Unfortunately, despite Mr. Macmillan's careful researches, there is simply no fuller information as to how Gregory moved from penury to opulence or how he came to make himself so enviable a position in the honours-tout business. Surmises as to a possible connection with the splendid world of company promoting are nothing more than—speculation. Unless some well-informed and candid person who knew Gregory and his milieu thoroughly kept a diary which posterity will some day read, there seems no chance that these questions will ever receive a satisfactory answer. All that can be said is that by 1919 Gregory was evidently fully engaged in his work of national importance, since a silly snob-advertising publication such as *The Whitehall Gazette* could only have existed as the trade journal of the honours business. And he continued to operate successfully until his downfall some thirteen years later. If one cannot exactly say that it was a short life neither can one say it was merry, but rather that it was pretentious and absurd.

In spite of Gregory's long line or lines of aristocratic ancestors and of his genteel upbringing and Oxford education there is nearly always something ostentatious or flashy or even vulgar in the anecdotes more or less admiringly related of him. One may cite as an example the over-smart clothes he always wore and the flashy jewellery which went with them. Real English gentlemen do not dress in that style, though it may be noted frequently as a symptom of those who share Gregory's deviationist penchants, a remark which might also be made about his intense interest in *Seven Pillars of Wisdom* with its homosexual passages which are piously committed to memory by the fraternity. This style of dressing may have impressed provincial war profiteers willing to allow their disinterested patriotic services to be recognised with a title, but would hardly recommend him to others.

Gregory's intrusive impudence never shrank from any attempt to impose himself on the great, and Mr. Macmillan tells of an occasion during a river excursion when Gregory managed to seat himself next to a Cabinet Minister, to whom he talked the whole way as if on terms of intimacy though in fact the politician had not the slightest idea who his un-wanted chatterbox was. That did not matter, because all Gregory wanted was for some of his dupes to see an ap-parently familiar conversation going on and to be impressed accordingly. He was a master of these scenic effects, as is demonstrated by the already mentioned "number ten" calls and the equally valuable deception of an acquaintance with some minor personage at Buckingham Palace which was cunningly exploited to suggest a more august frequentation.

His over-elegant clothes and jewels were no more evidence of good breeding than his collecting of expensive books he did not really understand was evidence of genuine culture, or even than the rather parvenu menus he drew up may be considered as evidence of a refined taste in food and wine. From Mr. Macmillan's descriptions of these traits and episodes one always feels the actor and the stage-manager at work in Gregory. He never really wishes to be something but merely to give the impression, the "stage effect" of being so. The same remark applies to the system of coloured lights in his office window with which he mysteriously (and quite unnecessarily, one would think) signalled to real or imaginary friends in the street, and to the various little tricks he devised to show off his supposed wealth.

Apparently Gregory knew F. E. Smith (the late Lord Birkenhead) to whom he always referred as "F.E." Now the use of the Christian names or initials of any known or notorious person is always an indication of the inferior and hanger-on.

M

The man's real friends in talking about him to strangers would call him "Lord Birkenhead" or "Birkenhead", whatever they might address him as in the intimacy of friendship. And then Gregory put out such silly, conceited stories to show off to his dupes! Thus, he remarked with apparent casualness: " 'F.E.' wants me to buy his yacht. But I don't want it; I've got four already." He certainly did own two Thames launches and may in addition have owned four yachts, but to hand out the information so directly and apropos of nothing in particular was as awkward as having a soliloquy in a modern thug play. Such a flimsy trick was surely more likely to cause amusement than awe? And the same thought is suggested by other tricks to display his supposed opulence. It seems unlikely that a highly intelligent man such as A. J. A. Symons would really be impressed by Gregory's producing a huge roll of bank-notes with which to over-pay for some Corvo scripts. And a leading London bookseller would surely have been (discreetly, of course) amused by Gregory's insistence that only one member of the firm was to know the amount of his current indebtedness and that the bill was only to be presented (for immediate payment) when it reached two hundred pounds. The wealthy man of affairs rather hides than parades his opulence in such up-stage attitudes. His ostentation is not a roll of five thousand pounds in notes but a complete absence of cash— everything he buys is on credit with instructions that the bills are to be sent to his office. As so often, Gregory, as the man of boundless wealth, remained the *cabotin* and could not help over-playing his part.

Yet, looking to the evidence published by Mr. Macmillan, we are forced to admit that these theatrical methods of Gregory's were amazingly successful in bringing him into contact with persons of quality and honour about town who would never have deigned to notice him if he had kept to the sobriety, restraint and modest self-effacement which seem more in accord with his real life as the Sir Pandarus of titles. In full accord with his love of display Gregory took over a West End night club and restaurant, which seems to have reached the acme of expensive vulgarity under the joint influence of Gregory and an Italian manager. The inevitable title for this should surely have been the Social Alpine Club, but Gregory naturally disliked an admission so open, and kept to the original and modest title of the Ambassador Club. The suggestion of exclusiveness, dignity and opulence is obvious and worthy of Gregory, but credit for it must go to the original name-giver, who was appropriately called or called himself 'Ritzie'—a slang word embodying a view of life which has woven old England's winding-sheet more effectively and disastrously than Blake's "harlot's cry".

How Gregory and his Italian restaurateur contrived to attract some of the well-known guests who unquestionably frequented the place is something of a mystery, especially since Mr. Macmillan says they ran it "in a flashy and extravagant way", and that at luncheon at any rate the service was very bad. In any case the 'club' lost money and had to be bolstered by Gregory's funds. Yet among the guests reported by Mr. Macmillan were Lord Birkenhead, King Manoel of Portugal, King George and Prince Paul of Greece, and the Prince of Wales—subsequently Edward VIII and Duke of Windsor. "He was known to the staff as 'Number One'," says Mr. Macmillan. But Gregory's greatest triumph with the Ambassador Club was when he succeeded in making it the scene of the annual Derby Eve Dinner for peers and M.P.s, though unfortunately these did not take place until 1931 and 1932, shortly after which Gregory was sent to prison. The Derby Eve Dinner had been founded by a Colonel Faber with the very natural and laudable belief that anticipation of a horse-race and a good dinner were a means of reconciling the political divergences of the most important people, at least for one evening. It is

an admirable example of that sage realism and genius for
compromise on which we so rightly pride ourselves.

After the death of Colonel Faber, the chairmanship of this
important annual dinner was taken over by Major-General
J. E. B. Seely. Unfortunately, we are not told how Gregory
persuaded the General to transfer the dinner to the Ambassador Club, but Mr. Macmillan tells us that Gregory
"met all the expenses of the dinner", which accounts for the
fact that the dinners were afterwards written up in *The
Whitehall Gazette* so lyrically and in such detail. The list of
guests at the Derby Eve Dinner of June 2nd, 1931, as recorded
by Gregory's high-class periodical, is most impressive, and
runs to one hundred and sixty-eight names. Here is the list of
those who sat at the chairman's table, if the placing is
correct:

"Major-General J. E. B. Seely (in the Chair); Sir Austen
Chamberlain, Mr Winston Churchill, the Duke of Marl-
borough, Mr J. H. Thomas, the Duke of Sutherland,
Viscount Craigavon, the Marquess of Reading, Major-
General the Earl of Scarbrough; Viscount Elibank, Mr J.
Maundy Gregory, Lord Jessel, Mr Ralph E. Harwood, Earl
Winterton, Lord Queenborough, Lord Bayford, Mr W.
Dudley Ward, Lord Pender, Marquis del Moral, Lieutenant-
Commander Sir Warden Chilcott."*

Mr. Macmillan states that if the guests had known that
Gregory was the owner of the Ambassador Club and that
he was paying for the dinner they would not have come. I
must say I think he overrates their innocence, lack of information and squeamishness. At the next dinner Major-
General Seely made a pointed and flattering reference in his
speech as Chairman to 'M.G.' and it needs no Burgess and
Maclean to tell us that this must have meant "Maundy
Gregory". Now if Gregory was so well known to the 1932

* *Honours For Sale* by Gerald Macmillan, p. 218. (Richards Press, 1954.)

guests that they would instantly take a reference to him
merely from his initials, it seems unlikely that they would be
in complete ignorance of his financial relation to the club
and to themselves. Among the other guests named at the
1931 dinner were owners and editors of newspapers. Could
they have lacked the information, and, possessing it, have
failed to pass it on? Are we expected to believe that not one
person present at that banquet knew that Gregory had for
years been the chief intermediary for the sale of honours, and
were they all utterly unacquainted with his flamboyant and
theatrical methods of obtaining customers? Of course in
1931-32 they knew there was an Act of Parliament forbidding
such deals—some of them had virtuously voted for it—but
how were they to know that Gregory would be so silly or so
unfortunate as to be found out?

This brings us to the crux of the Maundy Gregory
problem. Was he really a fraud in any serious or criminal
sense of the word? I am not of course referring to the charge
that Gregory poisoned his friend Mrs. Rosse in order to get
his hands on the £18,000 left him by her death-bed will—
money which he urgently needed. As a biographer Mr.
Macmillan was compelled to put before his readers all
the evidence he could collect, which he has done very
ably. The charge was actually brought against Gregory, but
it was by a disappointed candidate for the legacy. The fact
that the official investigation showed no grounds for taking
action should not be overstressed in view of the circumstances, though of course it is in Gregory's favour; but from
the narrative as presented I cannot see that there is much, if
any, circumstantial evidence against him. Others may feel
differently, but I personally feel unconvinced.

The fraud issue is quite different. He was prosecuted under
the Act of 1925, pleaded guilty, and was sentenced. The
very curious fact has been noted that Gregory is the only
person who has ever been prosecuted under the Honours

(Prevention of Abuses) Act, though it seems unlikely that he was the only person who ever infringed its clauses. On the other hand it seems as unlikely that the Act was passed for the express purpose of catching him as that no other person had ever assisted in bringing honour-seekers into touch with honour-sellers.

If the conscience of Parliament seems to have been so remarkably sluggish that it only discovered in 1925 that the traffic in honours ought to be punished, we must recollect that from the times of the Roman Republic the connection between wealth and honours, or wealth and social status, has been very close indeed. As a rule wealth is considered dishonourable chiefly by those who do not possess but would tremendously like to have it. Of course the modern persecution of the wealthy is not without precedent. From our schooldays we remember those dark stories of King John's dentists and the Jews. . . .

In discussing this topic of 'honours', whether historically or merely from the point of view of the *affaire Gregory*, it is as well to keep in mind some distinctions and reservations. The very phrase "sale of honours" is misleading, though due no doubt to the fact that in England we all speak loosely of "the Honours List", which includes both titles and orders, military and legal as well as political and civilian 'honours'. So far as the evidence goes, Gregory's traffic was in knighthoods, baronetcies, and a few baronies. There is no suggestion that he acted as broker for the sale of any of the very numerous orders and decorations sought after by a modestly blushing people, unless indeed there were some of Lloyd George's new-fangled Order of the British Empire—of which he is said to have distributed no fewer than 25,000 during his short reign. One must repudiate any suggestion that the military or legal titles and decorations—or indeed any of those for genuine service to the State—were ever bought and sold. They may have been, and certainly were sometimes or perhaps often, awarded by favour or routine or on erroneous reports—*humanum est errare*—but not for money.

Historically a distinction must be made between a property qualification for rank in the State and the purchase of rank or title from the ruler or rulers. In addition to the ancient distinction of patricians and plebs the Roman Republic graded its citizens into five classes based on a property basis, the poorer being exempted from military service on the cogent ground that they had nothing to fight for, not even a shilling a day. The 'knights', who came immediately after the governing body of senators (originally merely 'elders'), had to show they had an income of 400,000 sesterces (about £3,200 gold), but there is no suggestion that this 'knighthood' was ever sold by the Consuls or the Senate, which, considering the rapacity and greed of the Romans, is remarkable. But Roman 'knighthood' carried obligations—ten years' military service in the cavalry—as well as privileges and the access to high office. There seem to have been no purely decorative "titles of honour", but rather honourable nicknames, such as the rare *Pater Patriæ* or the sometimes abused military nickname such as 'Africanus' or 'Asiaticus'. An example which seems closer to the mere "title of honour" occurred after Pharsalia when the defeated and fugitive Cicero was permitted by Cæsar's magnanimity to retain his lictors and the title of *imperator*. It was perhaps the ironic tribute of consummate military skill to a fabulous vanity. Comparatively early in the Empire we find Claudius I accused of appointing his non-military favourites to a purely honorary command of a legion, which after six months entitled them to the rank of 'knights'; and he was even said to have sold such distinctions. Calumnies of Roman Emperors were endless, and the main significance of these rumours is that under the Roman Empire the "sale of honours" was considered a possibility. In the decadence of that Empire, after Constantine had 'orientalised' it and introduced such fulsome bureacratic "titles of honour" as *clarissimi, per-fectissimi, egregii, spectabiles, illustres* and so forth, there may indeed have been venality. These exuberant and—to our ears—absurd titles are an inevitable phase of decadent empires, akin to the pathetic effort to revive past glories by giving a little ruler a once great name, until the successor of Romulus and of Augustus ignominiously and pathetically expired in Romulus Augustulus. Yet it does not appear that the later Roman Emperors sold titles. Perhaps they had created so many that they were hardly worth buying, and then there was so much more to be made out of confiscatory taxation and stealing the property of wealthy men 'framed' on more or less false charges of treason or magical practices.

In dealing (in an appendix) with the topic of honours in the ages of chivalry and aristocracy Mr. Macmillan quotes an anecdote from the memoirs of the Duc de Saint-Simon, telling how a French noble when receiving the Collar of the Holy Ghost from Henri IV said: *"Domine, non sum dignus,"* and the King instantly replied: "I know that, but my cousin Soissons asked me to give it to you." *Se non è vero.* . . . Amusing as the anecdote is, it is not relevant to the sale of titles, for the Holy Ghost was an order like the Garter, and the award in question was not made for money but because of more or less corrupt influence in high quarters. No doubt it is hard to avoid the awarding of 'honours' to unworthy persons through corrupt influence in high places, but it is perhaps worth noting that the 1925 Act made no effort at all to check this form of abuse. And indeed it is hard to see how this could be achieved. *Quis custodiet custodes?*

For centuries the head of European aristocracy was France and not England, or Germany or Spain; and certainly few persons have been more deeply interested in the subtleties and precedences of peerage than Louis de Rouvroy, second Duc de Saint-Simon. He resigned his commission in the French Army because he did not think his military rank adequate to his aristocratic rank, and spent much time in lawsuits to determine rather minute points of precedence and ceremony, so that Louis XIV remarked that "since Monsieur de Saint-Simon had left the army he did nothing but inspect ranks." Yet in the family antecedents of this vainglorious noble Mr. Macmillan could have found a much more amusing and disillusioning story than that of La Ferté and his Collier de l'Ordre. Saint-Simon's father owed the dukedom, of which the son was so inordinately vain, to the prosaic, not to say ridiculous, fact that as a page to Louis XIII the elder Saint-Simon was the only one of the royal pages who during the *chasse* could sound the King's hunting horn (as apparently etiquette demanded) without spitting in it—a service anyone in the King's position would gladly reward with a dukedom. Moreover, during his embassy to Spain, the class-conscious Duc carefully investigated the origins of the Spanish grandees, and came to the interesting and significant conclusion that they were simply the descendants or imitators of the ancient *ricos hombres*, the wealthy men! Here again we find wealth as much as or more than valour or other merit as the basis of titles. If Saint-Simon was right, there is a certain analogy between the original grandees and the Roman 'knights' with their 400,000 sesterces a year.

Here again there is the essential difference between selling titles and awarding them to persons who have the immense merit of being rich. The King of France (as again we learn from Saint-Simon) unquestionably sold 'charges' (i.e. newly-created offices of State carrying a high salary) but did not apparently sell new titles of honour—he gave them to his mistresses. Yet under the *ancien régime* titles could be bought, for in many cases they went with an estate which an impoverished noble family was forced to sell to a *roturier* or *bourgeois*. (There is or used to be a popular belief in England that the earldom of Arundel goes with the possession of the castle —a delusion whose origin I have never seen explained.)

However, these sales were not always uncontested. Saint-Simon tells an anecdote of the wealthy Jewish banker, Samuel Bernard, who bought the barony of Rieux which depended on the États de Languedoc. They refused to recognise him as one of themselves, "not being noble in himself". Whereupon the vendor tried to establish a claim to enjoy the rights of the barony, but sentence was that the title went with the lands and he was ignominiously expelled. The upshot of this complex affair of honour was that Bernard's children, in spite of their protests, were forced to return lands and title to the vendor's son on repayment of the purchase price. Yet such had been Samuel Bernard's financial power at the height of his prosperity that at the end of his reign the Roi Soleil himself, harassed by money troubles, was forced to receive the Jewish banker and to speak graciously to him at Versailles—"*cette prostitution du Roi*", as Saint-Simon, still livid with rage, described it.

The story of titles and their sale in England is less pretentious. As everyone knows, the sale of titles began with that thrifty Scot, James I, who was far from being the pedantic nitwit of Whig propaganda-history. The King needed money for his wars with the Irish; the English country gentlemen had money, and were hungry for the 'honours' so steadily refused by Queen Elizabeth throughout her long and successful reign. So the King—or someone advising him—invented a new rank of hereditary carpet knights to be called baronets. Approved candidates could buy the title for a thousand guineas, a large sum of money at that time, and thus funds were raised for the liberation of Ulster. The coats-of-arms of descendants of the original purchasers quarter the red or bloody hand of Ulster heraldry. We are not told whether there were any contemporary go-betweens or Maundy Gregorys. Somebody must have told wealthy but untitled persons that the King was willing to sell his new-fangled baronetcies for a thousand guineas;

and somebody must have in turn told the King that such
and such persons were willing and able to pay that sum
for what cost him nothing at all. Possibly this has been
recorded, but I have never come across any account of it;
English history omits many details of interest.

This transmutation of gold into hereditary glory seems to
have taken place without any widespread protest or even
surprise in the King's lieges, though very likely it was jeered
at in clandestine pamphlets. As vidth and visdom were
firmly associated in the mind of the elder Weller, so apparently wealth and hereditary honours in the public mind of
the seventeenth century. It was equally so in the eighteenth
century, if we may credit a little story told in his recollections
by the Liberal M.P., G. W. E. Russell, a scion of that ducal
house and a fervent admirer of his party's great chief, Mr.
Gladstone. According to Russell, a newly-made peer in the
eighteenth century was accosted by a friend at his club and
asked for what reason he had been given this honour.
"Oh," he replied, "I heard that Tommy So-and-so had been
made a peer, and as my fortune is much larger than his I
wrote and pointed this out to Pitt, and a week later I was
promoted."

I must leave the responsibility for that historical anecdote
to Mr. Russell, but he tells another from his own knowledge
in his own time which is even more instructive. It concerns
the nineteenth-century descendant of one of the original
Ulster "red hand" baronetcies, who for some reason
imagined that he ought to be a peer and that his "political
services" deserved that splendid recognition. So an emissary
of the baronet (we might call the emissary the 'M.G.' of the
period) approached the appropriate Member, whom we
might call the Commissar of Party Funds since Russell omits
to say who he was. The Commissar heard Sir Vavasour's
ridiculous pretensions with impatience and dudgeon.
"Ho!" he said contemptuously, "you can tell Sir Vavasour

from me that if he wants a peerage he'll have to put his
Bloody Hand in his pocket."

G. W. E. Russell was a favourable example of the late
Victorian Liberal Member, a snob of course, and a bit
mealy-mouthed about his religious views, but on the whole
the kind of man one could trust in an emergency of no
particular importance in which he had nothing to gain or
lose. Though he takes up an obviously sincere moral attitude
on a good many points of principle and behaviour, there is
surely significance in the fact that he tells the tale of Sir
Vavasour merely as a funny anecdote, and without any
feelings or expression of disdain or horror at the inescapable
inference that the sale of titles through the Commissar of
Party Funds and a go-between was an accepted if not a
common occurrence. Is it possible that Mr. Gladstone knew
about this, presuming of course that Russell's tale is true?
One can easily imagine the sardonic cynicism of Disraeli
enjoying such situations, especially as he ended up by giving
himself an earldom for nothing—but Gladstone! Was it
hidden from him in a cloud of Homeric texts and revisions of
the Scriptures, or did he accept it without query as apparently he accepted the Buchenwald conditions under
which English convicts lived in Tasmania hoping for speedy
death, while denouncing the political prisons of the Kingdom
of Naples? We shall probably never know. It is one of the
great achievements of the British never—or seldom—to allow
their moral left hand to know what their worldly right hand
is doing.

If the handing out of a title in exchange for a more or less
secret but large contribution to party funds was taken as
lightly as Russell's anecdotes (whether true or not) indicate,
why, some quarter of a century later, was there this outburst
of moral disapprobation, followed by legislation and the
offering up of Maundy Gregory as a sacrifice of atonement?
To answer that question thoroughly one would have to go

far beyond the limits of a little sketch like this and, moreover, have access to much contemporary history which is still hidden in secrecy or propaganda. All that can be said is that the intense rivalries and enmities which came to a head in the political crisis of December 1916 left Lloyd George in the difficult and anomalous position of head of a coalition which lacked the support of many members of his own party, who incidentally and awkwardly kept control of the party funds. The sale of titles, mainly the minor dignities of knight and baronet, was the chief if not the only method by which a political war-chest could be collected.

It is a curious fact that the ardent "pro-Boer" who was very nearly lynched by a jingo Birmingham mob in a few years and under the stress of office and changed conditions evolved into an ardent imperialist, equally open-minded in grandiose plans of annexation and 'leadership' and in the high morality which was determined to exclude immoral France from any share in governing the Holy Land, despite existing engagements to the contrary. Such conversions are not necessarily insincere; they are part of the equipment of every statesman, who must necessarily change with changed circumstances. Lloyd George's conduct of the war was 'vigorous', and he was reproached with having introduced business men into the Government. I have never been able to see why the directors or managers of great industrial enterprises should be less capable of organising a war than scions of county families, lawyers, fox-hunters, trade union officials, and bureaucrats; or, if you are so diplomatically un-skilful as to become involved in a major war, why it should not be conducted 'vigorously'. It must be admitted that under Lloyd George the mental and moral tone of some publicists became low, not to say vulgar; though that was as much, if not more, the fault of the vulgarians who responded so excitedly to baser and baser appeals. And then, the combination of business and vigour undoubtedly resulted in a great deal of money being spent, much of which was virtuously earned by the heads of private enterprises. What more natural than that they should seek a national testimony to the excellence of their indispensable war work by the simple and gratifying process of becoming titled? And, purely as a coincidence, what more natural than that these same heroes of the home front should gladly make a little private contribution to the political war-chest of the statesman who had led us to victory, and, in doing so, had spent much of the capital owned by the once very wealthy England? After all, Lloyd George only did—or had done on his behalf while remaining "innocent of the knowledge"—what had evidently been done by his world-famous predecessors. No doubt he overdid it, but then his necessity was greater than theirs, and he had an unexampled amount of home-front heroism to reward. It is alleged that he found so many willing subscribers among his own compatriots that one great industrial Welsh town was nicknamed in the London clubs "The city of dreadful knights".

Granting that titles may have been handed out too freely by the Lloyd George régime to persons whose contribution to the war was that they had made a lot of money out of it, there may also have been a secret and even sublimely republican political motive. Pitt, we are told, deliberately "debased the peerage" by giving titles to persons whose main or sole merit was their wealth, his purpose being to sap the immense power and prestige of the eighteenth-century hereditary aristocracy. May not some such purpose have impelled Lloyd George, whose worst enemies would scarcely deny that he was a demagogue?

In any case it seems unfair to blame Lloyd George for whatever sins Maundy Gregory is supposed to have committed while operating on the titles market. Unless Gregory had some other lucrative occupation between 1910 and being called up in 1917 he must have engaged as an "honour tout" for years before Lloyd George became Prime Minister. Again, whether Gregory turned to the right by numbers from October 1917 until February 1919, or whether he made the world safe for democracy by listening at keyholes to what the Kaiser and Hindenburg said, it was Lloyd George who managed to dispense with his services in the field of honours during that period. And as Lloyd George fell from power in 1922, and Gregory continued to act as a go-between for at least another decade, he must unquestionably have found other patrons during the Bonar Law, MacDonald and Baldwin Governments, during which, however, the agitation against "the sale of honours" reached such a pitch that the Act of 1925 was passed. But if Gregory did actually negotiate for 'honours' to be bestowed in exchange for subscriptions to the party funds (whatever party it may have been), then the Commissars of Party Funds and the purchasers were equally guilty of a breach of morality.

Gregory was brought down by two mistakes or misfortunes. He had received a sum of £30,000 from an unnamed person on the promise that he would negotiate a title for the donor, and failed either to do so or to return the money. Gregory is said to have kept the money in the belief that the donor would not sue for its return because of the inevitable exposure. Here was something very much worse than a mere honours-brokerage. To keep the money and fail to produce the title was fraud; and to refrain from repayment on the calculations alleged was blackmail. Unfortunately for Gregory the unnamed purchaser died, and his executors and trustees had no scruples at all about suing for the repayment of the £30,000. Gregory tried to bluff it out until just before the case came on, and then caved in and paid.

We are led to believe that Gregory was financially ruined by the repayment of this £30,000. In which case he cannot have been the "very wealthy man" he is alleged to have been. He may have made a large income, but he must also

have spent or over-spent it in his exuberant method of
conducting his affairs. Unfortunately—apart from this one
sum of £30,000—there is no information as to what he did
earn, and we do not even learn whether the £30,000 was an
exceptional or a usual sum, and whether Gregory in other
cases had defrauded a purchaser in the same way. If he
'sold' only one title a month on the average, and received
only £1,000 for each, he still made £12,000 a year. (How did
he fill in his income-tax forms after 1925?) And he probably
made much more. His expenses of course were very high,
unnecessarily and extravagantly so. It is impossible to believe
that Gregory was the only mercenary honours-broker,
though doubtless he was the most successful and the most
flashy and ostentatious. The others must have operated, if
they did operate, in a comparatively drab secret squalor.
There is something engaging in the fanciful if spurious
splendour which Gregory contrived by skilful or at any rate
ostentatious stage-management to throw round his essentially
unheroic and indeed boot-licking occupation. He attempted,
like an artist, to give his life colour and prestige, to make
himself a remarkable character, as able to dazzle Corvine
banqueters with his gastronomic splendours as to act as
unofficial host to a large selection of both Houses of Parliament at an Eve of the Derby Dinner. Neither these nor the
other extravagances and ostentations which Mr. Macmillan
tells us about were necessary for Gregory's occupation.
Indeed, one would think that many of them were distinctly
an error, for the less such a person attracted public attention
the better. The dramatisation was due to the vanity of
the artist; and as the Black Maria took him off the field
of his glory he might indeed have exclaimed: *Qualis artifex
pereo!*

Gregory's second mistake was due to a miscalculation,
itself the result apparently of financial stress due to the
forced repayment of the £30,000. Gregory approached (and

made the mistake of putting into writing his willingness to provide a title in exchange for money) a person who was not interested in buying a title, who was indignant at the suggestion being made to him, and who had no hesitation about launching the criminal prosecution. When the news appeared in the papers we can well imagine the flutter it must have caused, not only among earlier purchasers who fondly imagined that the transactions leading to their entitlement were for ever buried in the oblivion of State secrets, but also among the Commissars of Party Funds and possibly even more exalted persons. If Gregory elected to plead not guilty and to give evidence, what might he not have to reveal? He must be persuaded to plead guilty, for summary conviction would not only ensure a light sentence but preclude further and most inconvenient enquiries. Even in disaster Gregory kept his head and the whip hand. It is said that in exchange for his plea of guilty and suffering the tortures of acting as librarian at "the Scrubbs", to be followed on his release by a strategic and permanent retreat to France, he was offered a life pension of £1,000 a year by representatives of both sides of his traffic. He retained sufficient impudence to insist on and to get £2,000. One can but applaud. With a change of scenario and a little luck he might have made himself a national hero.

Gregory's final years in France as "Sir Arthur Gregory" are of no interest, except that he continued on a reduced scale to make ostentatious gestures and to play the imitation grandee. He even continued to boast to his friends of accomplishments he hadn't got, but as the friends were mostly French they smiled sceptically and let him talk. What is interesting to note once more is that Gregory, the mere go-between, is the only person prosecuted under the 1925 Act, either at the time of his conviction or later. None of the principals on either side of the bargains he arranged was ever disturbed, but a scapegoat was discovered, punished, and discreetly banished to "agnostic, atheist France". Honour was saved.

Should there not be some memorial to this national character, who if not exactly a king-maker was by way of being a knight-maker and even a peer-maker? A full-length statue of Gregory might be put up in the archives of the College of Heralds, with the modest inscription: "*Si monumentum requiris, circumspice*". Or perhaps a bust, similar to that of Molière at the Académie Française, might be set up in the House of Lords with the inscription in English: "Nothing was lacking to his glory, he was lacking to ours."

SEVEN

Frauds or Not Frauds in Literature

I

If speech was given us to conceal our thoughts, as the tag tells us, then writing and subsequently printing seem to have been given us to falsify literature and history. The English are naturally very proud of Shakespeare, but how much is truly 'Shakespeare'? There are difficulties about the three parts of *Henry VI*, and about *Titus Andronicus*, *Pericles* and *Henry VIII*. *The Passionate Pilgrim* is a little piratical anthology of lyrics, most of which are not Shakespeare's. And there are apocryphal plays, completely rejected, such as *The Yorkshire Tragedy*. Spain's renowned *Don Quixote* was given a spurious second part by the enemies of Cervantes, who taunted him with his wounds and poverty, and boasted that they hoped to spoil his market for the genuine second part he afterwards published! France has no greater prose writer than François Rabelais, yet the authenticity of the *Cinquiesme Livre* has been a matter of debate for over a century.

These literary and historical frauds cover an immense range of time and quantity as well as of motive, from the most innocent of imitations and the accidental attribution of one man's work to another, through many intermediate stages, to that of downright forgery or, as in the case of Cervantes, malicious falsification. Who was 'Homer'? Nobody knows, and it is most unlikely anyone ever will know for certain. The assertions of scholars are really only brilliant inferences, conjectural and provisional. Even the text, which is said to be really more authentic than that of Shakespeare, cannot be the 'original'. It is piquant to learn that the cultivated Phocæans of Massalia (Marseille) especially prided themselves on possessing a text of Homer uncontaminated by the meddlings of Aristarchus, whose text is the basis of all later researches.

For centuries cultivated Europeans trustingly enjoyed what they thought were the poems of Anacreon, until modern criticism decided that we have only a few scraps of the genuine Anacreon—all the other poems which for so long passed as his were really clever imitations by minor poets of Alexandria and even Byzantium. It seems highly unlikely that these were ever intended to be taken seriously as the work of Anacreon. Poor taste, the fanatical destruction of ancient texts by ecclesiastics and wars, the blind worship of antiquity by the Renaissance, must account for the substitution of the imitations for the original. In its uncritical enthusiasm the early Renaissance mistook the *Hero and Leander* of the very late poet, Musæus, for the work of the mythical and very early Musæus. Bentley had to fight a one-sided battle against a coalition of malice and ignorance to prove what nobody now doubts—that the *Epistles* of Phalaris are spurious. Yet Bentley, though so obviously (now) in the right, had almost everybody against him, including Sir William Temple, Swift and Atterbury. And overwhelming as Bentley's arguments are, we find years after his death a Regius Professor of Greek maintaining that although "particular epistles" are proved spurious yet "the book may be authentic in the main, and an original still".

At the Renaissance one Annius of Viterbo published what he claimed were lost historical works of Cato, Archilochus, Manetho, Berosus and so forth. Nobody knows whether he was a forger or a mere dupe, whether he invented the books himself or credulously bought faked manuscripts from some unscrupulous person. Modern scholarship is quite certain that they are not genuine. At that time of intense but uncritical admiration for everything Greek or Roman, when the wealthiest Italians were ready to pay almost anything for "newly discovered MSS of lost works", the temptation to forgery of a poor scholar must have been very great.

Strange to relate, Christianity and the Church by accident, or in some cases intentionally, produced the greatest number of apocrypha, spurious writings and downright forgeries. Christian apocrypha may of course be no more than erroneous or heretical or spurious works condemned by the wisdom of the Church or of the Fathers. Yet it is staggering to learn that the names and, in some cases, fragments are known of some thirty 'false' Gospels, including the Gospel according to Judas Iscariot! That should be an extraordinary document, and if by chance a text turned up intact in some new papyrus find, it would surely be a world best-seller. Or it might turn out to be completely uninteresting. It cannot have been anything but a forgery, or an invented and catchpenny title. And as practically all the texts of the others are lost, nothing can be said about them. What would be worth knowing is how they came to be written, and why they were ever accepted.

The last question can be provisionally answered by reference to the amazing credulity of audiences, particularly in the Middle East. There, as elsewhere, people believe what they want to believe, but with a peculiar obstinacy and blindness to facts and irrefutable evidence which are stupefying. An example: during the 1914–18 War many of the 'notables' of Cairo (anti-British, of course, to a man) insisted that the Suez Canal was in fact held by the Turks, since we had lost it. They were taken out, shown the British guards and posts for miles, and announced themselves convinced that they had been wrong. Yet only a few weeks later they had returned to their former story, and were telling one another how the Turks held the canal! A Western Europe which has twice hailed the Russians as military saviours, and twice execrated them as destroyers of humanity and religion, can scarcely criticise. They can't be both, but that slight illogicality troubles few in Western Europe, from heads of States to the least expensive journalists.

Since we know nothing of the circumstances in which these Gospels were written, but only that the Church at an early date condemned them, we may perhaps be allowed the interpretation of a favourable kind that there was no intentional deception. After all, a sensational title may be attached to a book without the author's knowledge or consent; and "the Gospel according to Judas Iscariot" may well have been the invention of some early Levantine publisher more interested in circulation than in sanctity.

This explanation, however, will not meet the well-known case of the Edessa letters. Round about the year A.D. 200 somebody put into circulation what purported to be an authentic letter to Jesus Christ from Abgar Uchomo, King of Edessa, together with Christ's reply. Needless to say, no such correspondence took place; but as the forger or forgers remain unknown, conjectures as to motive are more than ever hazardous. The letters may have been manufactured to sell as "original documents" to some wealthy and credulous convent; but it seems more likely that the object was religious propaganda, perhaps part of the strange evolution whereby the Good Shepherd rejoicing over the lost lamb that was found eventually became the stern Kosmokrator threatening hell-fire at the Last Judgment. Or, though this seems highly improbable, it might have been a mere hoax by some learned non-believer to see how far the credulity of the faithful would extend. In any case, since there must have been an intent to deceive, the unknown perpetrator cannot be exonerated from the charge of 'forging' pseudo-historical documents. As is, or was, also pleaded in the case of the Josephus interpolation, the Abgar letters are excused as a "pious fraud". This is the worst excuse of all, for a 'fraud' can never be 'pious' and to make the plea is tantamount to endorsing that most fatal of immoralities—that "the end justifies the means".

Perhaps the most potent of all these now proven ecclesiastical forgeries was the Donation of Constantine, of which everyone has heard. This impressive-sounding document purported to be a grant from the Emperor Constantine to Pope Silvester of temporal sovereignty over the city of Rome, the whole of Italy and the western parts of the Empire. In addition the Emperor was also supposed to have granted the Pope more than was in his power to give anyone, namely supreme authority in all matters of faith and worship, and power over all other bishops. The authenticity of this document went unquestioned for centuries (except by a Chancellor of the Holy Roman Empire in the tenth century) and anyone can see how it might have been, and indeed was, used to support the medieval Papacy in its bid for world temporal power. Strange to relate, the first real blow against its authenticity was struck by a humanist, Lorenzo Valla, who in 1440 proved mainly on stylistic grounds that it could not have been written in the age of Constantine. Like most pioneers in the field of exposure, Valla received little but abuse (though the Pope at last magnanimously appointed him a papal secretary) and the controversy lasted for about two hundred and fifty years, when even the least scrupulous and noisy defenders were finally silenced. The Donation of Constantine is a forgery.

The debate went on, however, with the orthodox trying to prove that the document was not produced in Rome; but again on stylistic grounds it has been proved to emanate from the Papal Chancery somewhere between A.D. 750 and 800 and probably about 775. Its immediate purpose was to influence the policy of Charlemagne and to counter the iconoclastic heresy of Byzantium; though this is rather a probable conjecture than proven fact. The forgery is certain.

We have to remember that throughout the Dark Ages and the Middle Ages literary and other forgeries, even when perpetrated for gain, were apparently not considered so dangerous and despicable as with us. True, Dante puts the *falsatori* very deep in hell with horrid torments, but his individual examples are alchemists, persons who assumed disguise or false identity to get lovers, coiners of false money, Potiphar's wife who falsely accused Joseph, and Sinon who deceived the Trojans about the horse, but not forgers in our sense. Forgery was not made a statutory offence in England until 1562 and was not punishable by hanging until 1634. And unless money is involved in a literary forgery there might be some difficulty in proving a legal offence.

A curious example of a complex of forgeries by holy men in the Middle Ages is shown by the forged charters and papal bulls produced during the long dispute between the once famous and wealthy Benedictine monasteries of Aniane and Gellone in Languedoc. When Count Guilhemau Court Nez, the cousin of Charlemagne, retired from the world and founded a monastery at what is now St. Guilhem le Désert (then Gellone), he naturally applied for advice and monastic personnel to his friend Benedict, Abbot of the neighbouring Aniane; but since Guilhem was of the imperial house and wealthy he had no difficulty in arranging for his monastery to hold directly from the Holy See, subject to no other authority, even of the mother-house of Aniane. But in the fatal year 1066 a fire destroyed practically all the charters and other documents which guaranteed the independence of Gellone. Whereupon Aniane claimed jurisdiction over Gellone, and supported the claim with forged or interpolated documents, to which Gellone retorted with the like! Only a bull from Pope Urban II put an end to this unseemly competition of falsifiers, and established, or rather re-established, the independence of Gellone. Yet so successfully had the Aniane forgers gone to work that the monks of Gellone were careful to have their privilege confirmed by later pontiffs, while even so great a scholar as Mabillon was taken in and thought the independence of Gellone dated only from the bull of Urban II, whereas in fact it dated from the foundation by Count Guilhem in the beginning of the ninth century. It does not appear that any action was taken against the forgers in their lifetime. Many other examples might be cited, and all probably would have been defended on the "pious fraud" and "the end justifies the means" arguments. As not many of the laity could read and write in those times, the offence was necessarily limited to the clergy, which perhaps explains the tenderness with which the offence was treated.

Religious forgery was naturally a strong debating point with the early Protestants, who had no particular occasion for it; and commercial or banking forgeries naturally became a heinous offence in an immense trading community such as England. Forgery of bank-notes was very common in the early nineteenth century, though—to their honour be it said —some of the greatest bankers and brokers were instrumental in getting the death penalty for bank forgeries abolished. A unique petition for the abolition, which apparently decided the House of Commons, bore only three signatures—that of Nathan Rothschild, whose house annually discounted more bills than any other; that of Overend, Gurney & Co., who came next with thirty million sterling a year; and an M.P. named Sanderson, who was also a big broker. I have not seen this petition, but apparently it stated that they would far rather lose their money than cause any further death sentences for forgery. The inhuman ferocity of the English legal system was thus seasonably rebuked. If ever there was a class war it was the legal war of the English aristocrats

against the poor, and against the unfortunate and the minor
criminal unskilful enough to be found out.

2

If this seems a portentous exordium to a set of mere
literary 'forgeries', at least it tends to put them in their
proper perspective. Deplorable as the bad cases are, they do
not bring discredit upon literature as the too numerous and
successful forgeries of old and modern masters have tended to
discredit the art of painting—for if completely unknown
artists can produce pictures which pass as the work of the
greatest masters and fetch enormous prices, what is the real
cultural value of such an art and of the connoisseurship
which takes on such superior airs? Moreover, only a pedant
would maintain that literary 'forgeries' have anything like the
importance of those which struck at the economic life of a
nation. In the eighteenth century, the period in which these
literary frauds were mainly perpetrated, there was an
epidemic of a particularly mean kind of forgery. It sometimes happened that in finishing a letter a man left a considerable space between "your obliged, humble servant" and the
signature. If he were well-known or wealthy, and the letter
came into unscrupulous hands, the signature was cut off
very neatly and an acceptance written above it. The Abbé
Prévost was very lucky not to be hanged for practising such a
fraud on a London patron, and the practice became so
common in France that special legislation had to be passed to
repress it. 'Forgery' is really too serious a word for these
merely literary frauds, except in the case of Ireland and
Wise.

The eighteenth-century literary frauds of Macpherson,
Chatterton and Ireland are of course perfectly well-known
and have been exhaustively investigated, but it is not always

realised that they are related to one another and that they
may have been originally suggested by one or two, more or
less innocent, literary pastiches or hoaxes, and are condoned
to some extent by the lax standards of editorship shown in
such a once popular book as Bishop Percy's *Reliques*. The
situation was one which can hardly be repeated—a nation
where the upper classes were becoming more literate than
had been the case since the Great Rebellion; where there
was a slowly developing interest in, mingled with 'classical'
contempt for, the antiquities and literary remains of the
Middle Ages, added to an ignorance which would not be
found even in a schoolroom today. Ignorance, and its
liability to exploitation, were inevitable in the eighteenth
century, however inexcusable now after the devoted labours
of generations.

Our story begins with a poem written early in the
eighteenth century by the wife of a Scottish gentleman,
strange as it seems that any impulse to poetry should have
survived the fearful oppression of Scotch theocracy so
graphically denounced by Buckle.

Yet even under this prodigious discouragement poetry
continued to exist in Scotland, though nobody has ever
explained how it was that the Scottish Lady Wardlaw
preceded practically everybody in England in admiration for
medieval poetry. One can see how she might easily produce
"an altered and more delicate" version of *Gilderoy*, but not so
easily how she came to write *Hardyknute* with apparently no
suggestion or crude old ballad to work on. *Gilderoy* is said to
have been suggested by the hanging of Patrick MacGregor
(or Gilleroy) in 1638, and a contemporary ballad is said to
have been reprinted in London in 1650. As Lady Wardlaw
was not born until 1677 she can't have written these. And I
have never heard of any suggested original for her *Hardyknute*. That she concealed her authorship of these two famous
poems is natural enough. Writing poems was not con-

sidered particularly lady-like, in spite of the Duchess of
Newcastle, Mrs. Behn and the matchless Orinda. And
doubtless there was a touch of feminine malice and amusement in deceiving the superior males.

At all events she innocently produced the poem and said
she had "found it" (surely true enough if you consider the
basic meaning of *trobar*, Provençal for writing poetry) and
that it was on shreds of paper. At any rate it deceived two
Scottish lawyers, Lord President Forbes and the Lord
Justice Clerk for Scotland, Sir Gilbert Elliot of Minto. They
believed it was ancient, and helped to pay for its publication
in a folio sheet in 1719 while the real author was still alive.
It is sufficient to add that it deceived Thomas Gray and
Bishop Percy, though they thought they detected some
"modern touches" in it.

Now comes in the mysterious part of the affair. According
to Dr. Percy—and who are we to doubt the word of a pre-
late?—the second part of the ballad of *Hardyknute* was in fact
'discovered' by Sir John Bruce of Kinross, the real author of
the poem. He even quotes a letter from Sir John to Lord
Binning which says:

"To perform my promise, I sent you a true copy of the
manuscript I found some weeks ago in a vault at Dumfermline.
It is written on vellum in a fair Gothic character, but so much
defaced by time, as you'll find that the tenth part is not
legible."

The only fault to find with that quotation is that it does
not mention the first part of the ballad of *Hardyknute* as being
the text of the MS discovered in the vault. And Dr. Percy
does not claim that he had seen any of this himself, but says
that Sir D. Dalrymple "communicated extracts" from the
letter as quoted, and adds that Sir John Bruce (ungallantly,
one feels) "used Mrs. Wardlaw to be the midwife of his
poetry".

Of course, I can't answer for it personally, not having seen the documents, but every modern authority I have looked up (including W. P. Ker) is definite that the first part of the poem was written by Lady Wardlaw. In any case it soon became popular. It was reprinted in 1724 by Ramsay in his *Miscellany*, apparently as a genuine antique, and admitted to the famous *Reliques* in 1765. It was a great favourite with Scott, who learned it by heart as a boy and quotes it in *Waverley*; and the mystery so long kept up about its authorship may have suggested Scott's whim of denying the authorship of his novels.

I have suggested one possible motive for Lady Wardlaw's action, and here is another possibility. If she had been bored by the heavily learned talk of antiquarians (on the lines of Mr. Oldbuck's discourses on Roman camps), she might have thought she would try to play a joke on them with a faked medieval ballad. Finding the hoax succeed beyond her utmost hopes, she allowed the joke to go too far when she let the poem be published as a genuine discovery. Sometime between 1719 and her death in 1727 she evidently did try to reveal the facts, but by that time controversy had apparently started, and not everybody believed her. In any case it seems obvious that Sir John Bruce's statement applies only to the second part, which he did write, and that Percy's assumption that he therefore wrote the first part is mistaken. The final touch of mystery is given by the statement that (like *Gilderoy*) this poem may have been founded on ancient fragments transmitted orally; and a musician named William Thompson actually asserted that he had heard such fragments in his infancy before Lady Wardlaw's "copy was heard of".

So far as I can discover, nobody has ever passed any censure on Lady Wardlaw, but surely when she allowed to be published as a genuinely ancient poem which she had 'discovered' what was in fact her own composition, whether founded on ancient fragments or not, she was in a small way as much guilty of "literary forgery" as Chatterton and Macpherson? Evidently it didn't present itself in that light to her contemporaries or they would have said so. Perhaps the circumstance which altered the cases is that Macpherson and Chatterton were poor when they produced their works, and she was not. Mystery about authorship was not confined to Scotland in the eighteenth century, for "the ingenious Dr. Harrington of Bath" wrote a pseudo-ancient ballad called *The Witch of Wokey* (among other poems) and "withheld his name until it could no longer be concealed". And of course the frauds of the London booksellers, especially in hastily printing any trash they had on hand as the *Remains* of some eminent author just deceased, are too numerous and too well-known to be worth repeating. There has evidently been a great change, which most people will think also a great improvement, in the ethics of authorship and publishing in the last two centuries, and unless we bear this in mind we may easily be too severe in passing judgment on Macpherson and Chatterton—Ireland is another matter. If the production of her own work as ancient was not a fault in Lady Wardlaw, why should it be in them? Yet our toleration and encouragement of 'ghost-writers' are simply a new form of old literary fraud. Some eminent man feels that his views and ambitions would be advanced if he published a book; but he has "no time" for such unprofitable pursuits, and then perhaps his education as a writer has been a little neglected. On the rumour that a book of topical interest by such a personage might be obtained, large sums are offered by extremely successful periodicals, and smaller but still tempting sums by book-publishers. What is to be done? A 'ghost-writer' is called in, that is, a skilled and not particularly scrupulous journalist, who listens to and takes down in shorthand the remarks of the eminent personage, goes over any papers available, and produces an extremely snappy and saleable narrative which the eminent personage signs as "all my own work", while the 'ghost' is well paid and told to shut up. Sir Walter Scott's ethics were different:

"I do not see how my silence can be considered as imposing on the public. If I give my name to a book without writing it, unquestionably that would be a trick. But unless in the case of his averring facts which he may be called on to defend or justify, I think an author may use his own discretion in giving or withholding his name."

A *Short History of Ghost-Writing* would be interesting to read, but extremely perilous to write, unless indeed it were written by a ghost.

We need to keep all this in mind as "historical background" if we are to be as fair as possible to James Macpherson and the problem of his once-famous 'Ossian'. How much of 'Ossian' was genuine? How much, if any, of it was 'forged'?

3

James Macpherson (1736–1796) was a type of man very much deplored and despised by right-thinking John Bulls in the eighteenth century. He was a poor Scot who came to England to make his fortune—and made it.

This narrative is only indirectly concerned with Macpherson's successful career as Colonial administrator, Government-hired literary hack, London agent for the Nawab of Arcot (that hoary scandal!), Member of Parliament and so forth—ending up with the pleasing finale that he returned as opulent laird to the district where he had begun as a starved and despised urchin. He died a comparatively wealthy man, leaving money to each of the five illegitimate children he had had by various English women, thereby illustrating his dictum: "I hate John Bull, but I love his daughters."

Successes of this kind were unlikely to endear Macpherson to the London literary world, least of all to Dr. Johnson, who more or less starved until he got a pension, and who was so uncouth and unattractive to women that he had to marry an elderly and weighty widow. He was Macpherson's most bitter enemy, and also his least scrupulous. But then Macpherson was a handsome man, standing about six feet three.

Macpherson's parents were Scotch peasants of Inverness, and poor at that, living in the village of Ruthven, where he was born on October 27th, 1736, nine years before the Scottish rising for Prince Charles Edward. It is said that Macpherson's abilities were noticed at the village school, and that his father, despite his poverty, determined to educate the boy for the Scottish ministry. He went to King's College, Aberdeen; then moved to the cheaper Marischal College; and spent a little time at Edinburgh University. He taught in the village school, and began writing poems of very little merit, which would doubtless never have been published but for the fact that they were stolen and in the height of a controversy published by an honourable opponent. And in 1758 Macpherson contributed a poem to the *Scots Magazine*. Now, in the winter of 1755–56, when Macpherson was at Edinburgh University, this periodical published what is said to be the first English version of a poem in Gaelic, together with a letter pointing out that a great deal of Gaelic poetry was known in the Highlands and was often of high quality. There is no evidence that Macpherson ever knew the writer of this interesting contribution (a poor schoolmaster named Stone who died soon after this publication), nor even that he read the article. But Macpherson must surely have read it at some period, and probably early. What is worth noting is that Stone evidently had the eighteenth-century laxity in the matter of editing and translating, by which an ancient text was supposed to be adapted to "polite modern taste". (They

did that to Shakespeare in England and France.) Stone did
not publish the text, but it was found after his death. The
opening lines have been given literally by the Highland
Society, and in English run thus:

> "The sigh of a friend in the grove of Fraoch!
> A sigh for the hero in its rounded pale,
> A sigh which causes each man to mourn,
> And which makes each maiden weep."

And here is what Jerome Stone made of them:

> "Whence come these dismal sounds that fill our ears?
> Why do the groves such lamentations send?
> Why sit the virgins on the hill of tears,
> While heavy sighs their tender bosoms rend?"

Now, if Stone had lost his transcript of the original instead of
leaving it among his papers, and the poem or fragment had
only been picked up years later by someone else and probably
in a slightly different version, considerable detective work by
Gaelic scholars would have been needed to establish the link.
And of course at that time there were no Gaelic scholars in
our sense of the term. The language was known to the
Highlanders whose native speech it was, but officially Gaelic
was a despised and persecuted language, partly because it
was considered barbarous but mainly for political reasons—
the Highlanders were mostly Jacobites. The brutal harrying
of Scotland after Culloden is too well known to need stressing.
In addition to the executions, exilings, confiscations, disarm-
ing of the clans, the attempt was made to destroy their
language. The natural result was to arouse an interest in it,
but there are two points to remember in Macpherson's case.
Although he began early to note down fragments of Gaelic
poetry he heard from old people, he never knew the language

o

well. He was a classical, not a Gaelic, scholar; and the amusing thing is that he did not think very highly of the Gaelic poetry by which he became famous!

When he was twenty-two a change came in Macpherson's life. He was able to give up schoolmastering to become private tutor to a young man named Thomas Graham or Graeme, afterwards Lord Lynedoch. There is a touch of romance in the fact that one of Wellington's best generals was tutored by 'Ossian' Macpherson. It is said that, travelling with his pupil, Macpherson collected more Gaelic fragments and also met John Home, a writer of some reputation at that time and formerly a minister. Home, who knew no Gaelic, asked Macpherson to translate some of the poems or fragments of poems he had. Macpherson at first was very unwilling to do this, had to be persuaded, and took two or three days to make the versions. Home was extremely interested by what Macpherson brought him, and eventually took the fragments (in English) to Edinburgh, where they were seen by a then influential critic, Dr. Hugh Blair, who persuaded a reluctant Macpherson to produce some more translations. Other influential people, including Horace Walpole, saw and admired them; and in 1760 they were published in a slender volume with the portentous title: *Fragments of Ancient Poetry collected in the Highlands of Scotland and translated from the Galic or Erse Language*. This was in June 1760; and the publication was so successful that a subscription was raised for Macpherson to travel in the Highlands and Hebrides, with letters of introduction to lairds and ministers, to collect more poems. Thus the once famous 'Ossian' poems came to be written and published—*Fingal* in 1761, *Temora* in 1763, with smaller poems attached to each.

But at this point we have to acknowledge two apparently insoluble problems: (1) How far are the Ossianic poems authentic and really translations of Gaelic originals? (2) Why were prose poems which seem to us so vague, tedious and even

absurd such an immense and continuous success, in spite of
virulent opposition, not only in Great Britain, but on the
Continent? To the modern reader of 'Ossian' the latter
problem may well seem the more insoluble. One can but
record a few facts. 'Ossian' was translated into German by
Goethe, and everyone will remember the use he made of it in
Werther. Klopstock, Herder and Schiller greatly admired it.
In Italy it was translated by Cesarotti, Professor of Rhetoric
(later of Greek and Hebrew) in the University of Padua; and
Napoleon Bonaparte read and re-read the poems in the
Italian version, which formed part of his select travelling
library. Its French admirers included (after the Emperor)
Madame de Staël and Lamartine. Apart from Shakespeare,
Scott, and Byron, had any English-speaking author such a
Continental success until the publication of *Uncle Tom's
Cabin*? And Macpherson got there before the others, preparing the way even for Shakespeare, while Harriet Beecher
Stowe is clearly a character straight out of *Temora*. When
George IV (the illustrious Prinny) and Sir William Curtis
amazed the universe by appearing at Holyrood Palace in
vast kilts they paid tribute to 'Ossian' Macpherson as well as
to Sir Walter. Prinny indeed, like a good many of his
subjects, seems to have imagined that all Scotland was
organised into feudal clans with a touching reverence for
their betters. And all this could hardly have occurred if Macpherson had not achieved the seemingly impossible task of
making the Highlanders and their poetry popular.

Compared with this, the problem of the authenticity
shrinks into insignificance, and since it has been the subject
of a prolonged and unscrupulous controversy the difficulty
of arriving at the truth is made that much nearer impossibility. Indeed, it is impossible to settle the question of
authenticity now, for who now can say what Gaelic poems
were preserved by oral tradition in the Scotland of the
1760s? And the joke of the 'controversy' is that none of the

protagonists on either side knew Gaelic! Macpherson ad-
mittedly didn't know much, but he knew far more than they
did. Dr. Johnson, the London literary dictator, knew no
more about Gaelic than he did about Chinese, which had not
prevented him from proving to his toadies with a good deal of
snorting and shouting that the Chinese are barbarians. But
then he also said that the Athenians were barbarians. The
French had no manners and Voltaire was a bad writer. As
for the Scots, they had little literature and the finest prospect
they ever saw was the road which led to England.

In any case, the Great Cham had some reason to be
suspicious of literary Scots. In 1751 Johnson had injudiciously
sponsored a book by a Scot named William Lauder which
set out to prove that *Paradise Lost* was a plagiarism from
certain neo-Latin poets. Johnson was one of England's
greatest Latin scholars and was especially well read in neo-
Latin poetry; yet he failed to notice that the quotations made
by Lauder were grossly falsified by interpolations from
Paradise Lost translated into Latin by Lauder. This took
some living down, and must have left an additional anti-
Scottish rancour.

Of course Johnson was far from being the only distinguished person who had from the beginning denied the
authenticity of Macpherson's Ossian poems. Thomas Gray
was one. But Johnson was the literary dictator, and from the
beginning had treated the poems with contempt, being
particularly offensive about them to Dr. Blair, who had
sponsored them. Having brushed them aside, Johnson
naturally expected them to die of his displeasure. It must
have been particularly annoying for him then to find that this
Scottish upstart's work, so far from dying, continued to gain
readers as new editions were printed, not only in England but
on the Continent. Cesarotti's very popular translation came
out in 1763, and Johnson gradually perceived that the work
by the unknown Scot he had tried to squelch had not only

survived, it had become more widely known and admired than anything of his. There is some reason to think that the journey with Boswell to the Hebrides was undertaken at least partly to prove that Macpherson was a fraud. In his *Journal* Johnson insulted Macpherson, with such words as 'insolence', 'audacity' and 'guilt', and when Macpherson sent him a challenge Johnson pretended to think it a threat, bought his cudgel and wrote his famous letter about not desisting from detecting what he thought a cheat, from any fear of the menaces of a ruffian.

Nothing, of course, happened. 'Ossian' continued to sell more widely than ever, and Macpherson added to his other crimes that of receiving a pension from Government of £600 a year, while Johnson's was only £300. No wonder he listened eagerly to Boswell's malicious gossip about Macpherson's immorality and 'infidelity'—meaning atheism. But then Cesarotti's Italian translation of 1763 had been followed by a German prose one in 1764 and a German verse translation in 1769. Goethe began his translation in 1770. A Frenchman published a version of *Temora* in 1774. And *Werther* appeared. So where was Dr. Johnson's literary dictatorship? Whether Macpherson was a fraud or not, there is comedy—and what used to be called "poetic justice"—in the spectacle of the old Fleet Street pedant furiously dismissing to oblivion a book which had larger and wider circulation and received more admiration, the more Johnson disparaged it! The more he asserted that 'Ossian' was a forgery, the funnier was the situation where the Great Cham of literature could do nothing to harm it and only advertised it. Obviously, whether fraudulent or not, whether wholly translated or partly translated or wholly original, 'Ossian' at the time gave Western Europeans something they wanted; and dogmatic, surly 'criticism' received a permanent black eye. Whether they were right or wrong, the literary public of Europe could not be prevented by the London literary dictator and his allies

from reading what they wanted to read and from admiring
what they thought admirable.

Nevertheless, the controversy went on with acrimony long
after Johnson and Macpherson were dead and buried in
Westminster Abbey. The most sustained and virulent attack
on Macpherson's 'Ossian' came from Malcolm Laing, who
proved or tried to prove that they contained almost a
thousand plagiarisms from over eighty authors! It seems
unlikely that so young a man as Macpherson was in 1760
could have been so widely read or have found time to steal so
extensively in the short time that 'Ossian' was written; and
then Macpherson himself had pointed out some similarities to
the Bible, Homer, Milton and others. (Perhaps he put them
there.) Walter Scott wrote one of the most sensible and
impartial articles on the subject, but as late as 1816 he made
fun of the 'Ossian' enthusiasts in the talk between Oldbuck
and his Highland nephew:

" 'Then,' said M'Intyre, 'this is the answer of Ossian:
    'Dare you compare your psalms;
    You son of a——' "
"Son of a what!" exclaimed Oldbuck.
"It means, I think," said the young soldier with some
reluctance, "Son of a female dog:
    'Do you compare your psalms
    To the tales of the bare-arm'd Fenians?'
"Are you sure you are translating that last epithet
correctly, Hector?"
"Quite sure, sir," answered Hector doggedly.
"Because I should have thought the nudity might have
been quoted as existing in a different part of the body."

Johnson, and those taking his side, had constantly asked
for the 'originals', though what they would have proved to
people who knew no Gaelic it is hard to say. And what did
they mean by 'originals', since they had not troubled them-

selves to look at the transcripts Macpherson had left with his London publisher for anyone to consult? If someone had asked Johnson for the 'originals' of the Homer and the Virgil on his shelves, he could certainly not have produced the authors' MSS or anything but copies of copies produced centuries after their time. But when he was assured that fragments of the Ossian poems or of similar poems did exist in Gaelic MSS of a century or more, he insisted they must be forgeries too. Too late for him to know, there was discovered the so-called *Dean of Lismore's Book*, an early sixteenth-century MS containing about 11,000 lines of Gaelic poetry, including "twenty-eight poems of an Ossianic character". This does not prove Macpherson's 'Ossian' authentic, but it does prove that his poet and that poet's characters were known in the early sixteenth century. In any case, much if not most of Macpherson's 'originals' were bards and elderly men and women who had recited fragments from memory; he couldn't very well 'produce' them. Moreover, he would have been very dull if he had failed to see that the continued wrangling was a useful and gratuitous advertisement.

Is it possible to arrive at any fair conclusion? The Committee of the Highland Society in 1805 published an elaborate report with documents and affidavits and so forth. They reported that the story of Fingal and his poet Ossian (the Oisin of the Irish) had existed for ages in Scotland, and that until 'recently' many people could repeat long fragments of the poems. Fragments such as these can be traced, sometimes literally translated, in Macpherson, but no completely similar poem. Finally the Committee believed that Macpherson "supplied chasms and gave connections by inserting passages of his own, and that he added to the dignity and delicacy of the work by omitting or shortening certain incidents and refining the language", but could not say "how far these liberties extended".

In other words, Macpherson used and abused the extreme

liberty allowed an eighteenth-century editor of barbarous or popular poetry, even to the extent of re-casting, re-writing, adding to and inventing his material; but is this altogether 'fraud' and 'forgery'? In 1765, only five years after the first of the Ossian poems appeared, Dr. Percy published the *Reliques*, which shared the popularity of his Scotch predecessor. Without going into details, one can point out that Percy unhesitatingly cut, altered, amended and in some cases entirely re-wrote his originals, and that he included such well-known 'forgeries' as those of Lady Wardlaw and the ingenious Dr. Harrington. Though Johnson attacked him for his bad taste, he did not accuse him of fraud and forgery. To be sure, Percy had showed him the old MS book (rescued from the fire-lighter) which formed the basis of his heterogeneous miscellany; and Johnson could read English. Perhaps if Macpherson had taken a similar precaution by submitting his Gaelic notes and the translations or re-creations to Johnson before publication, he might have had a different reception. If Macpherson really was guilty of 'forgery' in any real sense there is pleasure in reflecting that he sat for many years in the House of Commons and received the final honours of the Abbey.

An irreverent young friend who did me the honour of glancing hastily through these Macpherson pages remarks that he fails to see what all the fuss was about—the unforgivable sin of Macpherson and Percy was that they resulted in Wordsworth!

4

In the series of British 'literary frauds', Thomas Chatterton is the only one whose name still is currently remembered, though it might be said with some show of truth that this is far more the result of posthumous hero-worship by romantic admirers than of the intrinsic merit of his work. He is something between the Infant Phenomenon and the Juvenile Delinquent of English poetry, and is remembered rather as the luckless precocious subject of a tragical episode in English literature than as a great poet or even as a poet. It is very hard to be just to him, for while the merits of his writings are uncertain, there can be no doubt whatever about his forgeries. The wide, not to say contradictory, diversity of opinions about him is the natural result of stressing some aspects of his life and personality and neglecting or passing over others. Those who at the time had their vanity wounded by discovering that he had duped them saw nothing but the Juvenile Delinquent, and easily believed that God had punished so atrocious a crime with starvation and suicide at the age of seventeen and nine months. The romantic reaction made a merit even of his forgeries—what skill! what imagination! what knowledge! what poetic genius!—and erected the Infant Phenomenon into a Greatest Poet, while sentimentalising his death in French tragedy and English painting. The marvellous boy! Where the truth lies between these extremes it is not easy to say.

Destiny or Providence might almost be accused of plotting Chatterton's temptation and ruin. How strange that a penniless boy of his gifts and temperament should have St. Mary Redcliffe, Bristol, as his childhood's playground, and old parchments from the muniment chest lying about his home, just at the time when the long scorn and neglect of the Middle Ages was ending, when pastiches of old poems were becoming fashionable, and when echoes of the great success of the *Reliques* and, above all, 'Ossian' must have reached him! In spite of his poverty and obscurity, the fatherless boy had access to periodicals as well as to books, and could hardly have failed to note that the more Macpherson was angrily denounced as a literary fraud and forger, the greater the success of his book. The fact cannot be proved, but there is evidence that he was an omnivorous reader as a schoolboy at

Colston's Charity School. It is stated, presumably on the evidence of his mother, that he read everything he could lay hold of, "works on religion, mathematics, heraldry, logic, poetry, navigation, travel and adventure, astronomy, physics and algebra, even cookery, music and the fine arts." There is probably exaggeration here, but even if he read only a fraction of what is asserted through being lent books, he would surely have had no difficulty in finding newspapers and periodicals a little out of date.

There can be no doubt of his precocity, since all he did was achieved by an age when luckier youths are beginning to think of a university. He was born on November 20th, 1752, and it is said that in 1763—at the age of eleven!—he wrote the fragment called *Sly Dick*, supposedly a satire on the charity school. Unfortunately the authority for the poem is a transcript by Sir Herbert Croft, who might conceivably have joined the now fashionable game of literary forgery by producing spurious Chattertoniana after the lad's death. If it really was written at the age of eleven, that is the only noteworthy aspect of the fragment. From Croft come another satirical poem *Apostate Will* and a *Hymn for Christmas Day*, both said to have been written before Chatterton was twelve. There seems to be no way of proving that these lines really were written at that tender age.

Chatterton's paternal ancestors had been sextons of St. Mary's, and so had access to the muniment room. His father, a schoolmaster, had used old parchments taken from the muniment chest to make covers for school books! Philistinism and vandalism are universal, but the carelessness and contempt shown to old documents and buildings in England during the two centuries after the Reformation are certainly unfortunate. The wonder is that anything survived. Chatterton, like other children, fled imaginatively from the real to a dream world, shutting himself up in an attic with the old documents his father had filched but not yet cut up, and with

books. In St. Mary's he had often seen the tomb of William
Canynge (restorer of the church and supposedly an ancestor
of George Canning), and from these various materials
Chatterton built up an imaginary Thomas Rowley, supposed
to have been patronised by Canynge. Here is the origin of
the "Rowley poems".

It is now proved that Chatterton's rather absurd jargon
(which took in practically all his contemporaries) was in the
main based on such reference books as Kersey's *Dictionarium
Anglo-Britannicum* and Speght's glossary to Chaucer. I have
not found any explanation of how a charity schoolboy had
access to such books, or how it came about that at so early an
age he had read Spenser. Although the poem was not
published until 1769, Chatterton is alleged to have written
Elinoure and Juga (a Rowley poem) at the age of twelve. It
contains these lines:

"No moe the miskynette shall wake the morn,
    The minstrelle daunce, good cheere, and morrice plaie;
No moe the amblinge palfrie and the horne
    Shall from the lessel rouze the foxe awaie . . ."

'Miskynette' and 'lessel' are words invented by Chatterton,
the first supposed to mean "a small bagpipe" and the second
"a bush or hedge"; but already this child is a far more skilful
forger than Ireland ever was, even though the 'echo' of
Gray's elegy in the lines is obvious to everyone. Whether he
really did write that poem at the age of twelve or whether it is
simply part of the legend manufactured by and for him by
himself and his uncritical adherents seems incapable of being
determined. What is certain is that Chatterton resented
school, and resented still more the humiliations of his life as
apprentice to a lawyer named Lambert in Bristol.

This, a worse servitude than the charity school, was
imposed on Chatterton in July 1767, before he was fifteen.

Today his position would be that of an office-boy, but no employer would dare to behave now as Lambert did to Chatterton. The boy was treated as a servant, made to eat in the kitchen and to share a bed with the boot-boy. Although Lambert could find him only two or three hours' legal work a day (he was not a successful lawyer), he forced Chatterton to sit at his desk from eight in the morning until eight at night, with an hour off at midday to eat and the hours from eight till ten at night for exercise! Is it astonishing that a gifted boy, whose most salient characteristic was a proud ambition, should not have been very ethically scrupulous in trying to escape from such vile servitude? There is a story—but how many such stories there are in biography!—that when Chatterton was a little boy somebody offered to have a cup made for him and to paint on it what the child wanted. He is supposed to have answered: "Paint an angel, with wings and trumpet, to trumpet my name over all the world."

Even before he left the charity school for Mr. Lambert's office Chatterton had used some of the old parchment from the muniment room to forge a pedigree for a Bristol pewterer named Henry Burghum. With considerable humour Chatterton 'deduced' this pot-manufacturer from an imaginary Simon de Seyncte Lyse or Senliz, who was either Earl of Northhampton, or the husband of Matilda, daughter of Waltheof, Earl of Northumberland, Northampton and Huntingdon. Along with this, Chatterton provided a poem called the 'Romaunt of the Cnyghte', supposed to have been written by one John de Bergham about 1390. Two other 'medieval' poems came along with other parts of the pedigree, and the pewterer Henry de Burghum showed his inherent nobility of soul by bestowing a largesse of five shillings on the discoverer of his aristocratic descent.

Chatterton was not sixteen when his ingenuity brought him to public notice under the pseudonym of Dunhelmus Bristolensis. There was a new bridge built, and Chatterton sent to a periodical called *Felix Farley's Bristol Journal* an account of "Fryars passing over the old bridge" in the time of Henry II, supposedly taken from an ancient manuscript but of course forged by him. This aroused so much interest that a deputation of Bristol citizens came to see the 'antiquary' and were somewhat baffled to find a very youthful office-boy. However, he faced up to them, told them the same tale he had told Burghum (i.e. that the bridge story came from documents taken by his father from the muniment chest), and instead of insisting on seeing all he had, the gentlemen merely urged him to look for more. Within a short time Chatterton produced a number of the Rowley poems. He was patronised by another pewterer, George Catcott, and, especially, by a surgeon, William Barrett. He sold Barrett a description of medieval Bristol and similar documents, with fantastic plans and drawings—all of which the credulous Mr. Barrett published in his *History and Antiquities of Bristol*. The credulity and ignorance of these 'learned' gentlemen would seem impossible if we did not realise the ignorance and credulity of a century which had accepted the enormous cheat of George Psalmanazar and was to pay for the clumsier Ireland forgeries of Shakespeare with enthusiasm, faith and money.

How did Chatterton go about the actual forging of these documents and poems which he drew from his imagination? A friend of his named Rudhall, a chemist, years after Chatterton's death "sold the secret" for ten pounds, which he gave to Chatterton's mother. According to Rudhall the boy gave a look of age to his parchments by holding them over a candle until the ink changed colour and the parchment was wrinkled and darkened, or he smeared the parchment with ochre and rubbed it on the floor to dirty it. The crudity of these methods measures the ignorance of those they deceived. But here we come on a distinction between even Macpherson and Chatterton, for however much Macpherson 'improved' and re-arranged and even added to the Celtic fragments, he did not deliberately manufacture falsely antique parchment 'originals' of his own invention and sell them for money.

In March 1769, Chatterton made a big mistake. He knew that Horace Walpole had written a history of painting in England, and sent him "for any future edition of your truly entertaining Anecdotes of Painting" a document of his own fabrication which he entitled *The Ryse of Peyncteyne in Englande, wroten by T. Rowlie, 1496, for Mastre Canynge*. Now, it is one thing to introduce a poem or a historical novel with some transparent tale of antiquity, and quite another to invent completely spurious facts of alleged historical value. Suppose Walpole had been silly enough to accept the *Ryse of Peyncteyne*, it would have made him and his book ridiculous and shaken his credit as a historian. A second letter from Chatterton aroused his suspicions, and Mason and Gray at once decided that the MSS Chatterton had sent were forgeries. It is natural to wish that such a man as Walpole, knowing the boy's extreme youth and poverty, might have helped instead of crushing him with what seems to have been a contemptuous reply, though Mason and Gray did nothing to help him.

It is hard to say what were Chatterton's motives in sending Walpole these forgeries, but his second letter suggests his naïve ignorance of the world and above all of the man he was addressing. By confessing his youth, his poverty, his servile condition and his hopes of "bettering himself" to such a snob as Walpole, he was asking for rebuff. Walpole was polite while he imagined his unknown correspondent was a gentleman of means; he was contemptuous and horrified when he found he was dealing with a poor boy whose vanity was as high-spirited as his own. While Walpole might justifiably have felt annoyance at the attempt to impose on him with the *Ryse of Peyncteyne*, it seems doubtful whether Chatterton's offence really called for such remarks as these:

"I should have been blamable to his mother, and society, if I had seduced an apprentice from his master, to marry him to the nine muses; and I should have encouraged a propensity to forgery, which is not the talent most wanting culture in the present age. All of the house of forgery are relations; and though it is just to Chatterton's memory to say, that his poverty never made him claim kindred with the richest, or more enriching branches, yet his ingenuity in counterfeiting styles, and I believe, hands, might easily have led him to those more facile imitations of prose, promissory notes."

The insolence of that needs no comment, especially since there is no evidence that Chatterton actually forged signatures, as young Ireland unquestionably did. Moreover the statement that "all of the house of forgery are relations" comes extremely well from the man who in 1764 published a spurious medieval novel as taken from an Italian work published in black letter at Naples in 1529, and who later, out of sheer malice, forged a letter purporting to come from the King of Prussia in order to annoy Jean-Jacques Rousseau. What was to prevent Mr. Walpole, if he should have lost his sinecures procured by political jobbery, from "claiming kindred with the richest branches" of forgery and from proceeding from a faked letter to a faked promissory note? From this we may perhaps deduce that in eighteenth-century England one difference between a forgery and a hoax in literary matters was that a hoax was purely malicious. George Steevens, the commentator on Shakespeare, used to print false Elizabethan information or documents (including a forged letter of George Peele) anonymously in some periodical solely for the purpose of misleading his rival commentator, Malone. It was Steevens who invented the myth of the upas tree which destroys all life for miles round, invented a story about Milton and two ladies to hoax his biographers, and 'planted' on the antiquary, Richard Gough, a forged tombstone of Hardyknute, engraved with the very drinking-horn which brought the King to his drunken end!

While Walpole and Steevens received mainly applause for their agreeable 'hoaxes', Chatterton, as everyone knows, was severely punished by Divine Providence for his impudent 'forgeries'. Throughout the summer of 1769, immediately after his attempt to arouse Walpole's interest, Chatterton sent contributions (under pseudonyms) to *The Town and Country Magazine*, *The Political Register*, *The Freeholder's Magazine*, *The London Museum* and *The Middlesex Journal*, whose editors were glad to print but not to pay for them. His protests brought only promises of future pay, but his determination to risk anything to escape from his office-boy servitude may easily be inferred from the fact that he wrote Lambert a letter threatening to commit suicide the next day, Easter Sunday, April 15th, 1770. This is interesting as showing that he had thought of suicide four months before he actually destroyed himself. If it was a device to get free from Lambert, it succeeded, for ten days later Chatterton was free of his indentures and, with a few borrowed pounds, set out to make his fortune as a free-lance writer in London. If the published note of some of the payments he received is authentic it shows how the boy was exploited by London editors and publishers. One item records the payment of ten shillings and sixpence by "Mr. Hamilton" for sixteen songs to be set to music. Yet less than two months before pride and destitution brought him to suicide Chatterton sent quite expensive presents to his mother and sister.

It is typical of this whole tragedy of mis-directed talents that the pride which made Chatterton refuse meals offered him in charity is denounced as conceit, whereas Johnson's throwing away the new pair of shoes put at his door at Oxford to replace the broken ones he was wearing is praised as laudable independence. But then Johnson was a Churchman, but Chatterton, like Shelley, an enquirer. Again, in the last fatal act of this depressing little drama, nobody would trust the boy for a loaf of stale bread, but he had no difficulty in getting plenty of arsenic "for an experiment". Some believe that the suicide was not determined solely by the despair of destitution and wounded pride but by Chatterton's realisation that the forgeries of the Rowley poems were detected, and that life would therefore be impossible for him. It may be so. Unquestionably, Ireland was persecuted all his life, and his efforts at writing books were unfairly depreciated. Yet how strange it is that nobody seems to have felt the slightest responsibility towards the brilliant boy that Chatterton undoubtedly was, however much we now feel that his poetic genius has been over-praised. Dickens, writing in *David Copperfield* of his own neglected childhood, has a passage of indignant eloquence on the total lack of any perception of the gifts which were his even as a child. A chance legacy to his father saved the young Dickens from despair, the factory and possible suicide. No legacy came to Chatterton, and he died by his own act, a blot on English literary history, and a pathetic little tragedy which after all these years is a wound to every sensitive heart.

5

The fact is doubtless without significance but it is a fact that the two persons in the eighteenth century who unquestionably were literary forgers both started life as clerks in a lawyer's office, while the worst offender in the nineteenth-twentieth-century epoch was a merchant in the City of London. Much more to the point is the question of how far this series of eighteenth-century literary frauds we are investigating was a matter of imitation. It seems unlikely that Macpherson did not know the *Hardyknute* story, and

P

he may well have wondered why what was a genteel hoax in the aristocracy was a criminal forgery with him. Chatterton certainly heard echoes of the 'Ossian' controversy, and may possibly have drawn his own conclusions from the fact that a book which was widely denounced as a 'forgery' was a great success, while the author did not succumb to the displeasure of his enemies and seemed (even in poor Chatterton's life-time) to be doing fairly well. But William Henry Ireland's forgeries were very largely the result of his admiration for Chatterton.

Another curious fact is that while Chatterton undoubtedly had literary talent and showed it in his Rowley poems, most of the 'authorities' and big-wigs decided (rightly) that the poems were forgeries and the allegedly ancient English spurious. Yet, although Ireland's forgeries were clumsier and his Elizabethan English so absurdly ignorant that one would think a schoolboy would detect it, the amazing fact is that Ireland made dupes of many persons supposed to be of high intellectual and literary standing. Chatterton's dupes were far fewer and less distinguished. Moreover, he appar-ently had no real accomplices, while Ireland had, yet none of Ireland's accomplices spoke out at first, which surely implies either that they were very stupid or "in on" the fraud? Unluckily, a considerable amount of the information about these frauds comes from young Ireland himself; and Malone, the Shakespeare scholar, who was the main critic of their authenticity, expressed strong doubts about a number of points and alleged facts in Ireland's *Authentic Account* and *Confessions*. He was not such a liar as Psalmanazar but he was more impudent than Chatterton, and his *Confessions* may well be as phoney as his documents.

The first character we have to consider is W. H. Ireland's father, Samuel Ireland, a queer coot if ever there was one. Malone was convinced that Samuel was his son's accomplice, but Malone had not had occasion to consider how often the besotted and conceited credulity of the dupe goes so far that it seems indistinguishable from complicity. To an expert such as Malone with his specialist's knowledge it must have seemed impossible that anyone could be taken in by such stuff, especially since Samuel Ireland made money out of it. But then numbers of most reputable and scholarly persons believed in them.

Samuel Ireland (whose birth-date seems to be unknown) had started life as a weaver, who developed some skill as an engraver, and opened a superior old curiosity shop which dealt in pictures and books and what are known as 'antiques'. He seems to have had an almost fanatical admiration for Shakespeare, and read the plays aloud to his family. He read other books aloud, including one which contained a faked set of letters between Martha Hay and her unsuccessful lover, the Rev. J. Hackman, who murdered her. The same book contained genuine letters by Chatterton. The son (born in 1777) was, like Chatterton, the 'apprentice' of a lawyer, in this case a man named Bingley; and young Ireland is said to have developed a strong admiration for Chatterton, which he showed by trying to write imitations of Chaucer. If they were as bad as his efforts at imitating Elizabethans they must have been pretty comical.

When young Ireland was seventeen he was taken to Stratford by his father, who seems to have behaved there with a considerable lack of discretion. They visited a man who was supposed to be a descendant of the poet's daughter, went of course to Holy Trinity, and bought bits of the famous mulberry tree from a carpenter who doubtless contrived to have an endless supply. At Clopton Hall they came on the seemingly inevitable hoaxer who saw the older man's mixture of Shakespearian idolatry and foolish credulity and caused him intense anguish by a tale of burning quantities of documents bearing Shakespeare's signature. There was evidently an even superior performer in the hoaxing line at

Anne Hathaway's cottage, for he or she sold Samuel the very
purse which William gave Anne and the identical oak chair
on which they sat to do their courting.

Now, if these tales of the Stratford visit are true—and
anyone may legitimately have doubts—then Samuel Ireland
was evidently a 'sucker' of the highest order, and one who
could be made to believe anything where Shakespeare was
concerned.

According to the tale, W. H. Ireland was started on his
career of literary forgery by discovering on a book-stall in
London a tract written by a member of Lincoln's Inn,
illuminated, dedicated to Queen Elizabeth, and bound in
vellum with "the Queen's arms" in gold on the cover. Her
arms were the arms of England, and it sounds very unlikely
even as long ago as 1794 that such a MS relic should be
knocking about for sale at a price which could be afforded by
the apprentice to a Chancery conveyancer. Young Ireland's
story is that he tried to forge a dedicatory epistle to this work,
using diluted ink. Dissatisfied with this, he showed it to a
bookbinder named Laurie and his apprentice, and they gave
him some of the colours used for marbling end-papers, which
being mixed together resembled ancient ink. He then re-
wrote his forged dedication (presumably on sixteenth-century
paper) with this 'ink', and somehow inserted it in the book,
which he presented to his father, who instantly accepted it as
genuine. In order to account for the fact that he could not
produce this earliest forgery, Ireland explained that he had
destroyed it when he reached more skill. It may be so, but
then what happened to the original Elizabethan book? The
whole story sounds suspicious, and designed at once to
exonerate his father and to give a plausible explanation of
how he came 'innocently' to 'hoax' his father by producing a
Shakespeare document for him.

Now, there existed a legal document, a mortgage, executed
by Shakespeare, which document had been presented by its

discoverer to David Garrick, while the text had been often printed and a facsimile published. Ireland says he made tracings from facsimiles of genuine Shakespeare signatures. At the office—where, like Chatterton in his office, he evidently was not given enough work—Ireland cut parchment from an old rent-roll, and on it forged what purported to be a lease, one of the parties being William Shakespeare. The legal language apparently was based on that of the genuine mortgage.

What was the motive here? According to Ireland, he would never have been so disrespectful as to try to hoax his father, let alone cheat him; he wanted "to please" him. The older man *was* pleased when it was given him by his son about Christmas time 1794, at once determined it was genuine, and in return insisted on his son taking some unspecified treasure from his shop. Now, here comes a little episode which, if true, is a striking example of how the dupe convinces himself. Young Ireland had put some genuinely old seals (stolen presumably from his master) on the forged document, and by a pure accident one of these represented a man running at the quintain. Samuel showed the deed to a respectable person called Sir Frederick Eden, who speedily decided for authenticity—the quintain meant "Shake-spear" obviously!

Unless, by chance, that forged document has been preserved, I must say I feel considerable doubts about it and its accidentally convenient seal. Still less convincing is young Ireland's account of all the persons who came to see it, and who put into his head the wish to continue his nefarious courses by significant hints that of course there would be more Shakespeare documents to come from the same source. This may be true, but sounds incredible, for if young Ireland had really come on any hidden collection of Shakespeare documents and MSS, surely the obvious thing to disarm suspicion would be to produce them all together, and not to bring them out one by one, allowing in each case the necessary time to think up and execute a forgery. Anyway, that is the excuse given for his continuing.

Yet in spite of such suspicions we have to admit the fact of a witness and an accomplice. A solicitor named Albany Wallis, who had discovered the Shakespeare mortgage, later expressed amazement that the similarity of language in the forgery had not been immediately noticed. So it must have existed. Moreover, the facsimile of the mortgage had been shown to Ireland by a young lawyer named Montague Talbot, who was just then transforming himself into a successful Irish actor. He instantly suspected Ireland, and taxed him with forgery, which of course Ireland denied. Talbot thereupon made a surprise call on Ireland at his master's office, and caught him at work on some other forgery! Amazing to relate, instead of denouncing Ireland, Talbot agreed to keep silent and became his accomplice. The reason given is the flimsy one that Ireland pleaded earnestly that his father would be so angry if told that he had been imposed upon! As if eventual detection, and far worse emotions for the father, were not inevitable.

Together this pair cooked up a fanciful story to account for the stream of forgeries young Ireland now began producing, and apparently not the slightest difficulty was experienced in finding credulous dupes, even among the most distinguished people. Apparently the story was not launched at once, but held in reserve to meet future questioning. And that such was bound to occur must have been easily foreseen when you realise that among the 'documents' Ireland produced in succession were Shakespeare's "Profession of Faith", a love-letter from him to Anne Hathaway with a lock of hair, letters to an imaginary "Richard Cowley", an actor, forged agreements and receipts (including one for £50 from Shakespeare to the Earl of Leicester), a letter from Queen Elizabeth to Shakespeare, and a promissory note for £5 from Shakespeare to John Heming.

These documents were crude and ignorant, and the marvel is that so many great 'critics' of the time were so very ignorant of Elizabethan English that they were taken in. Ireland is said to have borrowed his pseudo-antique jargon from Chatterton, and if so he did Chatterton a wrong. However imperfect Chatterton's Wardour Street imitations of medieval English, they were at any rate based on dictionaries and Speght's glossary to Chaucer. Ireland does not seem to have done any particular research, and deceived the mighty *literati* of the age by the simple device of writing the English of his time with many letters doubled and superfluous 'e's'—which adds point to Lamb's remark that Chatterton was obviously one of the "mob of gentlemen who wrote with 'e's'." Conceive the impossibility that the Queen's Majesty of England would write a letter to a common player, who was only saved from the status of a rogue and a vagabond by the fact that he was a minor servant of the Queen's own servant, the Lord Chamberlain! And here is the opening of the valuable historical document:

"Wee didde receive your prettye verses good Masterre William through the hands of our Lorde Chamberlayne and we do complemente thee onne theyre great excellence. Wee shall departe fromm Londonne toe Hampstowne forre the holydayes where wee shalle expect thee with thy beste Actorres that thou mayeste play before ourselfe toe amuse usse . . ."

The signature to this absurdity was traced from one of the authentic specimens of the Queen's elaborate calligraphy. Apparently it was at first as credulously accepted as the preposterous "Profession of Faith", whose dupes included the classical scholar, Dr. Parr, and the Headmaster of Winchester, Dr. Joseph Warton. According to Ireland, Dr. Warton said (he did not contradict it afterwards): "Mr. Ireland, we have very fine things in our Church Service, and our Litany abounds with beauties; but here is a man has distanced us all!" It seems impossible that the headmaster of a great Public School could have made such a statement about the obvious piffle that the 'Profession' is, yet, so far as I can discover, the episode has never been disproved. He must have read Thomas Warton's *History of English Poetry*, and one would think that the very numerous excerpts of ancient English given there would have enabled him to reject the document on linguistic grounds alone. As for Dr. Parr, he was one of the twenty distinguished signatories to a document later drawn up by Samuel Ireland which proclaimed their belief in its authenticity.

The production of this "Profession of Faith" resulted in so many pressing questions that Ireland now 'released' the improbable tale he had cooked up with Talbot. According to this artless fiction, Talbot had found and given Ireland the 'lease'. After much urging Talbot introduced Ireland to "the party" who had originally owned it, and searching this 'party's' rooms in London found other documents. The greater number, however, came from the country, "owing to the papers having been removed from London many years ago." At this time Talbot was in Wales, and Samuel Ireland wrote to him asking for his testimony. If Talbot really did reply as is stated, the careless impudence of his tale is only less remarkable than the credulity of those who accepted it. According to him these Shakespeare papers belonged to a Mr. H., who had made it a condition that his name should never be mentioned. Talbot inferred that Mr. H.'s ancestor must have been an actor in Shakespeare's time, and Mr. H. did not want this known as he was now an aristocrat! The reason why Mr. H. had given these unique and valuable documents to a juvenile delinquent in a lawyer's office was that in searching the pair had "discovered a deed, which ascertained to the party landed property of which he had then no knowledge."

Later it appeared that the ancestor of Mr. H. was John

Heming, and Ireland very nearly gave himself away by forging a promissory note from Shakespeare to Heming, and Heming's receipt. Albany Wallis again appears on the scene, for he went to Samuel Ireland and showed him that the signature of John Heming (of which he had an authentic example) was quite unlike that produced by young Ireland. The tale by which Ireland got out of this awkward situation is as amazing as the rest of the story. After taking a good look at the authentic signature, he went off and forged another receipt with a more passable imitation. He showed this, and then told Wallis that Mr. H. had easily explained the confusion. There had been, in fact, two John Hemings; one of them was the short John Heming of the Curtain Theatre, and the other was the tall John Heming of the Globe Theatre! Now, as it seems impossible that the Headmaster of Winchester could have made the remark attributed to him about the 'Profession', so it seems impossible that a London solicitor could for a moment have been taken in by this impudently transparent office-boy's lie. Yet apparently he accepted the tale, and young Ireland quietly substituted the newly-forged receipt for the detected old one—and nobody observed it!

So many of these 'documents' had been 'found' that in February 1795 Samuel Ireland opened a public exhibition of them. I cannot discover whether he did or did not take money for entrance to this exhibition, but if he did, then the affair had already gone beyond the 'hoax' stage, 'hoaxing' being as frequent an excuse for frauds as the defaulting clerk's excuse that he intended to repay the stolen money as soon as his difficulties were ended. In any case, both the Irelands were profiting—whether they were confederates or not—by the praise and notoriety they received, which are often far more important than money to a certain type of impostor. Indeed, in his later days young Ireland protested vehemently that his fraud was not undertaken for money, and that the little he had received was of no importance to him. And it is the fact that his father made a good deal more out of the frauds than he did. The type repeats itself.

If Ireland had been content to stop there, the debate might have continued for some time, even though he was certain to be exposed in the long run; but he lacked the cunning and knowledge of the world of the more successful crook who knows exactly how far he can go without arousing suspicion and how to stage plausible stories without accessible witnesses. But in his ignorance and conceit Ireland quite literally 'staged' the exposure of himself, his father and his forgeries. He began to 'discover' manuscripts of Shakespeare's plays! He began with the MS of *King Lear*, and had the stupefying impudence to 'improve' on the text both in the poetry and the alleged indecencies. He then 'found' some improved pages of *Hamlet*. What Malone, Ritson and other Shakespeare scholars felt, thought and said when they found such trash widely accepted as the real Shakespeare can hardly be imagined, especially as they came to realise the difficulty of making an ignorant public understand the difference between newspaper propaganda and truth.

Fortunately, Ireland undid himself, and spared them all trouble but that of valorously thrice-defeating the already self-defeated foe. Basing himself on nothing more solid than the fact that a print of Vortigern hung in his father's house, he produced in two months an allegedly authentic Shakespeare tragedy of nearly 3,000 lines on that subject. And Talbot wrote from Dublin the complete lie that *Vortigern* had been found among the other Shakespeare 'documents' belonging to that mysterious and aristocratic 'party', Mr. H. The MS was exhibited by Samuel Ireland, and was supposedly praised by many who read it. Sheridan was taken in, and though the manager of Covent Garden tried to get the performing rights, they went to Sheridan and Drury Lane. The agreement was drawn up by Wallis the solicitor (who must have been one of young Ireland's accomplices) with an advance of £300 to Samuel Ireland, who gave £60 to the "onlie begetter". An invitation came from the Duke of Clarence (afterwards King William IV) for the Irelands to visit St. James's Palace and bring the Shakespeare documents. Mrs. Jordan, who had a part in *Vortigern*, was present at the interview, and seems to have displayed more faith in the documents than the Duke.

It is very strong indication that the majority of people, in spite of the many criticisms, still believed in the authenticity of the "Shakespeare documents" including *Vortigern* that the play was actually produced at Drury Lane as late as April 2nd, 1796. The date, however, has its significance. Although the Prince of Wales (later George IV) had also seen the documents and had behaved with his customary politeness though he was noncommittal, some of the Drury Lane cast had the gravest doubts about *Vortigern*. Probably they had read the *Miscellaneous Papers* which Samuel Ireland had been foolish enough to publish at the end of 1795, which must have strengthened their instinctive professional feeling that *Vortigern* was a fraud. John Kemble was especially suspicious, and it was he who suggested the first performance should take place on April 1st, which Samuel Ireland insisted on being changed to the 2nd. Mrs. Jordan remained loyal, but Mrs. Siddons and Mrs. Palmer found excuses to throw up their parts, when they found that Kemble had chosen as companion piece a short play called *My Grandmother*! Phillimore is said to have parodied his part and to have 'died' so that his legs stuck out when the curtain fell, whereupon he removed them amid universal laughter. But it was Kemble apparently who killed the play by the tone in which he produced the line:

"And when this solemn mockery is ended,"
which he repeated—and the rest of the play was treated as a farce by the audience.

That really was the end of the "Ireland forgeries". Of

course, investigations followed, and young Ireland published his *Authentic Account* in December 1796. Samuel Ireland died, more or less in despair, in July 1800. His son survived many years, and published his *Confessions* in 1805. Except where they can be confirmed from other and independent sources both documents must be regarded with suspicion. The best that can be said for them is that W. H. Ireland tries to exculpate his father, but might not even that have been a calculated playing for sympathy? "See, he wasn't so bad after all, he defends his father." The man who could forge Shakespeariana to that extent is not entitled to be believed merely on his word.

But the wonder is that any educated person was ever deceived by such crudities. However much we may have degenerated from our ancestors, it must be admitted that we know more about the sixteenth century than the late eighteenth century did. Today a similar set of forgeries would hardly take in even Sir Winston Churchill and the Boy Scouts.

6

The angry controversies and public scandal of the Ireland forgeries put a stop to the eighteenth-century series of innocent, not so innocents and fraudulent literary impostures. For a long time the nineteenth century in England was virtually free from such literary frauds, though in France they abounded. The great chasm cut in French history and society by the Revolution, the destruction and dispersal of documents of all kinds, led after the Restoration to a state of affairs where there was great temptation to forge the letters and memoirs of historical personages, particularly of the epoch just before the Revolution. As the Goncourts discovered, paintings, drawings, works of art and furniture as well as interesting documents dating from the *ancien régime* could be bought very cheap. But as interest in the period increased, so did forgery, and there were, for example, whole collections of letters attributed to Louis XVI, Marie Antoinette and Madame Elizabeth which were practically all spurious.

In the mid-nineteenth century there was another and milder Shakespeare-forgery scandal due to John Payne Collier, a barrister who had written for *The Times* and become librarian to the Duke of Devonshire. For motives which are obscure, but seem to have been nothing more than a foolish wish "to make a name" for himself spuriously among Shakespearian scholars, Collier forged emendations to the plays in "an old hand" on a genuine Second Folio of Shakespeare's plays. However, there is a possibility that Collier himself was deceived and these "old hand" notes were made by some other deceiver. But he unquestionably tampered with documents at Dulwich College, even to the extent of forging Shakespeare's name, so that his folio emendations seem very suspicious.

Yet the period overlapping the nineteenth and twentieth centuries produced a typical epilogue to the older and cruder literary forgeries, in what might be described as rare book forgery made profitable and honourable. The Great War of 1939–45 has obliterated the J. T. Wise scandal, though there must be many who remember the dismay and consternation caused in respectable circles by the publication of Carter and Pollard's *Enquiry into the Nature of Certain Nineteenth Century Pamphlets*. The usual attempts were made to pick minute flaws in this work, but the main contentions were far too well documented to give a chance to any but temporary and one-sided objections. Many of the details are arid and technical; but purely as an enquiry the book will always stand high in the literature of exposure. The merit of the

book as patient investigation will remain even if any interest
still attaching to Wise should disappear. Of course if Wise
had been 'well-connected' the battle might have been waged
much longer and more bitterly; but he wasn't.

T. J. Wise was a self-made man, born in 1859, who rose
from a humble clerkship to be a prosperous City of London
merchant in the essential oils business—a partner where he
had started as office-boy. No satisfactory explanation has
been given as to how it came about that even in his twenties
much of Wise's time outside office hours was devoted to
book-collecting, not from the point of view of literature but
from the value of books as curiosities and rareties—first
editions, association copies, corrected proofs, unrecorded
private printings, pamphlets and trivia by famous authors.
It was Wise who succeeded in turning the interest of collectors,
particularly of wealthy Americans, from the older type of
book to the nineteenth-century English. Both his flair and
his influence must have been remarkable, for, be it said on
his side, his Ashley Library collection, formed entirely by
himself, was sold after his death to the British Museum for
sixty thousand pounds, and is said to have been worth more.

Wise was the genial friend of numerous men-of-letters of the
successful clubman type, writers whose literary reputation is
perhaps due as much to social contacts as to talent. However, through his membership of the Shelley and Browning
Societies he had some acquaintance with Browning and
Swinburne, and was on terms of intimacy with such minor
literary figures as Buxton Forman and Edmund Gosse.
Through these personal relations with living writers, his
library, his ten-volume catalogue of its contents and his
bibliographies, Wise established himself as unquestionably
the most eminent parasite on the market in supposedly rare
and valuable modern English books. He did not limit
himself to the nineteenth century, but made excursions into
others, particularly the Tudor-Stuart epoch.

How artificial and inflated even the Elizabethan prices were in relation to actual public wish to read the books was revealed to me in the 1920s. Somebody in England—it may have been Wise, but I don't know that it was—sold to America for high prices some minor Elizabethan prose works of the Nashe, Greene, Dekker kind; and, misled by newspaper publicity about the money, a British and an American publisher clubbed together to issue facsimile reprints. I bought the facsimile reprints because I wanted to read them, and wrote a review of them for a New York literary paper. I was told, I know not how truly, that mine was the only 'popular' review published in New York; and that hardly anyone there bought exact facsimiles of books whose originals had been sold for thousands of pounds! Surely the real benefactors to literature were not the people who lavished thousands for the mere possession of rareties, but the publishers who risked their money—and I fear may have lost some of it—to bring the books to those who really wanted to read them?

Curiously enough, Wise's career began by his issuing facsimile editions. For some reason he was asked by the Shelley Society to arrange for and see through the press facsimile reprints of the first editions of *Adonais*, *Hellas* and *Alastor* for members of the Society only. Now, anyone can understand why Shelley enthusiasts would like to own such facsimiles, and since they were plainly marked as such, the reprints were perfectly legitimate; but it is said (I don't know on what evidence) that these innocent reproductions gave Wise the idea for the many fraudulent 'editions' he issued over a number of years and foisted on the libraries and the book-collectors. It may indeed be so, but it is not true to say that these 1886 Shelley facsimiles were the first issued in England. By mere chance I happen myself to possess a facsimile reprint of George Herbert's *The Temple*, which was first published 1876 and subsequently reprinted. Now, this

reprint is issued as such books should be, leaving no chance
for even the most unwary to be deceived. Long before the
exposure of Wise had made everyone wary, both publisher
and printer of this Herbert facsimile seemed to have realised
the possible danger, and to have taken every precaution.
Nobody could possibly suppose that this was the genuine
first impression. Now, what Wise did was the exact opposite
of this honesty. By persuading the printer to leave his name
off these books, Wise invented, printed and sold as first
editions of famous or rare works by well-known writers what
were simply ante-dated reprints. He did not forge the text,
he forged the edition; what the enlighted modern collector
was prepared to pay for was the edition, not the text,
as my little experience with the Elizabethan facsimiles
showed.

Wise put out so many of these 'forgeries' that the reader is
referred to the Carter and Pollard book, which like so many
interesting books is out of print (and expensive if found)
when trash abounds. For my purpose it will be enough to
give a brief account of one of his most daring and successful
efforts, namely, his forgery of a non-existent, privately-
printed and very limited 'first' of E.B.B.'s *Sonnets from the
Portuguese*. The exploitation, whether for gain or bibliophile's
prestige or both, of the sentiment evoked by the Browning
elopement and the sonnets is characteristic of Wise's
cynicism.

The *Sonnets* were written in London by Mrs. Browning
before her marriage in 1846. Not long after the marriage she
dropped a vague hint about some love sonnets, which Robert
misunderstood, and instantly hurt and dismayed her over-
sensitive spirit by some loftily disapproving remark about
people who wear their hearts on their sleeves. She of course
instantly retired into silence and kept her sonnets hidden.
The misunderstanding continued until after the birth of their
son in 1849, and Browning did not see the poems until at last

his wife showed him them in that year. The poems were first printed in the 1850 edition of Mrs. Browning's *Poems*.

This version is that of Dr. Furnivall, President of the Browning Society, who had it direct from the poet. That testimony unsupported might be questioned, but passages from Browning's letters at different dates independently confirm it.

In 1890, soon after Browning's death, the poet William Sharp ("Fiona Macleod") published a *Life* in which he stated "on indubitable authority" that Browning first saw his wife's Sonnets at Pisa in 1847. Furnivall at once queried this, and gave his version. However, in 1894 Edmund Gosse re-affirmed the 1847 Pisa version, which turned into a "very pretty" story; and when republishing his essay in 1896 in his *Critical Kit-Kats* he published this declaration in his preface:

"In particular, in two instances, that eminent poet who for many years honoured me with his friendship, Robert Browning, laid upon me as a duty the publication of what I have written. What is here found, in matters of fact, regarding the Sonnets of his wife and the incidents of the career of Beddoes, comes with the authority and is presented at the desire of Browning."

This version was accepted by Edward Dowden in 1905 and by Alice Meynell in 1929. Yet the correct version was known in London, for under the date September 3rd, 1888, William Allingham noted in his diary:

"Browning told Miss Swanwick he knew nothing about the *Sonnets from the Portuguese* till two or three years after his marriage, when his wife showed them to him. He said to her, 'If I consulted my personal wishes I should keep these all to myself, but as the guardian of your literary fame I must counsel you to publish them.'"

So far there is nothing here but a clear-cut instance of what constantly occurs in biography, namely, contradictory dates and versions of the same episode. The precision with which Sharp and Gosse give their version, and especially Gosse's declaration, make it highly improbable that they were guilty of carelessness. And it is still less probable that they were guilty of deliberate misrepresentation. The only possible explanation is that Browning gave out two contradictory stories—one to Sharp and Gosse, and the other to Furnivall and Miss Swanwick and various correspondents. It is not possible that Gosse could have made so definite a statement if it was unfounded, yet it is equally impossible that Browning, who kept his faculties to the end, could have forgotten an episode so intimately connected with his emotional life. And that perhaps gives the clue. Like most other generations, the Victorians had a great deal they wanted to hide from the public, and to that end they invented and tried bitterly to enforce a theory of 'delicacy' and 'reticence', of distinction between what was 'public' and what was 'private', with the result that most Victorian biography is tainted with humbug. Browning gave Sharp and Gosse his "pretty story" version in order to hide the fact that he had wounded his wife's feelings by his lack of comprehension.

The "pretty story" as told by Gosse is to this effect: One morning in Pisa, in 1847, Mrs. Browning thrust into her husband's pocket "a packet of papers", telling him to tear it up if he didn't like it. He found he had been given "the finest sonnets written in any language since Shakespeare's". Mrs. Browning did not want to publish, but she was eventually cajoled into sending them to her friend, Mary Mitford, who published them in a small volume in a very limited edition: *Sonnets* by *E.B.B. Reading Not For Publication* 1847.

That "small volume" was a forgery by T. J. Wise. There never was any such edition. And—there is no way out of it—Gosse was duped by Wise.

According to Wise, he 'discovered' some copies of this edition in the possession of a Dr. W. C. Bennett (who died soon after), who had been an acquaintance of Miss Mitford. But Wise had a good deal to explain. Gosse does not say for whom the 1847 limited edition was intended, but in 1896 Wise's close friend, Buxton Forman, printed the highly improbable explanation that E.B.B. had them privately printed to show her husband. How did it happen then that no copy of the 1847 edition existed among Browning's papers, that his son had never heard of the publication, and that he had inherited forty-three of the originals? Wise explained that by saying that "years later" Miss Mitford had returned these forty-three originals. He adds that when she gave Dr. Bennett the copies of this edition she inserted in one of them the manuscript of the sonnet *Future and Past*. Wise stated that he paid £25 for this copy, and bought another of the unbound copies. He then "hurried the good news" of his discovery to his friends, Buxton Forman, Edmund Gosse, R. A. Potts, Stopford Brooke, J. Morgan, W. B. Slater and 'others', who of course were delighted to buy copies of this unique and hitherto unknown edition at ten pounds a time.

Here we come again on the puzzling psychology of the dupes, who instantly accepted Wise's improbable story and eagerly handed over their ten-pound notes, which of course went into Wise's pocket. No doubt they were duped by the persuasiveness which is part of the stock-in-trade of the successful business-man, especially since it was to their interest to believe and to propagate a story which sounded romantic and let them in on the ground floor of a nice little investment. One of those copies sold in New York eventually for $1,250.00, about £250 in those days. I must repeat that the original ten-pound notes did not go to Bennett, but to Wise. In view of the sale prices later recorded he must bitterly have regretted not asking more, though of course he

had an unknown number put aside for later and anonymous
sales on the rising market.

But should not such shrewd men as Gosse and Forman
have suspected something? The tale put out through Forman
that the *Sonnets* were printed for the purpose of showing them
to Browning seems very lame. Even lamer was the story that
Miss Mitford "years later" returned the originals to Bennett.
In those days of uncertain mails and police censorship in
Italy, how could the Brownings have risked sending the
originals through the post? Why not a fair copy? Then, why
send them to England to be printed, when, as Byron, Shelley
and Leigh Hunt had proved twenty-five years before, it was
perfectly easy to get English poems printed in Pisa? Wise's
lame excuse is that an Italian or London printer would have
been 'impolitic', because "privacy would have been impossible". Why a Reading printer was more private than a
Pisan printer he does not condescend to explain. And if
Mrs. Browning really wanted so complete a secrecy, why
send the poems to another woman, when her devoted male
cousin Kenyon was available? And why did Miss Mitford
not hand the undistributed copies to Browning, instead of
giving them to a distant acquaintance whose possession of
them after many years was miraculously discovered by the
astute Wise? Not one of these expert bibliophiles seems to
have known that Browning's library contained no copy of
this edition. Not one of them seems to have consulted
Browning's son, who would surely have heard the story from
his father, and in fact eventually confirmed the 1849 Bagni di
Lucca version.

Strong as all this evidence is against the authenticity of the
edition 'discovered' by Wise, fanatics obviously could still go
on arguing, could refuse to admit the facts, and could go on
trying to put up a case for Wise. Unluckily for them and
Wise, the scientific and technical tests devised by Carter and
Pollard proved beyond any possible doubt that the alleged

Miss Mitford Reading 1847 edition of the *Sonnets* was a fraud. The book, which has a title page dated 1847, is printed on paper which is conclusively proved not to have been manufactured before 1874 and most probably not in any quantity before 1883. The type used for the *Sonnets* is identical with that used by Wise for a facsimile of Matthew Arnold's *Alaric at Rome*—of which, by the way, he also issued a spurious edition.

Now, this particular type was specially designed for the printers Richard Clay & Sons, and was not used by them in this form before about October 1883. When in 1933 the two enquirers put the facts before the then representatives of the firm (who of course had changed) they instantly agreed that the *Sonnets* must have been printed by their firm. But then the enquiries came on a sudden and unexpected check. The London manager who dealt with the forger had died in 1929; and all the ledgers and correspondence of the firm had been destroyed in 1911. Why? Other printing firms kept their records, and there was certainly no paper shortage in 1911 as there was in 1917 and 1940–45.

How many copies of this spurious 'first' did Wise print and sell? He accounts for eight, but leaves us to infer that others went to friends to whom Wise "hurried the good news". That leaves the total conveniently vague. The enquirers give a list of seventeen copies known to exist in libraries (nearly all American), and nineteen others whose ownership was not known in 1934. Herbert E. Gorfin, who had worked for nearly twenty years in Wise's City office before setting up as a bookseller, sold an unspecified number on commission. He also paid Wise four hundred pounds for a number of forgeries, 'suspects' and piracies and a few genuine books— but the Browning *Sonnets* do not occur in this list, as Gorfin was only allowed to sell them on commission. If $1,250 was paid as a top price in a New York sale-room for a copy, Wise would surely have asked and received more than ten pounds for the copies Gorfin sold for him on commission. It is impossible to know how much Wise netted by the sales of this and his other forgeries; but they must have amounted, all told, to a considerable sum.

The extent of Wise's frauds is indicated by the amazing fact that no less than fifty-four of his publications are listed by the enquirers as forgeries, 'suspects' or piracies; and of course suspects are obviously forgeries which cannot be conclusively proved to be such. Since 1934 the investigations of Mr. Wilfred Partington have added another twenty-four. If Wise cleared a hundred pounds on the average for each of these (not to mention others which may be proved forgeries) he didn't do so badly.

Among the authors whose work Wise misappropriated in one way or another are Matthew Arnold, Mr. and Mrs. Browning, Dickens, George Eliot, Kipling, William Morris, D. G. Rossetti, R. L. Stevenson, Swinburne, Tennyson, Thackeray, Wordsworth and Ruskin. It is worth noting that, although the work of some of these was still protected by copyright when Wise died, no attempt was made (so far as I can discover) to force his estate to pay compensation to the heirs. On the other hand a good deal of superfluous pity has been expended on the 'collectors'. But the most curious and interesting part of this affair from the point of view of the "psychology of dupes" is the fact that during the better part of half a century there seems to have been virtually no suspicion of these frauds among the well-known writers who collaborated with Wise, the experts in first editions, the bibliographers and bibliophiles. There were one or two exceptions, the most important of whom were Ruskin's editors, who proved by collation that four of the "Ruskin pamphlets" published by Wise were forgeries—information which they published in the notes to their great collected edition. The information went wholly unnoticed, for such expensive books are produced for display, not for reading.

Wise's Ashley Library of course contained, among a great number of other perfectly genuine and valuable books, all his forgeries, displayed as genuine and boasted of as rareties and 'discoveries' in the eleven-volume catalogue published between 1922 and 1936. Each volume had an introduction by a well-known man-of-letters and bibliophile: Richard Curle, Augustine Birrell, Edmund Gosse, John Drinkwater, E. V. Lucas, A. E. Newton, R. W. Chapman, Alfred W. Pollard and Sir John Squire. All of them taken in by a dealer in essential oils! It is perhaps worth noting that during the War of 1914–18 a consignment of oils to Wise's firm was held up by the Royal Navy at Gibraltar. There exists a letter from Sir Edmund Gosse to Wise saying that he would put the matter personally before Sir Winston Churchill and thus certainly get the cargo cleared.

Wise's motives have been differently interpreted, from those who think that he was merely out for money and the prestige of "discovering unknown rarities" down to Bernard Shaw, who thought Wise only a practical joker. Well, Wise was not the only "practical joker" sponsored by Shaw in defiance of elementary ethics. There are certain engravers who from time to time play the practical joke of abandoning their unremunerative occupation for specialist work, which usually causes action by the police. Who would listen if they put up the defence Shaw made for Wise? "Oh, but we're just having a practical joke. Lots of people like to collect these crisp Bank of England notes, and we've been giving them what they wanted. Where is the harm?"

Of course the analogy is not exact, since Wise's motives for his illegal action were not wholly financial. As a 'mere' business man he must surely have enjoyed a good deal of private mirth in his successful taking in of so many pompous intellectuals and expert 'collectors'. Moreover, his prestige as a discoverer of rare books must have helped to raise the prices he asked as a hidden book-dealer pretending to put his friends on to "good things". He was a fraudulent parasite on the parasites of literature. The genuine reprints issued by Wise and his friend Clement Shorter overlooked any neglected contemporary literary talent. It was a discreditable episode, but Wise has the last laugh—at Yankosachsen moneyed intellectual snobbery, pretentiousness and credulity. I rather like him for that.

Note: This book was already in type when another of Wise's feats was revealed. Among the books in his library bought by the British Museum were rare and expensive Elizabethan editions, defective when he bought them, but completed by him with pages from other copies. It now turns out that he or an accomplice stole these from complete copies belonging to the Museum. Thus, he not only wantonly damaged national property, but made the nation pay his heirs for it. A splendid example of effrontery.

EIGHT

Postscript: Général Cambronne

OR L'IMPOSTEUR MALGRÉ LUI

Some are born frauds, some achieve fraud, and some have fraud thrust upon them.

Notoriety and money are the usual objects of the first two categories, sometimes separately, mostly in conjunction. The more or less bogus achievement of power through notoriety might be studied in a frank and well-documented analysis of almost any successful politician. Unluckily the documents are usually lacking, and frankness is dangerous with such characters. Those who have fraud thrust upon them are generally more or less blushing heroes, victims of their country's jingoism, credited with mighty but supposititious deeds either to magnify a victory or to divert attention from a defeat in war.

The Battle of Waterloo produced several silly legends about himself which always annoyed the Duke of Wellington, such as that he was 'surprised' or that he said: "Up, Guards, and at 'em." Naturally, the more remarkable frauds of this kind were on the French side—they needed them. The most celebrated, phoney, and unkillable of these is the myth of Cambronne and his famous or infamous *mot* which is still firmly believed by about ninety-nine per cent of the French nation.

Before coming to Cambronne perhaps a word may be said

in defence of Marshal Grouchy, whose reputation, memory and descendants have most unjustly suffered for a century and a half. The myth wavers and is not altogether consistent, since in some versions Grouchy is a *traître* who refused to obey the Emperor's orders to march to his aid, while in others he was a fool and a blunderer who arrived too late. At all events every Bonapartist and most other Frenchmen, taken in by the propaganda of the day, have made Grouchy the scapegoat for the Emperor's mistakes and miscalculations on that memorable and fatal day. Let us try to see what Grouchy really did, and what were his motives.

Early in the morning of the great battle, Grouchy decided that his duty, in accordance with his general instructions, would be to advance on Wavre to keep the Prussians engaged and if possible drive them back, shattered as they were from the defeat at Ligny two days before, while he maintained touch with the Emperor. Just about ten o'clock, about an hour before the opening bombardment at Waterloo, Grouchy received a despatch from the Emperor which, to his great satisfaction, ordered him to do just that. When Grouchy's men had started their march, the distant rumble of the Waterloo cannonade was heard, and some of Grouchy's staff suggested that their Corps (some 33,000 men) ought to follow the ancient rule and "march to the guns". Grouchy disagreed—the Emperor knew what he was about; scarcely an hour before, he had ordered the march on Wavre; their duty was to obey. Even if between eleven a.m. and noon Grouchy had halted, turned about and marched to the guns, it is rather doubtful if he could have arrived in time to be of much use, even if unmolested. The two Prussian Corps of Pirch and Bülow, though delayed for various reasons, had started at dawn and did not get into action until after four p.m. And if he had tried a flank march he would either have bumped into some of Blücher's two Corps or more likely have been attacked in flank by the Wavre Prussians under Thielmann.

It was about one-thirty p.m. when Napoleon realised that the troops who could be seen advancing at a distance of about six miles to his right were part of the Prussian Army. The Emperor, like Grouchy, had not foreseen this move. A despatch of course was sent at once to inform Grouchy, with orders to attack Blücher's force at once. This despatch crossed one from Grouchy (timed eleven a.m.) to say he was marching on Wavre as ordered. It gives some idea of the distance between the two sections of the French Army to know that the cavalry officer bearing this despatch and riding at full speed was three and a half hours on the way, and Grouchy did not get it until five. None of Grouchy's men could have reached the Waterloo battlefield until long after dark when the issue had been decided, while many of his men were already fighting their way across the Dyle river. On the morning of the 19th Grouchy attacked again, drove back the Prussians to his front with great gallantry, when he suddenly received the appalling news of what had happened the day before at Waterloo.

Realising the imminent danger to his Corps, Grouchy broke off the action at once, and made a masterly retreat, saving nearly all his men from being cut off by Blücher and bringing them safely back to France—the only disciplined and intact remnant of Napoleon's Army that was left. To his amazement and rage, Grouchy found that instead of being praised for saving his army so skilfully he was being denounced as a blunderer or a traitor by Napoleon's propaganda in order to salvage a little of the Emperor's damaged reputation. Waterloo was lost by Napoleon, who was outwitted and outfought by Wellington and Blücher (the two generals who weren't afraid of his reputation); it was not the fault of Grouchy.

The Cambronne incident is a mere anecdote in com-

parison with Napoleon's tragic mishandling of his detach-
ment, but it is as widespread and as persistent as the Grouchy
injustice. When the rout of Napoleon's Army came and
most of them were, in Stendhal's phrase "running away like
frightened sheep," three battalions of the Old Guard formed
square and held out long enough for the Emperor to escape,
first by carriage, and then on horseback as the village of
Genappe was crowded with fugitives. According to the tale,
an English officer called to these troops of the Old Guard to
surrender, and Cambronne is supposed to have replied:
"*Merde!*" or in more dignified versions: "The Guard dies
but does not surrender." This, no doubt, was a very noble
sentiment especially for civilian consumption, but it is a little
unfortunate that the words "The Guard dies but does not
surrender" were attributed by the unwary propagandists to
Cambronne. Let me invite the reader's attention to a brief
supplementary letter to the Waterloo despatch, giving the
latest news for the information of Lord Bathurst at the War
Office:

Bruxelles, June 19th, 1815

My Lord,
    I have to inform your Lordship, in addition to my dispatch
of this morning, that we have already got here 5,000
prisoners, taken in the action of yesterday, and that there are
above 2,000 more coming in to-morrow. There will probably
be many more.
    Amongst the prisoners are the Comte de Lobau, who
commanded the 6th Corps, and General Cambronne, who
commanded a division of the Guards.
    I propose to send the whole to England, by Ostend.
                    I have the honour to be &c.
                                        Wellington.

Reminiscing long afterwards, the Duke related that when
he got back to G.H.Q. about ten p.m. he found these two
generals standing, hat in hand, at the entry. Now, it has long

been the custom of a British Commander after a victory to invite any captured general to dinner. "By God," said the Duke, "I thought they had behaved so badly I wouldn't invite them. So I sent them to report as prisoners to the King of France at Ghent." By "behaving badly" the Duke only meant that they had broken their military oath to Louis XVIII, which he chose to regard as a bar to hospitality. As a matter of fact there was another and far more powerful motive for what might seem a little churlish in so great a gentleman. Wellington wanted to be free from any outsiders' company at dinner. Nearly all his staff officers had been killed or wounded; Colonel Gordon was dying in a room at G.H.Q.; the Military Secretary, Lord Fitzroy Somerset, was badly wounded. Among his generals, Picton was killed, Uxbridge, Cooke, Alten, Halkett severely wounded. Ponsonby also was killed, though Wellington didn't know it. The Army had lost six hundred officers, many of them his personal friends, most of them known to him. Every time the door opened during dinner he looked up quickly, hoping one of the missing had arrived.

There was no military disgrace attached to the capture of Lobau and Cambronne. On the contrary. They were captured simply because their men held out to the last— Lobau's in Planchenoit, and Cambronne's between the battlefield and Genappe. Both had done their duty and more. Many years later M. de Cambronne was ennobled and took his seat in the French Upper House. In the course of one of his speeches he asked leave to deny most earnestly and categorically that he had ever uttered the famous sentence or the still more famous word. His speech was entered in the records of the House of Peers, and no doubt reported widely in the press at the time. Chateaubriand, who was also a peer, must have heard it. In any case he quoted it as a footnote to his *Mémoires d'Outre Tombe*, though, strange to relate, I find no mention of it in the most recent edition. You would think that the authority of the General himself and the publicity given by a famous book which every educated person in France still reads would have killed the legend. Not at all. Only a short time before these words are written I saw in a French newspaper a peppery and patriotic article by a more than usually ill-informed journalist (which is saying a lot) which was based entirely on "the spirit of the *mot de Cambronne*". Well might jesting Pilate ask his question.

Note, though, that this is really a legend, which has existed for a hundred and fifty years in spite of the utmost efforts of its hero or victim to contradict it. But if Cambronne himself had fabricated the story, and if he had persuaded two or three veracious journalists or biographers to spread it while himself pretending that he had not given them the story and indeed while forcing them to say that he had not collaborated in their 'stories' or books, then it would not be a legend—it would simply be a successful lie.